Effective Intervention for Atypical Dyslexics:

How to Teach Nonresponders when Phonics and Whole Word Intervention Just Don't Cut It

AMANDA TAN SWEE CHING

CONTENTS

Foreword   Pg 5

Introduction   Pg 8

Chapter 1:   Pg 21
Domains for sucessful literacy acquisition

Chapter 2A: Pg 56
When 'nonresponders are just responders who need more help

Chapter 2B: Pg 65
Types of nonresponders and their associated characteristics

Chapter 2C: Pg 74
Main principles and considerations to approach nonresponders

Chapter 3:   Pg 96
Single-syllable word instruction for type As

Chapter 4:   Pg 118
High-frequency word instruction for type Xs and Ys

Chapter 5:   Pg 169
Type Y case studies: The 4 (plus 3) heavenly kings

Chapter 6:   Pg 242
Multisyllabic word nonresponders

Afterword   Pg 259

FOREWORD

Phonics works.

After all, it is backed by research. Those who benefit from it do well and see measured progress.

Phonics falters.

We understand that some kids have a more severe form of dyslexia - that progress may be way slower than others. However, there is a difference between slow but steady progress, and no progress due to a lack of receptivity.

Phonics does not work – or only works partially – for such students. Such variation in receptivity towards intervention is expected. There are definitely students who are not receptive to mainstream phonics intervention. After all, the special needs industry is where the population has diverse needs.

Parents of nonresponding children feel stuck. They know that the intervention does not work but the experts themselves claim that it does, that all these children just require more time and reinforcement. Recommendations of a whole-word approach seems to fall flat too when they turn out to be ineffective.

Not only the parents feel the heat. Some practitioners may also realise that their students are not responding to phonics or whole-word intervention. Attempts to help them become futile and said practitioners become frustrated. They become disheartened. They feel, and I would quote them, 'useless'.

Despairing parents and practitioners alike start to look for alternatives. However, the route to finding an effective intervention method is slow and treacherous. For one, the variety of approaches out there is bewildering and every solution seems different from the rest. They neither have funds nor time to try everything out. It is exhausting. In addition, there is a prevailing norm that deems alternative methods to be 'unscientific'. Feedback from people who do not seem to understand the desperate situation of these parents and practitioners seem to discourage any attempt at trying out 'alternative' methods. A certain alternative approach may seem promising but the naysayers radiate scepticism and cynicism in the name of 'protecting' consumers from getting scammed.

The naysayers may mean well... but seriously, it is aggravating.

If you are reading this book, I assume that you are most likely a parent or a practitioner who is trying to gain some understanding into the world of nonresponders (or "treatment resistors"). Or perhaps, you are an individual who is interested to know more about this field and is willing to accept ideas beyond the homogeneous message touted by the mainstream.

While this book is not a holy grail that promises solutions for all nonresponders, it seeks to offer you some understanding and direction on how to guide your child or student. It will offer explanations on (1) the difference between phonics intervention, whole-word intervention and alternative intervention, (2) the different types of nonresponders, (3) the learning style of each type of nonresponder towards literacy acquisition, and (4) some preliminary intervention methods.

I hope that by the end of this book, you can determine the difference between the types of nonresponders. Perhaps, you will be able to see the similarities and differences among all intervention approaches – mainstream or alternative methods – and realise that the callous dismissal of alternative approaches as a scam is ultimately the inherent unwillingness or inability to deeply reflect on information.

Apart from genuine scams, every intervention approach suits a certain population of dyslexics (or individuals with Specific Learning Differences (SpLD)). However, it takes deep expertise and understanding to be able to advise and provide the right intervention approach to the right individual with dyslexia or SpLD.

It is a lack of open-mindedness and an arrogance to claim that there is only one approach of tackling a problem. Yet, it is very human to use our own experience and assumptions to make generalisations of social situations and societal developments. Unfortunately, this makes things that fall outside our realm of experience to be incredibly difficult to accept, increasing the likelihood for insensitive disregard. Nonresponders form the minority rhetoric. This means that the experiences of nonresponders fall outside the experiences of the majority who have benefitted from phonics.

In opposition to mainstream, I am of the belief that anecdotal evidence holds as much importance as statistical evidence. Probably due to my learning style, cognitive processing and medical issues, I am allergic to the term "placebo effect". I know that certain phenomena are indeed due to a placebo effect. However, the exponential number of times this term gets thrown around by experts and the public alike as a form of dismissal is a problem of epic proportions.

For others to disregard a person's experience without bothering to understand the context is a devaluation of the person's experience and a subtle discrimination of the highest order. Any experience that is deemed out of the norm is always viewed as an exception and thus, not significant. When there are claims that a certain approach works, the onus is on us to find out why the approach works (alongside with identifying the commonalities and differences between this approach and that of others) rather than to blindly trust in the mainstream approach that is commonly validated by parents or practitioners who are simply seeking quick fixes and solutions to their child or client's predicament.

The research world is skewed in such a way that research is catered to the majority and its responsivity towards the needs on the ground becomes slow. As such, these alternative approaches serve to cater to that need quickly at the expense of "scientific validation". This results in a disparity between the sentiment on the ground and what is touted to be the gold standard.

At the end of the day, the root to understanding – like every other out-of-the-box solution – merely requires a perspective shift. 'Merely' because you do not need to fork out tons of cash nor cross your fingers and hope that an approach works. However, this 'merely' is a rather tall order.

It is very difficult to gain this shift in perspective and thoroughly understand the underlying principles of an approach unless you break new ground and realise that in many occasions, effective solutions are deemed to be wrong not because they are 'unscientific'. Rather, it is just that science has yet to catch up.

INTRODUCTION

In 2011, I was accepted into a role that required me to provide both intervention and educational support to students with the diagnosis of dyslexia. As a fresh hire into the school, I went through an Orton-Gillingham training programme that placed emphasis on a structured and sequential phonics intervention in tackling the phonological deficits of students with dyslexia.

When I first started out, the phonics intervention programme was indeed effective for the students under my care. Some progressed quickly while others required more time to process what was being taught. Nevertheless, there was a general sense that things were working out.

Three months into my job, I met the first student who proved me otherwise.

This student had been on the programme for more than a year. Using the phonics concepts that were previously taught to him, this student could spell the four letter consonant-consonant-vowel-consonant (CCVC) and consonant-vowel-consonant-consonant (CVCC) words (e.g. plan, bend). He could also spell words ending with letter combinations (e.g. think , stung).

At the magic-e concept (e.g. shame, slope) however, he crashed spectacularly.

He was randomly putting the letter 'e' behind certain words with no understanding of when the letter 'e' should surface in words despite having been taught the rule.

I quickly realised that something was amiss.

The source of his problem did not originate from his Attention Deficit Hyperactive Disorder (ADHD). He paid full attention and tried his best during work. He was very bright as he could remember and apply certain previously taught concepts readily without much prompting.

However, the magic-e concept seemed like his nemesis. He concentrated and tried his best but he still made the same spelling mistakes of the same word or concept lesson after lesson despite my reinforcement. This situation continued for half a year. It was very obvious that things were not working out.

His parents came to the same conclusion. Unsurprisingly, he had hit a wall with his previous teacher and was stalling in his progress when he came to me. His parents felt like they had invested enough time in a programme that did not yield the results that they were hoping for.

As frustrating as it was to fight a losing battle, I decided to try and find a solution within half a year. I tried to segment the words in different ways, increased repetitions and gave him chunks of sound instead of isolated sounds (e.g. instead of /f//l//a//p/, I taught him /fl/ /ap/).

Nothing seemed to work. The inevitable came after half a year and the student left the programme.

Within the same time of teaching that student, I received two more existing students of similar profiles. They had been on the programme for more than a year and were similarly not making much progress with their literacy.

Student number two humoured me by going through the motions of attempting all that phonics intervention, all while being aware that whatever that was being taught had no impact on his literacy. He was in my class because his mother told him to attend and he was polite enough not to disrupt the class out of boredom.

At the age of twelve, he attempted his national exams with a reading and spelling age of about seven. He used his superior intellect to be exam smart and managed to do so well for his exams that he qualified for a highly coveted spot in a sports school that placed emphasis on the academic performance for all applicants.

To say that his mother and I were dumbfounded would be the understatement of the century. According to him, his reading strategy revolved around guessing the word via its overall shape through a process of elimination and hunches before guessing the meaning of the word using the context of the sentence.

I was immensely proud of him. He also proved once more that my intervention was ineffective.

And then, there was Warren.

If my first student was the trigger for me to find a solution, Warren evoked that urgency... that desperation within me to seek for a solution like a man possessed.

Fortunately, not only was I attracted to problem solving and analysis, I had the perseverance to experiment repeatedly. In addition, I did not have issues with my self-worth when I taught students who had a history of not responding well to instruction.

I had been told that some teachers did not like to teach underperforming students because they felt like 'failures' when the students showed no improvement. In the teachers' own words, they "don't know why the students don't know". The feeling of guilt became unbearable and such students either get passed around to the other teachers or the teachers quit the industry altogether.

Armed with my determination, love for problem-solving and a constant urgent reminder that came in the form of Warren, I set off to find my solution.

Firstly, I coined the term 'nonresponders' to describe those students who were not responding well to the phonics intervention programme.

Then, I gathered as many nonresponders from my colleagues as possible. The nonresponders under my care swelled in number and they could not be any more different from one another.

My initial observations revealed that they had differing literacy competencies and learning styles. Some preferred visuals while others hated them. Some had an inclination towards auditory input while others had no specific preference. Everyone had varying degrees of literary competency and stalled at largely different parts of the phonics intervention programme. The only commonality was that they were crashing early into the phonics intervention programme but even then, some managed to apply bits of the phonics sounds into their spelling without much difficulty while others rejected it entirely.

Back then, the available help beyond phonics was largely on the behaviour modification level. There exists a chasm between behaviour modification and targetted literacy intervention for nonresponders. Afterall, the former attempts to incorporate even more structure into an intervention while has to cater to the nonresponders' inability to conform to structure.

In that year, I tried all ways and means to make some real progress towards solving this mystery.

But one year on, I was still none the wiser.

Exploring the Literature on Alternative Methods

Throughout this period of time, I spent every available moment trawling the net for alternative approaches, for any academic research that offered a different perspective from the usual phonics intervention. Every proposed method seemed to work with a few nonresponders but was unable to be universally effective for all the nonresponders under my care.

- ## *Audiblox*

"Audiblox is a system of cognitive exercises, aimed at the development of foundational learning skills. Audiblox develops and automatizes the foundational skills of reading, spelling, writing, mathematics and the skills required in the learning of subject matter." (Cognitive Exercises for Learning Disabilities, n.d.)

The problem with Audiblox was that it was working on the weaknesses of my students. The website rightfully held no promises and stated that progress might be evident after long periods of hard work and dedication. At that point in time, a sizable portion of the nonresponders that I met were disillusioned and demoralised. Any mention of hard work and more failure in the short term would mean that I would have a revolt on my hands. That, together with the fact that there were logistical and time constraints in my class, meant that such a touted and acclaimed programme had been – regretfully – sitting in my cupboard ever since the day of purchase.

Source: http://www.audiblox2000.com/audiblox-01.htm

- ## *Child's 1st cards*

Child's 1st cards embed the meaning of high-frequency sight words (e.g. could, are, play) into the words itself. Essentially the word becomes a picture. It is advocated as a literacy resource for right-brain learners.

I adored the way that the cards were created as it made sense. Showing normal sight word cards with no visuals is like continuously showing blobs of ink to a non-reader who has to guess the word via the overall shape of the 'blob'. It worked incredibly well for my students who responded to phonics. However, it was a different story for the nonresponders.

This was not to say that the cards were completely ineffective. However, the effectiveness of the cards fell dramatically when it came to the nonresponders. For those whose sight words knowledge were greatly lacking, they did not have great retention of the words on the cards as they only remembered the pictures but not the words. As such, they were unable to reproduce the correct spelling of the words and inaccuracies prevailed.

It may be argued that such sight word cards cater to people who do not respond to phonics as these cards are more 'visual' in nature. However, I would like to state that there is a difference between my group of phonics nonresponders and what is perceived to be a nonresponder by others. This important distinction will be reiterated in chapter 2.

Source: https://child1st.com/

- ***Books: "Visual-spatial learners" by Alexandra Shires Golon , "Right-brained children in a left- brained world" by Jeffrey Freed, M.A.T., and Laurie Parsons & "Upside-Down Brilliance" by Linda Kreger Silverman***

All the books touted a spelling approach that was similar to Child's 1ˢᵗ – embedding a picture into the word to promote understanding and word retention. Golon (2008) also included a checklist to determine if a child is visual-spatial. According to Freed (1998), the truly visual-spatial ones can remember and verbally spell a long, colour-coded word (e.g. existentialism) forward and backward. They can even identify the position of letters (e.g. "This word has twelve letters. What's the ninth letter?").

It felt like this spelling method was suitable for words with multiple syllables. However, the problem was that nonresponders had an immense difficulty in ensuring consistent and accurate spelling of single-syllable words. In addition, not all nonresponders were receptive to learning mutli-syllabic words just by colour coding each syllable.

Moreover, I was – and still am – a teacher in a phonics programme. I had a curriculum and a specific teaching technique to adhere to. Deviating drastically from the curriculum and technique was simply not permitted among the teachers – much less a new hire like me who was still undergoing training. Even when I made the decision to deviate when necessary, there were far too many words that the nonresponders needed to know for this method to be practical.

At that point in time, I had yet to thoroughly understand the material and had incorrectly prioritised the fact that the ability to verbally spell long words backwards was the hallmark of a visual-spatial individual. None of my students, then, were able to spell long words backwards. I could see that some students were visual-spatial but quite a few were not strongly visual-spatial. Some were not visual-spatial at all. On top of that, I noticed that a few of the nonresponders did not see pictures in their minds and were strongly auditory inclined.

- *Book: "The Gift of Dyslexia" by Ronald D. Davis and Eldon M. Braun*

Ronald D. Davis is said to have both severe dyslexia and autism (About Ron Davis, n.d.). His methods include (1) controlling and "switching off" perceptual distortions through an individual's mind's eye, and (2) the prevention of confusion, which will once again trigger the perceptual distortion (coined as 'disorientation'). Prevention includes mastery of letter symbols using concrete methods (shaping letters with clay) and being aware of trigger words (words with abstract meanings, or multiple meanings).

His book was intriguing. At that point in time however, I had not met any student that fit the description of his clients. They did not seem to demonstrate that degree of perceptual distortion. The description of the orientation counselling was mind-boggling. In addition, I had yet to realise how crucial it was to understand the nature of the trigger words.

The Davis method is deemed to be 'controversial' by sceptics as the ideas and principles of the Davis method are the most radical among all of the alternative approaches. It is deemed as the antithesis of phonics intervention.

Regardless, I did not doubt the book.

- ***Other materials***

To add on to the list, I also looked at many other programmes (e.g. Lindamood Bell) and read many books including the following:

- o "The illustrated Book of Sounds and Their Spelling Patterns" by Sarah Major

- o "Reading Reflex" by Carmen McGuinness and Geoffrey McGuinness

- o "That's the Way I Think: Dyslexia, Dyspraxia and ADHD Explained" by David Grant

- o "The Dyslexic Advantage" by Brock L. Eide M.D. M.A. and Fernette F. Eide M.D

- o Overcoming Dyslexia" by Sally Shaywitz, M.D.

- o "Decoding Dyslexia" by Jennifer Poole

- o "Reading by the Colors" by Helen Irlen

- o "Learning with a Visual Brain in an Auditory World" by Ellyn Lucas Arwood

- o The Turner & Hope Method

  - - "DYSLEXIA or BEING RIGHT BRAINED" by M J Turner & Karen Hope
  - - "14 STEPS TO TEACH DYSLEXICS HOW TO SPELL & READ" by Karey Hope deGraaf
  - - "Teaching the Dyslexic Student: SPELLING AND LANGUAGE ARTS" M J Turner & Karen Hope

- o "Developing Ocular Motor and Visual Perceptual Skills" by Kenneth A. Lane, OD, FCOVD

- o "When the Brain Can't Hear" by Teri James Bellis Ph.D.

I trawled through many case studies on clinical intervention of severe neurological impairment – alexia, agraphia, visual agnosia and aphasia – that are in direct association with literacy and language impairments. Thereafter, I began to search for detailed accounts of individuals who experienced severe distortion of their reality due to an onset of neurological impairment (I found it essential to find out how these individuals perceived the world). As such, I began to read books that included the following titles:

- o "My Stroke of Insight " by Jill Bolte Taylor

- o "The Man Who Mistook His Wife For A Hat: And Other Clinical Tales" by Oliver Sacks

- o "Visual Agnosia" by Martha J. Farah

Admittedly, I did not make it known to the parents that I was referring to clinical books on neurological impairment because labelling their children as "neurologically impaired" or a 'clinical' case was undoubtedly a touchy subject.

However, I was of the firm belief that by understanding the experiences of individuals who were deemed as the most extreme of cases, I would be able to generalise their experiences to individuals with drastically milder forms impairments but were nonetheless still some of the most severe nonresponding students under my care). In addition, I believed that the solution was probably embedded in the world of neurological research. Unfortunately, these highly coveted information from medical and neurological research did not percolate to education that easily.

Regardless, I was accumulating so much information but said information existed in isolation. I was unable to see how each piece of information interacted seamlessly with each other. I lacked the decisive factor, the final piece of the puzzle to make sense of everything.

Breakthrough

A year later, a new manager was recruited. The overall environment became relative more supportive towards learning experimentation. New colleagues entered and support for my quest to find the solution grew.

March saw the entry of a 15-year-old boy, Zeak, into my class.

At that point in time, he was easily the most severe case the centre had ever seen. This naturally meant that he was eventually transferred to me after at least a year of ineffective phonics intervention.

He struggled to spell three to four letter words like 'ham' and 'spit'. His phonics application to words was laborious.

After a couple of lessons, I decided that there was no harm asking him to complete the visual-spatial survey that was featured in the book written by Alexandra Shires Golon and Linda Kreger Silverman.

He maxed it out the checklist – a first among all my nonresponders.

Spurred by his results, I made him spell a long word – 'celebrate' – after allowing him to look at the colour-coded word for as long as he wanted.

He could spell the word 'celebrate' forward and backwards after staring at it for a mere three seconds. He could even identify the letters that were beside the second letter 'e'.

Just like what the books had said.

But that was strange. None of my students maxed out that checklist nor had they shown such astounding visual spatial abilities that were comparable to Zeak's. In addition, Zeak's ability to remember long words backwards did not solve his struggles with single-syllable words and word retention.

However, having analysed Zeak and the rest of the nonresponders at length, I could establish the similarities and differences that Zeak had with my other nonresponders. It was that very instance that everything fell into place and a comprehensive understanding of the nonreponders was established. I saw the commonality between them and a viable way to teach all of my nonresponders.

I rushed to find one of my colleagues who was steadfast in my support to find a solution. Upon explaining my ideas to her, my colleague tried it out on her student who was a nonresponder.

It worked like a charm – there was receptivity and retention.

I could still remember her looking so energised as she taught her student – a stark contrast from her previous resigned attitude due to her student's lack of receptivity.

Her student similarly looked intrigued and energised – the first time in years.

Against the backdrop of her excited chatters, I was aware of this ecstasy that was quickly overwhelming me.

It had been nearly two years into my job. One year and four months since the start of my quest for a solution.

I had finally – *finally* – found my answer.

Moving Forward

Following my breakthrough, I had a year of further exploration and refinement. I welcomed more nonresponders from my colleagues. At my peak, I had about 16 nonresponders out of 36 students. That was a whopping 44% of my students. Unlike what research had claimed, these students formed a large minority in my caseload.

While an approach for nonresponders may seem like to be a radical alternative that is deemed unacceptable by phonics purists, it is not as radical as it seems. After so many years, I realised that this approach is simply a more comprehensive framework that is in direct response to the many cognitive problems – apart from phonological awareness – that students with learning difficulties face. Any individual that champions a sequential, rule-based phonics approach to be the main approach in addressing the needs of all students with dyslexia is simply not factoring the degree of interference that the other problems or co-morbidities can present in a student's literacy acquisition.

Unlike phonics responders, nonresponders are diverse in nature. The amount of initial preparation work I had to do was phenomenal. In addition, I had some challenging moments that required me to cope with vastly different needs within a class. Initially, I had to handle a class of five students with very different needs. Having one phonics responder and four nonresponders, who each had distinct needs and required individual attention, in one class was not a feat for the faint hearted. I was exhausted, to say the least.

Regardless of the challenging moments, all of the nonresponders showed varying levels of receptivity and progress in their literacy interventions.

All, but Warren… and Nathan.

Layout of this Book

This book consists of six chapters. Each chapter builds on the content of the previous chapter to present knowledge in a cumulative fashion.

- **Chapter 1: Domains for successful literacy acquisition**

It is crucial to understand how both internal and external domains contribute to successful literacy acquisition. This chapter provides a detailed account of all aspects of the internal domain, which comprises of the language, sensorial (perceptual) and sensorial (storage) domain. [The external domain, also known as the mechanical domain, refers to the type of intervention. The external domain will be the object of focus from chapter 3 to 6.]

- **Chapter 2A: Differentiating phonics responders and nonresponders**
- **Chapter 2B: Types of nonresponders and their associated characteristics**
- **Chapter 2C: Main principles and considerations to approach nonresponders**

Not all students who do not seem to be responding to instruction are nonresponders. To complicate matters, not all nonresponders are the same. Chapter 2A, 2B and 2C explore (1) the difference between phonics responders (who just require more targeted instruction) and nonresponders, (2) the different types of single-syllable word nonresponders (type A, B, X, Y) and their associated characteristics, and (3) the main considerations required to shape instructions for nonresponders.

- **Chapter 3: Single-syllable word instruction for type As**

This chapter modifies an existing phonics technique – onset and rime – to suit learning needs of type As. In addition, this chapter provides the justification that that while type Bs resemble type As, they actually require instruction meant for type Xs and Ys.

- **Chapter 4: High-frequency word instruction for type Xs and Ys**

This chapter comes in two parts. The first part introduces the concept of the three tracks of impairment before analysing the degree of effectiveness that certain techniques have on type Xs and Ys. The second part introduces the concept of disinclination and its effects on shaping the different learning styles of type Xs and Ys.

- **Chapter 5: Type Y case studies: The 4 (plus 3) heavenly kings**

This chapter provides case studies on the most severe type Ys that I have taught to date. These case studies include the "Four (plus three) Heavenly Kings" – Zeak, Sean, Xian, Warren, Sophia, Nathan and Sam.

- **Chapter 6: Multisyllabic words nonresponders**

The types of multisyllabic word nonresponders differ from the single-syllable word nonresponders. Single-syllable words phonics responders may also demonstrate nonresponder tendencies in response to multisyllabic word phonics instruction.

This chapter explores the different types of multisyllabic word nonresponders and recommends the intervention method for each type of multisyllabic word nonresponder to cater to the diversity of needs and learning styles.

Disclaimer

This is a system purely for literacy acquisition – how to read and write. It does not cover language intervention (i.e. what if the student cannot understand what he or she is reading or writing) nor does it cover mainstream academic instruction. Those are huge disciplines and it is not within the scope of this book to cover them. If you are interested in the concept of visual thinking and understanding, I would strongly recommend the works of Ellyn Lucas Arwood. She is a Speech and Language Therapist and her books provide one of the most enlightening takes on visual learning and understanding.

CHAPTER 1

DOMAINS FOR SUCCESSFUL LITERACY ACQUISITION

Before discussing about the teaching strategies for nonresponders, it is important to understand the different domains that contribute to successful literacy acquisition.

In my opinion, the language, sensorial (perceptual) and sensorial (storage) domains make up the three internal domains within a person.

The language domain refers to how a person understands his or her world.

The sensorial (perceptual) domain refers to how a person perceives the world using his or her senses. In this case, it would specially refer to how the person sees or hears written and spoken words respectively.

The sensorial (storage) domain specifically refers to a person's ability to remember and retain how a word looks like.

The external domain comprises of the mechanical domain, which is the type of intervention that the student receives. The mechanical domain must resonate with the students' internal domains in order to witness successful literacy acquisition.

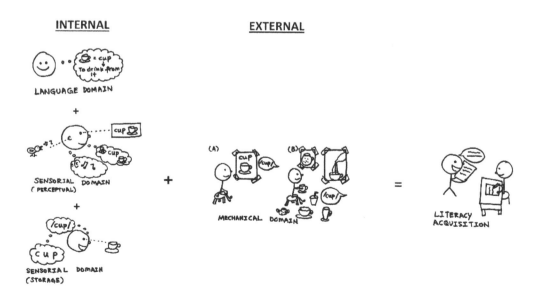

Components of internal domains at a glance

Each internal domain consists of the following components:

1. **Language domain**
   - Degree of receptivity to abstract concepts
   - Clear definition and distinction of words / concepts

2. **Sensorial (perceptual) domain**
   - Processing visual information
     - Common complaints
     - Visual span
   - Processing auditory information

3. **Sensorial (storage) domain**
   - The thing about memory
     - Long-term memory and short-term memory
     - Working memory
     - 'Sight' memory and orthographic memory
     - Auditory memory

This chapter provides a detailed account of the language domain, sensorial (perceptual) domain and sensorial (storage) domain. It will also focus on the atypical functioning of the internal domains. Thereafter, chapter 3 to 6 will explore the mechanical domain, which deals with the types of interventions that are suitable for nonresponders.

1. LANGUAGE DOMAIN (meaning making)

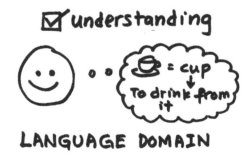

☑ understanding

= cup
To drink from it

LANGUAGE DOMAIN

1st component		2nd component		
Receptivity to abstract concepts	**+**	Clear definition of words / concepts	**=**	Understanding of reality (retention of concepts taught)

For individuals to understand their reality and the information that is taught to them, they need to be receptive to abstract concepts and have clear definitions of words or concepts. Should either of these components be missing, a person will fail to understand and problems will arise.

In the classroom, it means that the student will not retain the words or concepts that are taught despite repeated emphasis by the teacher. When it comes to social behaviour, some students may act inappropriately due to a lack of understanding of social norms.

The section devotes itself to an in-depth analysis of the components of the language domains for literacy acquisition.

• 1st component: Receptivity to Abstract Concepts

The degree of a person's receptivity to abstract concepts shapes the way said person engages in meaning making of their reality. When I analyse the learning behaviour and comprehension abilities of others, I am always measuring their degree of receptivity towards 'abstract' concepts as everyone's perception of what is 'abstract' is different.

In my opinion, when a person is unable to comprehend certain input and gets confused, the person deems information from that input to be abstract. As such, lack of comprehension to input equates to the perception that the information is too 'abstract' and the information has to be made less 'abstract' in order for understanding to set in. My Speech and Language Therapist colleagues term it as the "Step up. Step down." technique. The "Step down" portion indicates that should information be pitched at a level that is beyond the student's capacity for abstract concepts, no learning will take place.

While this concept of receptivity towards abstract concepts applies to any setting, I will specifically focus on vocabulary acquisition.

The simplest form of the word is usually one that has a direct representation of reality. It has a "concrete representation" as *the word literally describes reality as it is.*

However, when a word starts to bear lesser and lesser resemblance to what is directly represented in reality, the word becomes more and more abstract.

For example, what are you wearing right now?

Most people, if not all, would give the following answer:

It is a direct representation of reality as people see clothes in their closets and in boutiques. The eventual definition that a person may come to understand the word 'clothes' would be the following:

Pieces of fabric or cloth that I am wearing = clothes

By having a clear definition of the word, individuals demonstrate understanding by being able to read, spell and use the words correctly in daily speech.

Then, the word 'attire' appears. It bears lesser resemblance to the simplest form of the word. This means to say that the word 'attire' does not directly equate to 'clothes'.

You do not point to the shirt that you are wearing at home and say that you are wearing an 'attire' as it refers to clothes that are worn in a more formal setting. Hence, these words are context dependent. The word 'attire' is more abstract as compared to the word 'clothes' because it bears lesser resemblance to the simplest understanding of the word.

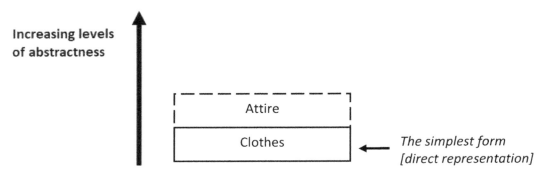

Abstract words can come in many forms. They are usually words that are context-dependent (e.g. attire), broadly encompass many other forms of the word or are simply words that are low in frequency (e.g. garment, raiment). In my opinion, words that have higher levels of abstractness are also known as 'jargons'. Words that are not the simplest form may also be defined as jargons.

As we move up the spectrum of abstractness, 'garment' would be deemed as more abstract than the word 'attire'. At the very least, the word 'attire' has a more direct representation in reality. In particular, a person who has more difficulty with abstract concepts may be able to remember the word 'attire' because the term "school attire" or "work attire" directly represents clothes worn in the school or work setting.

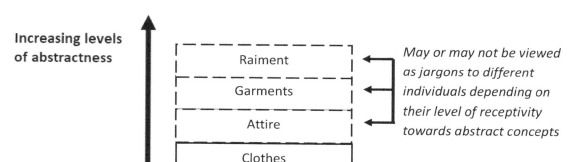

'Garments' do not have such a direct representation, unless you refer to the word 'undergarment'. However, a person with very low receptivity to abstract concepts may only remember 'underwear' or think that 'undergarment' refers to "clothes under their clothes". (This need for rigid definition will be elaborated in the section that features the 2nd component of the language domain.)

The point that I am trying to make is that the number of words that a person can understand depends on the degree of receptivity a person has towards abstract concepts. The more a person is receptive to abstract concepts, the easier it is for that person to remember jargons.

We generally understand higher-level vocabulary by building upon the simplest understanding of the word that is representative of reality. We also must have the ability to accept that higher-level vocabulary are more ambiguous representations of the simpler word. A person that has extremely low levels of receptivity towards abstract concepts is only able to accept the simplest form of the word. Any attempt to teach the student higher-level vocabulary with similar meanings – synonyms – will not be successful.

Let's imagine a person with such low levels of receptivity to abstract concepts that even the words 'clothes' is a jargon to him or her. To that person, the word 'clothes' is not a direct representation of his or her reality. Upon seeing what he or she is wearing, the person would say 'shirt', 'shorts' or 'skirt'.

(Certainly, there may be cases when a person is only able to remember the word 'clothes' and not 'shirt', 'shorts' or 'skirt'. This means that the person is unable to tell the different between 'shirt', 'shorts' or 'skirt'. As everything is made of cloth and the position of said cloth on the body does not seem to hold any meaning to this hypothetical person, we can say that this person has a problem with establishing clear definitions between the words. In other words, this problem is due to the atypical functioning of the 2nd component of the language domain.)

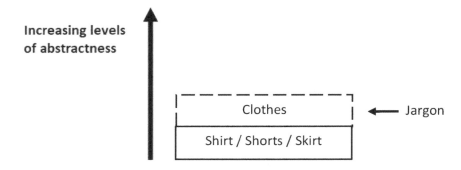

It might seem far-fetched to think that there would be a person who does not know how to read or spell the word 'clothes' because he or she does not understand the word. The problem surfaces when different people have varying definitions of what is deemed to be abstract. What one person may view as the norm or basic may be perceived as abstract in the eyes of others. As different people perceive their reality differently, a person's understanding of information may vary from that of others.

Let me give you a real example of how this idea of perception, though simple, could influence and alter the way my students perceive words, resulting in an adverse impact on literacy.

We would assume that the word 'address' is straight forward – it means where a person stays. However, one of my students does not deem the word 'address' as a direct representation of his reality. In other words, the word 'address' is deemed as abstract to him. As a result, he could not remember the meaning nor remember how the word is read nor spelt.

It may be argued that explaining the word 'address' as "where you are staying" may be elaborating the meaning for him. However, "where you are staying" still does not indicate a direct representation of his reality. The answer to "where you are staying" is the name of the town or district that he resides in. As such, the simplest form of the word 'address' that describes a direct representation of reality would be "words on the letters that are sent to my parents".

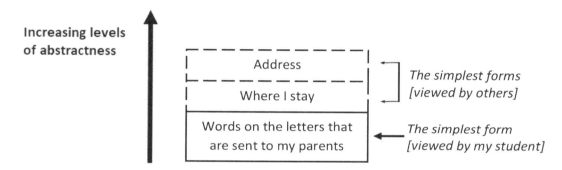

From this example, it demonstrates the problem of the differing levels of receptivity to abstract concepts and what is deemed to be abstract in the first place.

Should a teacher view the word 'address' as the simplest form that reflects a direct representation of reality, the teacher would not be able get through to the student. As a result, the student does not comprehend every time the teacher says the word 'address'. Even when the teacher attempts to explain 'address' as "where you stay", the student would either give the teacher a blank stare or feign understanding of the word.

o   *An informal test for basic receptivity towards abstract concepts*

Everyone knows that some people are able to understand abstract concepts a lot faster than others. Some people deal with information from various fields – like physics, quantum mechanics, programming, finance – like fish to water while the typically-population struggles to gain a basic understanding of it.

It is known that such fields contain technical knowledge that requires more abstract understanding. It is also accepted to be commonplace if a person does not comprehend such subjects because they are specialised bodies of abstract knowledge.

However, when I talk about basic receptivity to abstract concepts, I am referring to what is deemed to be acceptably abstract to the typical population.

An informal test of receptivity towards abstract information can be performed by simply observing the way students learn new concepts.

Let's take studying for example.

Usually, students who have greater receptivity towards abstract concepts either understand jargons quickly or just proceed to memorise the study material even if they do not understand. When they are confronted with concepts that are difficult to understand, they will simply move on and proceed onto other concepts

I would say as a disclaimer that learning without understanding is not the ideal way to study. However, there are situations – like exams – when the speed of learning takes precedence over the luxury of learning via understanding. This is why students try to spot questions and memorise answers.

Students who demonstrate lower receptivity towards abstract concepts will usually require an explanation for everything. They would like jargons to be explained in the simplest terms possible. They want abstract concepts to relate to real life examples. They will be unable to – or take much longer to – memorise information. Any attempt at moving on without understanding a prior concept will result in utter confusion, in which such confusion pervades and affects associated concepts.

Take for example the formula of pi when the teacher teaches the concept of circles. For example, a student may ask the following question when the concept is taught:

"Why does pi equate to 3.142?"

Some teachers may just reply, "Just accept that pi equates to 3.142."

A typical student will just accept it and proceed to recall that pi equates to 3.142 in their math questions. However, a student who has lower levels of receptivity towards abstract concepts needs an explanation to remember. However, that student will be forced to move on and will continue to find it very difficult to remember that pi equates to 3.142 because the student has derived no understanding from it. They may not be able to attempt any math questions on circles due to their inability to understand pi and the subsequent formulas relating to the calculation of the area and perimeter of circles.

Sometimes, it is difficult to find an explanation to justify why a concept is done in a certain way. As such, teachers create stories from embedded pictures or mnemonics in order to justify why things happen in a certain way.

Let's take the symbol '8' as another example.

When a child learns the meaning of number '8', the teacher or parent will take eight things and count in increasing order from 1 to 8 in order to reinforce the value of number '8'.

Thereafter, the symbol '8' is shown as a symbolic representation of eight things. A child who is receptive towards this relationship of using an abstract symbol '8' to represent the direct reality of eight things will establish this connection.

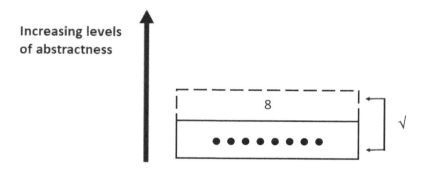

Overtime, the symbol '8' will be deemed as the simplest form – a direct representation of reality.

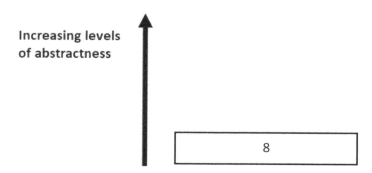

A child who is not receptive of such levels of abstract knowledge will not accept that the symbol '8' represents eight things. They want to know the reason behind why eight things are represented with the symbol '8'. It does not make sense to them as the symbol '8' is not a direct representation of their reality – they see eight toys (not symbols of '8') scattered around them.

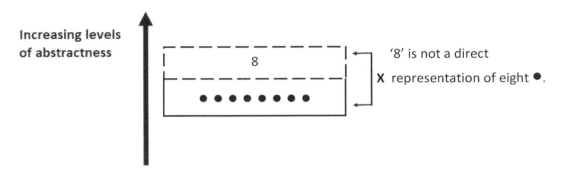

As such, this child may exhibit the following behavioural patterns:

- Not remember how the number is written
- Interchange numbers – this is assuming that the child has no visual processing issues (e.g. writing the symbol '8' as any other numerical symbol the child can think of)
- Unable to demonstrate number sense (e.g. 8 + 4 = 2)

In order to provide a justification as to why the abstract symbol '8' represents eight dots, teachers may incorporate both the eight dots and the symbol '8' in a story, illustration or some other engaging form.

Doing so helps the child to establish meaning or what is termed as a "lexical connection". The closer the story or illustration is to the child's experiences or reality, the more directly related the story or illustration is to the child and the retention rate increases accordingly.

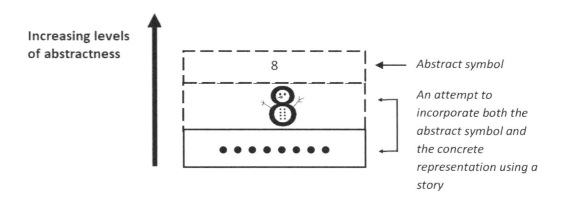

Increasing levels of abstractness

8 ← *Abstract symbol*

An attempt to incorporate both the abstract symbol and the concrete representation using a story

However, there are students who reject all stories or visuals as a form of explanation. They want logical explanations. Stories and visuals seem like a 'farce'.

An ex-student of mine had very low receptivity to abstract concepts that did not have a logical explanation. At the age of 6, she could not understand why '1+1+=2'. It took her six years to accept it. At the age of 17, she could not remember mathematical formulas, chemistry symbols or equations. She went through a tough time and was not able to cope with her national exams.

- **2nd component: Extremely clear definition of words / concepts**

At 10 years old, a student of mine read the word 'ride' as 'drive'. He also read the word 'pond' as 'lake', 'sea' or the name of any large body of water that he can remember. He would also be unable to read other words of similar meanings.

Individuals – like my student – who have very low receptivity to abstract information require very clear definition of what a word means. Certain words have similar meanings which may cause confusion among people who have difficulty in determining the distinction between the words.

Let's take the words 'water' and 'pond' for example.

water

pond= stores small to large bodies of water

The student understands that the word 'pond' is a place that stores a body of water. The word describes smaller bodies of water like the school pond to larger bodies of water like ponds at the national parks. The distinction is clearly made. The student sees the word 'water' and reads it as /water/. The student sees the word 'pond' and reads it as /pond/.

The problem arises when another word 'lake' with a meaning similar to the word 'pond' emerges. Where is the distinction? Sure, there may be subtle differences to the words in terms of size but how large should a body of water be before we start considering it to be a 'lake' instead of a pond? There is simply no clear and simple visual distinction between the words.

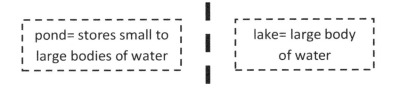

As such, the student experiences confusion. In some cases, the students are able to sound out the word 'lake' and read it as /lake/ while being perpetually confused about its meaning. There are other cases where the students look at the word 'lake' in confusion and are unable to read it despite much exposure to the printed word. Then, there are those who look at the word 'lake' and read it as /pond/.

In all cases, the spelling of the word 'lake' and 'pond' are affected due to the lack of thorough understanding of the words. The students will either be struggling to read or spell the word 'lake' despite much guidance or not be able to recognise the word at all.

Thereafter, other words like 'sea' and 'ocean' that describe large bodies of water may surface. An attempt at explaining the word 'sea' may entail descriptions such as an extremely large body of water with a sandy beach. This description will be acceptable to students who frequent the seaside. However, students who have visited lakes with sandy beaches will dispute this claim.

Coupled it with a student who cannot tolerate any sort of ambiguity – those who require simplified yet precise real-world word distinctions – and the teacher will have a ball of confusion on his or her hands. In the worst-case scenario, the student will either be unable to recognise any word or will read the words 'lake', 'sea' and 'ocean' as /pond/.

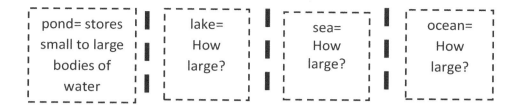

The same is true for a homonym (the same word with multiple meanings). For instance, the word 'flat' has two commonly accepted meanings.

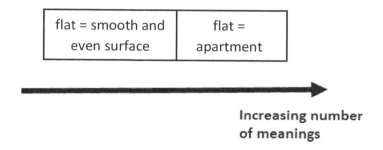

Both definitions are clear and distinct. In addition, both are concrete representations of reality. The student should be able to accept both definitions.

However, for homonyms like the word 'pound', students may understand that 'pound' refers to beating or boxing something repeatedly with great force. An instance would be when they see someone using a meat pounder to tenderise the meat by pounding repeatedly with great force. (Then again, that is assuming that students are aware and are able to accept of the distinctions between 'beat', 'hit' and 'pound'.) However, struggling students may not accept its more abstract meaning as a unit of measurement.

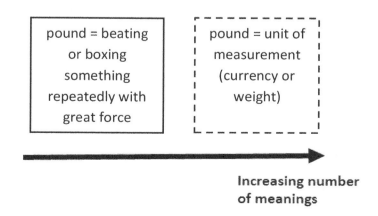

o   *Why does this matter?*

You may ask, "So what if the students don't get the meaning of words? That's vocabulary. I am teaching literacy. I can focus on word recognition and spelling first before the vocabulary sets in. Vocabulary takes a while to develop anyway."

This is indeed true for typically-developing students. They can easily remember a new concept or new word even if they do not fully understand it. They can tolerate ambiguity and are receptive to abstract information. By repeating – or memorising – something that they do not understand initially, the abstract information just "sinks in" and they are able to retain it for sustained period of time regardless of their level of understanding.

Students with dyslexia who respond very well to phonics intervention also display similar learning behaviour. While they need to understand that words are constructed from sounds, they are highly receptive to the abstract concept that each letter or phonogram contains a sound.

They break down the word into individual sounds before reading the word. Thereafter, they are taught the meaning of the word. The subsequent repetition of the word and its meaning cements the word into the students' brains. As such, there is this belief of literacy first before vocabulary – while vocabulary is important, students with dyslexia are able to learn how to read the printed word using phonics before or alongside vocabulary acquisition.

Nonresponders do not have such luxuries.

I will have to disclaim that not all nonresponders have issues with the language domain.

However, nonresponders who have issues with it most probably have a particular strand of language impairment. As there are many strands of language impairment, I usually informally term this particular strand as "the-world-exists-in-black-and-white-not-grey" language impairment.

[There are definitely many students with mild dyslexia who have this strand of language impairment without experiencing any literacy issues. However, one of the focus of this book is on nonresponders whose literacy acquisition are affected due to this strand of language impairment.]

Under the language domain, what the nonresponder struggles with is not merely the inability to acquire vocabulary easily. Rather, it is the pervasion of perpetual confusion due to the inability to make meaning of their world.

The world is grey as it is filled with overlapping meanings, inferences and nuances. It is so confusing to them. In order to survive in this world of perpetual confusion, nonresponders with this strand of language impairment demand that the world exists in black and white. Everything that they understand must be physically and visually represented in the real world with extremely clear and simple definitions that leaves no room for ambiguity. Otherwise, they will "shut down".

Such students demand the following:

1) *Words must have clearly defined categories. There should not be overlaps in the meaning of words.*

For instance, students are taught that the word 'many' is meant for countable things while the word 'much' is meant for uncountable things. In a bid to promote understanding among the students, examples are cited.

Hair is uncountable as it takes too much effort to count them – hence the phrase "so much hair". On the other hand, the things on a table – however messy it is – can be counted. As such, there exists the phrase "so many things".

Such instruction, however, does not alleviate confusion among some students. There is no clearly defined boundary between the words 'many' and 'much'. In other words, there are still overlaps in the meaning of 'many' and 'much'. Students who are confused may ask:

"Why can't it be 'so many hair'? You can count hair. All you just need to do is invest effort. What does it mean by too much effort? Exactly how effort is considered to be 'too much effort'?"

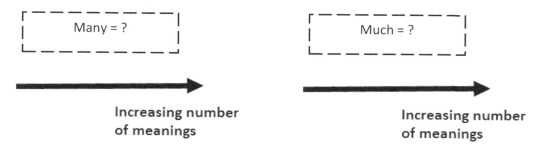

In order to alleviate confusion and start constructing meaning, the teacher has to state a rule to clearly separate the meaning of both words.

"If you are unable to finish counting anything in 10 minutes, it becomes uncountable."

There will definitely be points of contention when it comes to any attempt at imposing a defined boundary on abstract terminologies. That being said, a fixed unit of measure establishes clear definitions and boundaries between the two terms.

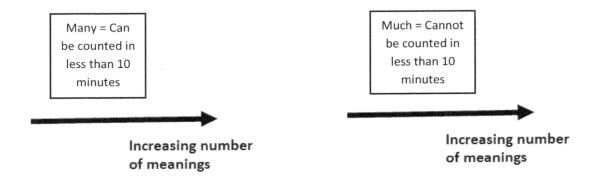

Many = Can be counted in less than 10 minutes

Much = Cannot be counted in less than 10 minutes

Increasing number of meanings

Increasing number of meanings

2) *Words must be literal and its meaning must be straightforward (Jargons are not straight forward)*

The second reason as to why certain individuals are unable to accept the multiple meanings of a word is because some meanings are more abstract in nature and are not directly representing of their reality.

Let me provide another real-life example. A student understood the word 'race' to be 'competitive running'. However, he did not understand that the term race also meant a group of people sharing the same culture and language.

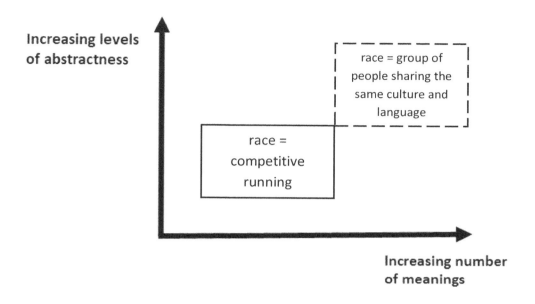

Increasing levels of abstractness

race = group of people sharing the same culture and language

race = competitive running

Increasing number of meanings

While there is marked progress in viewing different 'races' (or "ethnic groups") according to different cultures, societal stereotypes persist in attaching the concept 'race' to a person's skin colour. However, colour was not a good distinction for the student as he found that even people within the same 'race' came in different shades of colours. In addition, he was confused as there was no fixed definition and boundaries using a person's skin colour to determine the distinction between, for instance, a Japanese and Korean.

He attempted to use spoken language as a form of distinction between people of different races. He argues that when a Chinese only speak English, said Chinese should not be a 'Chinese' but a 'Caucasian'. As such, all purely English-speaking people are 'Caucasians' while purely Mandarin-speaking people are 'Chinese'. His attempt to create clear definitions and distinctions opened another can of worms.

3) *The world has no grey area – only black and white. Situations are only either right or wrong. There is no in between.*

Not all individuals who require clearly defined boundaries for abstract terms view their world in absolute terms. However, for individuals who do perceive their world as such, they are known as the more extreme cases whose need for clearly defined boundaries extends not only to abstract terms in learning but their entire world view as well.

Once, I wore stockings to class. My thirteen-year-old student was intrigued as it was the first time that he saw a person wearing stockings. Upon enquiry, he learnt that I wore stockings with a skirt for that day because all my pants were in the wash.

That established his definition for me. When I wore stockings from then on, he would always assume that all my pants were in the wash. This notion persisted regardless of my explanation that I also wore stockings for aesthetic purposes.

That inability to understand grey areas would, of course, spread to more abstract, real world concepts.

He could not get his head around the concept of mercy killing. From his perspective, ending a life is killing, and killing is bad. Using highly relatable and publicised examples from the medical world, I spent half an hour going through concepts of suffering and he agreed that sometimes, putting people out of their misery is an act of kindness. He nodded sagely after that half an hour and went, "But isn't killing bad?"

In another real-world example, albeit a more serious case of "the-world-is-black-and-white", a fourteen-year-old girl read in the newspaper about isolated incidents of theft and outrage of modesty committed by a maid and a construction worker respectively. She started despairing that her personal security was in serious danger, that she could not trust any maids or construction worker in future.

She could not understand that the behaviour of one person did not represent the entire group. As she also had what I strongly suspected to be pragmatics impairment, that despair resulted in an even more inappropriate body language, expressions and gaze. Merely thinking about that isolated incident would cause her entire body language to radiate fear, her expression to become distrustful and panicked, and her body fraught with tension as if she was going to hightail out of the school.

- *Repercussions from the lack of understanding (underdeveloped language domain)*

So what is the deal with 'understanding'? Don't people just remember things that they do not understand? So what if they do not understand? They should just accept it and move on with their learning.

When a person can just accept and remember a term or concept without much understanding, that person's receptivity towards abstract concepts is high.

However, people with low levels of receptivity towards abstract concepts are unable to accept this state of confusion. More importantly, the inability to understand could arrest a person's cognitive facilities. Such effects of confusion – Ron Davis terms it as 'disorientation' – manifest in different ways and intensities.

Here are some real-life examples of the mild, intermediate and severe levels of confusion that have manifested in different people.

Mild

I consider myself to have some mild receptive language problem. This problem ends up causing many misunderstandings with other people throughout the course of my life.

One of the misunderstandings centred on the most mundane of things – bowls and plates.

In my mind, I have clearly defined meanings of what I attach to plates and bowls. Plates hold rice and noodles while the bowls hold soups. It is the physical structure of both bowls and plates that affirms my reality. After all, a plate looks structurally unsound to hold liquids. As compared to plates, bowls are suitable as the sides of the bowls are raised significantly. I linked the definitions of the plate and the bowl to their physical properties.

While preparing for dinner one day, my mother said, "Get me the bowl to put my rice."

I have known for more than twenty years that my mother prefers a bowl to hold her rice. But time and again, my cognitive processing would stall as I paused all of a sudden and doubted her desired utensils.

You know that it is a receptive language disorder – albeit mild – when such a mundane thing made me pause.

I kept staring at the bowl and plate. On one hand, somewhere in the distant part of my mind, I knew that my mother uses the bowl to put her rice. But my reality (language concept) dictated that a plate was for rice and a bowl was for soup. While the physical structure of the bowl is structurally sound to hold rice as well, my brain – at that abrupt moment – decided that the world (or rather, utensils) existed in absolutes, in black and white.

At that moment, I did not – could not – accept the crossing of functions between the plates and bowls. At that moment, my brain was unable to accept that a bowl was able to hold both rice and soup.

My mother's preference of using the bowl to hold rice challenged my reality. It compelled me to think that perhaps, my mother meant the plate instead.

I was stuck in a dilemma. On one hand, my mother could not stand 'stupidity'. Asking her a question to confirm her preferred utensils even after staying the same house for more than twenty years was certainly the catalyst for her tirade about my 'stupidity'. On the other hand, if I chose not ask, this utterly awful feeling of uncertainty and confusion would continue to overwhelm me and it was a horrible, horrible feeling.

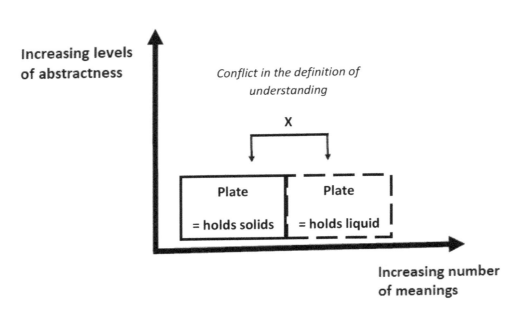

You may ask, "Why don't you just grab anything – be it a plate or a bowl – and present it to your mum? Just don't think and grab something randomly."

I just could not force myself to grab something. This indecision of a seemingly mundane thing just stalled my decision-making capabilities there and then. I could not just randomly grab one of it and shove it towards my mother, hoping that it was correct. I *had* to know so that there and then, my understanding of my reality – or what is reality – is affirmed.

In the end, I decided to just *check*. Enduring another tirade of hers was a good exchange for getting rid of that awful feeling of uncertainty.

I asked. Tirade triggered. Indecision dissipated.

Plate for rice. Bowl for soup. Mum is exception. Affirmed my understanding of reality.

I established clear distinctions.

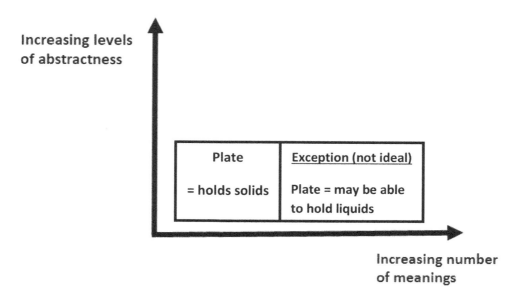

In my defense, I do not have this problem every mealtime. I am largely okay with remembering this exception in my world. However, when I have not been helping out in the kitchen for a long time, I tend to forget about this exception. As such, I am faced with my dilemma again every time I resurface in the kitchen after a period of absence.

This is why I consider myself to be a mild case. I can get over it (and can accept exceptions readily) but from time to time, I have to remind myself lest I revert back to my old ways. It is just like going for therapy to remind myself the right way of doing things but when I stop my therapy for awhile, I tend to 'forget'.

Another misunderstanding occurred over the lever tap in my bathroom.

This tap controlled the volume of water that was directed to the toilet bowl. Turning on or off the tap would restrict the volume of water accordingly.

One day, my mother asked me, "Did you close or open the tap?

I did not understand what she meant. I would have understood if she said 'turned on' or 'turned off' the tap. At that moment, the word 'open' signalled the dismantling of the water pipe in order to look at the interior. It was illogical.

I hate it when words are not specific in meaning because I get easily confused. When that occurs, my attempt to alleviate that confusion usually backfires as the things that I say there and then do not make much sense.

As such, I asked her if she meant that the water was flowing through the tap or not. In attempt to provide more detail to aid understanding, I even told her the direction that the lever handle was facing.

You can imagine how her reaction was like.

Moderate

Once, I had a student, Sheryl, who needed extremely clear boundaries to function. In addition, she needed to understand everything and was unable to remember anything that she could not understand. Exceptions were the bane of her life and it took her a herculean amount of effort to move on. For instance, it took her six years to accept – not understand – that $1 + 1 = 2$. Even then, the confusion that persisted due to the lack of understanding had widespread repercussions to her processing speed, decision making skills and academic performance.

Not only was Sheryl unable to remember formulas and symbols, she also constantly struggled with the ambiguous and abstract words in her academics. This was especially apparent when she attempted her Chemistry experiments.

Sheryl always failed her Chemistry experiments. She would spend the entire hour reading just the first paragraph of the question paper. It was not because she did not know how to conduct the experiments. Rather, she could not move on due to the ambiguous and abstract words in the question.

"Heat the test tube for **about** one minute."

She constantly lamented about the meaning of 'about'? Is it 1.01 minute? 59 seconds? 59.3 seconds? It threw her world out of the loop. She could not move on. Her reality was being threatened.

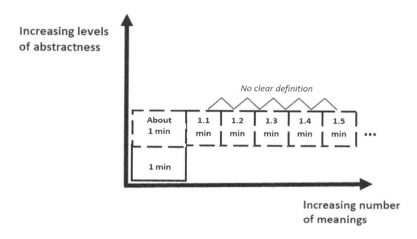

The story took a pretty dramatic turn. The contents of her test tube were boiling madly and Sheryl's classmates were pretty alarmed. They started to yell at her as the situation looked really dangerous, demanding that she should stop heating the test tube that very instant. However, Sheryl refused to stop heating it and she yelled back at them that she had to continue heating because "the question said about one minute" – all while being utterly confused as to what exactly constituted "about one minute". The definition was not clear and in that state of confusion, she persisted with heating.

As such, the contents of the test tube exploded onto her classmate.

Even when Sheryl knew that it was dangerous, she still went ahead with heating the test tube. She was compelled to rid herself of the confusion despite the apparent danger.

Severe

One of my students, 10-year-old Sean then, entered the school with severe levels of confusion. For me, I had trouble dealing with concrete objects or actions that were not specific to its function or had overlapping function. Sheryl's confusion – triggered by an incredibly wide range of vague and abstract terms, and her desire to gain thorough understanding of everything – overrode her sense of well-being. However, both of us were aware of the confusion that was surfacing and thus tried to engage in futile attempts to mitigate the confusion.

In contrast, individuals with severe levels of confusion do not know that they are confused about the basic properties, characteristics or functions of concrete objects or actions.

Severe levels of confusion come in various forms. In Sean's case, his confusion was already apparent the moment he started speaking.

In an effort to bolster his confidence, I asked him to explain to me how he was able to remember "so many things". His reply was as such:

"This one go to my neck and the smart one is in the neck. But I switch it. I can remember anything, but under here [below his neck] is nothing – no smart thing. It's all our lungs and here are say things one right? I got two things. Say …and play – watch movie over here and everything is here. Another one is do everything. The 'do' one is in my neck and play is in my brain. Test, I switch it [exchanging the places of 'doing' and 'playing']."

The audio recording stretches for another few minutes and it never fails to make any Speech and Language Therapist that I have met intrigued. This is a textbook case of severe language impairment but let us just focus on conceptual confusion.

Sean had wrong language concepts and he was not aware of it. He did not understand how information was stored and retrieved in the human body. In fact, he was confused over the function of a brain and a neck. However, Sean still explained with much confidence about his ability to remember information.

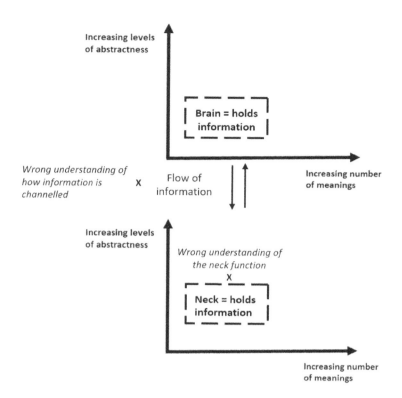

○ **Note**

Sometimes, confusion persists. Other times, confusion is momentarily. Sheryl and Sean's confusion persisted. My confusion, on the other hand, was momentary. When I think back about those moments of confusion, I have no idea why I was confused in the first place. It was at that point in time that I had a fleeting moment of confusion.

However, the duration of confusion is not the only determiner of its severity. The frequency of confusion is also another important determiner.

At the age of 13, one of my students had fleeting moments of confusion. However, he had frequent moments of fleeting confusion as he got triggered by anything that he did not understand. Science questions were a minefield of triggers and he frequently got confused just by looking at the illustrations or reading a sentence.

For instance, he was presented the following science question:

"What is the body of the fish covered with?"

With much concentration and focus, he wrote the following:

"The body of the fish is covered with feathers."

Upon reading his answer, I covered his written answer and proceeded to verbally repeat the question. This time, he replied, "The body of the fish is covered with scales."

I asked him why he wrote such a strange answer and he gave me a blank look as he was also unable to comprehend why he had written such an answer.

Unlike Sean, Ron goes in and out of confusion frequently.

Like Sean, Ron's degree of confusion is severe as he was confused over the basic characteristic of a fish.

Like Sean, Ron – amid confusion – thought that his written response was correct.

o   ***The trouble with understanding the link between language and literacy acquisition***

Many teachers are unable to understand how language has a direct impact on literacy acquisition due to several reasons:

(1) The diversity of students with special learning needs does not match the teachers' homogeneous perception of learning. Literacy acquisition (learning how to read and spell) and language acquisition are kept in dichotomies as the former is deemed as a basic skill while the latter is deemed as a higher-level skill that deals with curriculum and testing.

(2) Many teachers have high levels of receptivity towards abstract concepts. Such teachers are able to remember information even if it does not make sense to them. Thus, such teachers may feel that even if the students do not understand what they are being taught, the students can be taught to remember the abstract information first before understanding sets in overtime with more exposure. Such is the basis of more mechanical ways of instruction like drilling and repetition.

(3) A lot of students who have language impairment may misunderstand the world but are still able to read and write. Reality provides many examples:

Two students may fail to respond to literacy intervention but only one grapples with language impairment. Then, another student with a diagnosis of language impairment is able to respond to phonics intervention very well. Among the nonresponders, vastly diverse behaviour characteristics and error patterns are observed. The teacher will be confused. As such, his or her understanding of what language impairment and nonresponding behaviour becomes murkier.

This is why the teacher should not attempt to dichotomise the students' learning needs between language and literacy. Instead, the teacher should measure the learning needs according to a universal yardstick of a student's receptivity towards abstract concepts.

2. SENSORIAL (PERCEPTUAL) DOMAIN

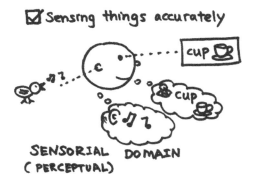

The ability to perceive our reality accurately is of prime importance for the proper daily functioning of an individual – and this includes accurate literacy acquisition. It is important to see and hear clearly and accurately.

- **1st component: Processing visual information**

It is common for students – both phonics responding and nonresponders – to complain about sensory related issues (especially those that are related to visual processing). Such affected regions result in an inexhaustive list of visual and other sensory processing related complaints:

- Symptoms of visual stress (e.g. word animation, blurring, eye irritation)

- Auditory processing issues (yes, auditory processing issues)

- Hyper or hypo sensitivity to external stimulation (e.g. light and sound)

- Copying errors

- Visual spatial problems (e.g. inability to judge distance)

- Figure-ground problems

- Inability to visualise [leading to all sorts of executing functioning problems related to planning and execution]

- Inability to remember the sequence of letters in a word correctly (e.g. Able to remember the letters in a word but not how they are positioned in a word)

- Inability to remember how the words are read or spelt [even if they have seen the same word seconds ago]

- Perceiving words of the same colour (especially black) as an incomprehensible blob of ink

- Complaints relating to peripheral and eccentric gaze

  - Students who have a wider field of vision may get distracted by information in their periphery. For instance, they may be distracted by the first and third sentences in a passage when they are reading the second sentence. They may also be distracted by letters in other words when they read laterally.

There are number of reasons why such symptoms occur:

- Both eyes are unable to synchronise properly (eye tracking and teaming)

- The lenses in the eyes are unable to change its shape effortlessly between near and distant objects (accommodation).

- There is an imbalance between the peripheral and central vision. Too much emphasis is placed on the clarity of an object (central vision) at the expense of the detection of motion and subconscious visual processing (peripheral vision). This is especially so when the student has existing undetected problems with their peripheral vision but the optometrist keeps emphasising the central vision by prescribing thicker and thicker lenses that only gives the students a headache.

- Retina receptors are affected – information through light becomes distorted and information to the brain is also subsequently corrupted

- Visual pathways from the eye to the visual processing parts of the brain are affected.

These symptoms and reasons adversely impact a student's literacy acquisition. With regards to understanding the literacy acquisition of nonresponders however, the concept of visual span proves to be of prime importance.

- *Visual span*

Visual span is the length of the word that a student is able to remember effortlessly without external aids like colours, pictures and stories to promote word retention. Typically-developing students or phonics responders with developed orthographic processing abilities have very wide visual spans. They literally look at a single-syllable for a couple of times before they are usually able to remember the word regardless of the length. According to my observations, the 'sweet spot' for *most* nonresponders is three letters (e.g. put, pot). Four letter words (e.g. most, bend, trip) are also acceptable to *most* nonresponders after a certain age. I am emphasising the word 'most' because students with a certain strand of language impairment are only receptive to words with distinct word meanings. The length of the word is not their primary problem.

- **2nd component: Processing auditory information**

Some students may pass their hearing test but are unable to listen to sounds the way that society expects them to hear. Their brains process auditory information atypically and thus interprets information inaccurately. Other students have certain auditory processing disorders that does not allow them to discern sounds clearly.

Once, I had an experience that was similar to the inability to discern sounds clearly.

I know this will sound very gross. I added too much ear oil into my ear years ago, which resulted in the backflow of ear wax towards my ear drums. It nearly sealed off most of the sounds that I could hear.

Everything sounded the same – muffled and soft. When someone was talking to me, I could only look at their lips and made futile guesses whatever they were trying to say. Regardless of the number of times I had my colleagues to repeat the letters, I could not discern the letters 'b', 'd', 'p'. Letters 'm' and 'n' sounded the same as well. I could not hear the letters that made softer sounds – 'p', 'f', 'h', 't'. I could not even hear the last sound or last few sounds of the words. If someone said the word 'band' when I was looking at their lips, the most I could discern was /ba/ or /pa/.

As such, my ability to figure out what was being said via auditory means was extremely low. I had to frequently get the context of the situation and guess the word that was mentioned. Even then, when I said the word out loud, it sounded like the homogeneous, muffled mess that was every other word.

My experience is similar to individuals who have auditory processing issues.

It was through this experience that I learnt an important lesson. Phonics instruction is only effective for students who do not have auditory processing issues. Should a student have mild auditory processing issues (e.g. unable to distinguish between 'b' and 'd'), sound discrimination and phonemic awareness interventions are useful compliments to the phonics intervention that the student is receiving.

However, there are some students whose auditory processing problems are more extensive. For instance, extensive auditory processing problems could come in the form of the student complaining about auditorily similar letters and words. This is when it becomes counterproductive to use any sound-based training to teach the student as it causes fatigue and confusion to build up exponentially. For such students, the purpose of sound-based training is only to train them in discriminating sounds marginally better than before. Literacy acquisition has to be sight-based. You cannot use phonics and hope that the student will be able to make much literacy gains using a method that focuses on his or her weakness.

○ **Note**

What if a student has both visual and auditory-processing disorder? That is the worst-case scenario. (Technically, the worst-case scenario is already triggered when a student has very severe visual processing disorder.) The student will not experience any literacy gains.

3. SENSORIAL (STORAGE) DOMAIN

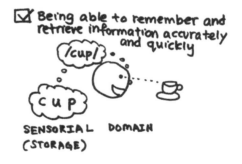

● **1st component: The thing about memory**

The thing about memory is that very vague terms that are thrown around in attempt to describe why students with dyslexia – or any other special learning needs – are unable to remember certain types of information. The psychological report may indicate that the student has very poor working memory. But what does that even mean? It does not help that the report is flooded with other numbers and jammed packed with jargons like "forward digit span" or 'WISC' that does not seem to make much sense.

Parents may exclaim in bewilderment – or frustration – at their children's queer memory. Their children are unable to remember 'simple' things (e.g. bringing along his books, washing the dishes) but are able to remember life events that have occurred many years ago regardless of its significance. It may seem so insignificant (e.g. "When I was in preschool, I dropped my ice-cream cone along that pavement.") and the parents have no idea why such 'meaningless' events are remembered but not 'simple' things like bringing their clothes to the wash.

- *Long-term memory and short-term memory*

There are two routes to channeling information into a person's long-term memory. Information can be channeled either by (1) understanding or (2) repetition.

o Information that is meaningful and understandable goes straight into the long-term memory.

o Information that is abstract and not readily understandable is stored in the short-term memory. With constant repetition, the information gets transferred into the long-term memory.

   - Typically-developing individuals will mistakenly assume that this process is called understanding. That is incorrect. The ability to remember repeated actions or information without the need for justification or in-depth explanation is not called understanding.

Ideally, we should be acquiring information by understanding in order to store important information into our long-term memory. In reality, we do not always have that luxury to understand everything around us because we simply do not have that much time. As such, we have another way of remembering information – using our short-term memory. With enough exposure (repetition), the information transfers into the long-term memory. This means that even if typically-developing individuals do not understand the information that is presented to them, that information will be remembered for a longer period of time with enough repetition.

However, students with learning difficulties have poorer short-term memories. As such, their long-term memory becomes their relative strength as compared to their short-term memory 'weakness'. They would often prefer to rely on their long-term memory to remember information. This explains why they seem to remember personal events that occurred long ago but are 'forgetful' about mundane, everyday things. If the short-term memory 'weakness' is not significant, the student still has both routes of the long-term memory that are made available to them. The student is still receptive to concepts and approaches that are more abstract in nature. In addition, the student will be receptive towards even more practice and repetition – that is characteristic of many intervention approaches for students with learning difficulties – to bridge the gap in their short-term memory 'weakness'.

Students whose short-term memory is significantly poorer than their long-term memory are unable to utilise the route to the long-term memory via the short-term memory. Regardless of the repetition and reinforcements, their short-term memory is not enough to hold the abstract information long enough for the repetition to set in. Simply put, to invest such a large amount of effort to ensure the translation of that bit of abstract information into the long-term memory is not only inefficient but ineffective as well. The students will make very little progress as they are either unable remember the information or able to merely remember the information mechanically without knowledge on application. Only the long-term memory route – understanding for information retention – is available to the student.

- **Working memory**

Many students with learning difficulties learn by understanding. It is a necessity for these students to understand information. Not only do they want to understand, they also desire to have a part in creating information. Memorising or remembering anything without understanding will only trigger confusion. Most of the time, information that has no meaning gets dumped out of the brain instantly. Their short-term memory is not comparable to their typically-developing peers.

Working memory is a person's super short-term memory. It is short-term memory to the short-term memory. It is like the RAM of a computer that is in charge of holding abstract information long enough (ranging from seconds to minutes) to free up cognitive resources to work and analyse such information. It is utilised all the time. For instance, we utilise it in attempt to remember a telephone number when we do not have anything to record the number on. We also use it when we attempt to remember a series of items that we would like to order from the menu. Psychologists often attempt to stretch the limits of their clients' working memory by, among other tests, getting them to recite a string of numbers forward and backward.

The working memory is usually one of the first to be sacrificed in individuals with chronic or neurological illnesses. Students with learning difficulties may also have compromised working memory. For those whose working memory are intact or just slightly compromised, handling abstract information like phonics is not much of a problem.

However, the poorer the working memory, the lower the students' receptivity to abstract information and by extension, phonics. Phonics is a highly abstract system and it requires an avenue to manipulate many abstract sounds, rules and sequences simultaneously. That is a nightmare for students with poor working memory.

- **"Sight memory" and orthographic memory**

The words "sight memory" gets thrown around freely.

"The student uses his sight memory to remember."

"It's ok if he doesn't use phonics. He uses his sight memory anyway."

So what exactly is "sight memory"?

It is a generic term to describe an individual's ability to remember how to read and spell the word after seeing it for a few times. In essence, phonics instruction is carried out with the assumption that the student has enough "sight memory" to support him or her. Phonics instruction is a method to aid beginners in understanding the formation of the word. However, solely relying on phonics is neither an effective nor efficient approach to building an individual's long-term literacy competence. If there is only reliance on phonics, spelling inaccuracies will surface as a result (e.g. 'bread' can be spelt as 'bred' or 'brad'). In addition, the student will spend more time sounding out each sound and it affects the efficiency of reading and spelling each word. That is why phonics instruction works on the assumption that the student can wean off phonics eventually. It is assumed that the student's "sight memory" takes over as he or she progresses towards being more proficient in reading and spelling.

The technical name for "sight memory" is actually known as "orthographic memory". It is the ability to recognise word forms – the ability to determine what is a real word and non-real word (e.g. 'tail' vs 'tial; 'school' vs 'skool'; 'meet' vs 'mit') and the associated patterns of words (e.g. letters 'm' and 'k' can never be placed together – there is no such word as 'mkae'). Orthographic memory is an exceedingly important aspect of literacy acquisition.

The macron has 'longer' contact point.   *The breve has a 'shorter' contact point.*

That was why, she declared with the satisfaction of someone who had finally saw the light, short and long vowels are termed as such.

I was just exasperated that she was spending so much brain energy on a jargon that could have been easily replaced with another word that has more direct meaning. Such a colossal waste of her time.

Model: Progressively simplified mode of instruction

Tiers of increasingly simplified mode of instruction for low functioning phonics responders / non-readers receptive to phonics

Typical mode of instruction	MINIMISE THE USAGE OF JARGONS			
1) Phonemic Awareness:			**Universal simplification**	
• Blending • Segmenting	Interchangeable		*Use of visuals and stories for each word (for meaning making) to increase automaticity and retention over time.*	
2) Consonants and vowels				
3) CVC	**One step simplification**	**Two step simplification**	**Onset-rime colour-coding in word families**	
4) Beginning blends: CCVC double blends	*Explicit onset and rime instruction*	Word families		
• 'l' blends – bl, cl, fl, gl,pl,sl	e.g. s ip	e.g. –ip family	e.g. –ip family	
• 'r' blends – br, cr, fr.gr,pr,tr	cr ab	sip	sip sip	NONREPONDERS TERRITORY
• Other blends – sw, tw, squ	cl am	lip	lip lip	
4) CCCVC triple blends	gr ub	hip	hip hip	
• spl, scr, str	sl um	nip	nip nip	
5) CVCC / CCVCC ending blends	sw im	rip	rip rip	
• -ft, -nt, -nd, -mp, -lt	str ap	flip	flip flip	
(except –pt & -ct)	squ id	clip	clip clip	
		slip	slip slip	
		grip	grip grip	
		drip	drip drip	
		trip	trip trip	
		strip	strip strip	

The above model summaries the different tiers of increasingly simplified mode of instruction for lower-functioning phonics responders or non-readers who are receptive to phonics intervention.

Typical mode of instruction

- **Phonemic awareness**

When a child is at the beginning stages of literacy, the teacher is supposed to introduce blending and segmenting activities as a pre-primer to phonics instruction. Blending activities teach a student that sounds of letters come together to form a word during reading (e.g. /g/ /r/ /a/ /b/ = /grab/).

Segmenting teaches the student that a word is able to be broken up into individual sounds in order for the students to spell the word.

The following concepts are presented in order for the student to be equipped with the most basic of phonics tools to form more basic words that do not have much spelling complexity:

- Consonants (C) and vowels (V)

    Vowels (V) – a , e, i , o, u – are introduced. This is followed by consonants (C) [letters that are not vowels].

Thereafter, the simplest of phonetically-regular words are introduced first.

- CVC [Consonant – vowel – consonant]

    - Examples: cat, hug, pen, hop

    Beginning blends

- CCVC [Consonant – consonant – vowel – consonant]

    The initial two consonants have a fixed set of patterns. They are presented as 'l' blends, 'r' blends and other double blends. (Please refer to the model.)

    - Examples: drag, skip, step, drug

- CCCVC [Consonant – consonant – consonant - vowel – consonant]

  The initial three consonants have a fixed set of patterns. They are presented as triple blends. (Please refer to the model.)

  - Examples: strip, scram

Ending blends

- CVCC [Consonant - vowel – consonant - consonant]

  Now, attention is paid to the back of the word. The last two consonants have a fixed set of patterns. They are presented as ending blends. (Please refer to the model for the blends.)

  - Examples: jump, lift, sand, mint

- CCVCC [Consonant - consonant - vowel – consonant - consonant]

  Now, the double blends are incorporated with the ending blends.

  - Examples: stand, stamp, blunt

- CCCVCC [Consonant - consonant – consonant - vowel – consonant - consonant]

  - Example: strand, sprint

  Lastly, the triple blends are incorporated with the ending blends.

Simplification of instruction

Should a student fail to respond to typical instruction, the teacher or educational therapist should progressively simplify their instruction. The following points demonstrates the progressive steps of simplification:

1. Universal simplification

If a student is unable to respond to such instruction, the teacher should actively attempt to simplify the jargon used in the instruction, shorten the rules or convert abstract and technical-sounding rules into stories.

2. One-step simplification: Explicit onset and rime instruction

Instead of breaking the word into individual sounds, the word should be segmented into onset and rime. Onset and rime ensures that there are only two auditory chunks for the student to remember. This is preferred to the segmentation of the individual sounds that will overwhelm the students' memory.

When breaking a word into individual sounds take too much time

It is fine to break the word up into individual sounds if the student is in grade 1 or 2 as there is an expectation that they will increase in their reading speed of words instantly in time to come. If the student is much older, say grade 6 for instance, such laborious reading is not going to be effective for the student. This is especially so when the student is delayed in his or her reading by so many years. What the student needs is a more efficient way of reading and spelling as many words as possible in the shortest amount of time. Spending anything more than a split second to read each word is too time consuming.

It will be worse if the student spends a lifetime to decode the word, only to read it wrongly.

15 seconds later

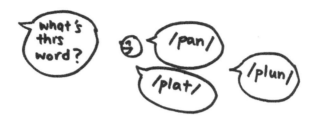

Reading the word wrongly after taking a long time to decode

3. Two-step simplification: Word families

In order to ease the load on the working memory even further and ensure the ease of retention, words should be presented as word families. This is to allow the back of the word (the rime) to stay consistent as the initial blend changes. This way, the student is able to free up more working memory to tackle reading and spelling as they are able to see the pattern between the words.

○ *Note*

Most nonresponders do not see such patterns. If left to their own devices, they are likely to remember many words in isolation with relatively little association between each word in the word family.)

4. Final round of simplification: Colour coding onset and rime in word families

This is the last line of defence to classify the child as a partial phonics responder. Even after onset and rime instruction, alongside with ensuring that the words are presented as a pattern as word families, the student still draws a blank and word reading is still laborious.

The student may have some form of visual perceptual issue. They may view the words as a whole mash of black ink or the student may have no idea where to 'cut' the word.

They may be able to blend 2 letters together...

but they may not be able to discern that 'pl' is in a word due to visual perceptual issues.

They cannot tell what the pattern is as they require colours to differentiate between onset and rime.

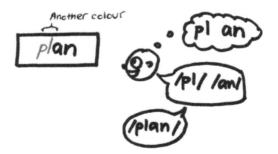

They can read the word if the word is colour-coded.

If the student does not meet the last line of defence (the final round of simplification), then welcome to the world of nonresponders.

CHAPTER 2B

TYPES OF NONRESPONDERS AND THEIR ASSOCIATED CHARACTERISTICS

COMPARING RESPONDERS AND NONRESPONDERS

Phonics nonresponders

Phonics responders

LEVEL OF LITERACY ABILITY

RECEPTIVITY TO ABSTRACT CONCEPTS

High functioning
sight word
readers

High functioning
phonics
responders

Mid-functioning
phonics
responders

Type A.1 – Partial
Able to segment
sounds till CCVC level
competently
Type A.2
Strong visual
(picture) memory

Type B
Adequate reading
ability, but low
spelling competence

Type B
Very low levels of
reading and spelling
competence

Low functioning
phonics
responders

Type X

Type Y

* A non-reader is defined as a
student who is unable to read or
spell almost any word due to lack
of prior instruction or exposure.

Non-reader

PROPOSED TYPES OF NONRESPONDERS
(according to breakdown in single-syllable words)

Highest rates of spelling accuracy ← → Lowest rates of spelling accuracy

A	B	X	Y
A.1 *Phonics receptivity:* • Able to utilise phonics to ensure high spelling accuracy till the CCVC word level • Uses their strong visual memory to remember words beyond CCVC *High frequency words:* • Reads and spell most words on the list **A.2** *Phonics receptivity:* • Low / No receptivity to phonics • Solely relies on their visual memory to achieves high of spelling accuracy *High frequency words:* • Spelling accuracy of words on the list is not as high as reading accuracy	*Phonics receptivity:* • No receptivity to phonics • Solely relies on their visual memory • Exhibits high spelling accuracy and word retention with words that contain real-word rimes • Demonstrates poor receptivity in recalling words with non-word rimes **Example of real-word rimes**: fl <u>at</u>, sl <u>am</u>, pl <u>an</u>, gr <u>in</u> **Example of non-word rimes**: fl <u>ap</u>, st <u>ab</u>, gr <u>ip</u>, sl <u>um</u> *High frequency words:* • Spelling accuracy of words on the list is not as high as reading accuracy • Requires type X and Y high frequency word intervention	*Phonics receptivity:* • Extremely low / No receptivity to phonics *High frequency words:* • Unable to accurately read and spell most words on the list (primer) *Characteristics:* • Heterogeneous group of individuals with distinct learning needs and difficulties • Shows signs of co-morbidities that have a direct impact on their receptivity towards literacy acquisition • Demonstrates significantly lesser inertia as compared to type Ys • Retention is evident with effective instruction (Does not require much reinforcement)	*Phonics receptivity:* • No receptivity to phonics *High frequency words:* • Unable to read or spell most words on the list (pre-primer) *Characteristics:* • Heterogeneous group of individuals with distinct learning needs and difficulties • Shows signs of co-morbidities that have a direct impact on their receptivity towards literacy acquisition • Demonstrates significant levels of inertia • Retention surfaces after the initial period of inertia with effective intervention • Requires more reinforcement for retention

There are four relatively distinct groups of nonresponders. With reference to the model and tables on pages 65 and 66 respectively, chapter 2B attempts to provide an in-depth explanation of the differences in characteristics between the various types of nonresponders.

Type A

If given the appropriate form of intervention, type A nonresponders tend to attain the highest rates of accuracy for spelling among the nonresponders. They have the potential to rival their peers who are receptive to phonics intervention in terms of literacy competencies.

Type A nonresponders can be categorised into two subgroups – type A.1 and A.2. The subgroups are characterised by different learning styles.

Type A.1

- **Receptivity to phonics**

Type A.1 nonresponders look like they are receptive to phonics because they are indeed partially receptive.

They possess the ability to discern up to four units of sounds in a word. As such, they are able to use phonics to spell words so long as words are four-letter CCVC words or shorter. Type A.1 nonresponders will be able to break the words down into sounds and spell it accordingly. More importantly, type A.1 nonresponders can look at the CCVC words that they have spelt inaccurately and self-correct. It is also important to note that among all the nonresponders, only type A.1 students can truly remember double blends and apply them in their spelling (e.g. 'fl', 'gl', 'fr', 'gr').

Attaining high spelling accuracy of CCVC words using phonics may seem pretty insignificant in the entire scheme of things (there are literally thousands of words beyond CCVC word level). In the nonresponder world, however, such accuracy using phonics is literally worthy of an applause.

However, type A.1 nonresponders are unable to spell words with accurate consistency should any word fall out of the CCVC spectrum. Firstly, they are not very receptive to silent letters. For instance, they will be confused with words like 'shake' vs 'shak' or 'plan' VS 'plane'. They also may not be able to remember if the word match is spelt as 'mach' or 'match'. Secondly, words that entail spelling rules do not make sense to them regardless of the amount of repetition or explanation. For instance, the rule "magic-e makes the vowel say its name" (and therefore a letter 'e' should be included in words like 'shake' or 'plane') does not mean a thing to the nonresponders.

More importantly, they tend to struggle with words that consist of more than four letters (and do not have the CCVC sequence). Using sounds to spell these words are no longer effective as such words either fall out of the usual four-letter auditory threshold that the students are comfortable with. This includes words that sound similar. For instance, these students may interchange the last letter of the words 'thing' and 'think'.

Type A.1 nonresponders use their visual memory for these words. However, they require colour-coding to 'break' the words visually into smaller parts in order for their visual memory to retain such words easily.

- **High-frequency words**

Type A.1 nonresponders are able to read and spell most words on the high-frequency word list, except for a few visually-similar words that are shown in the following examples:

o 'their' and 'there'

o 'when' and 'went'

o 'through', 'thought' and 'though'

Type A.2

- **Receptivity to phonics**

The commonality among all type A.2 nonresponders is that phonics instruction is simply not effective.

Type A.2 nonresponders have no receptivity to phonics at all as they are either unable to segment sounds in a word or deem such segmentation to be illogical. They rely entirely on their visual memory for all words, including CCVC or shorter words. Like type Bs, Xs and Ys, type A.2s nonresponders perceive each word to be distinct. As such, they do not remember words via rime patterns observed in the word family. This is because remembering words by patterns do not involve a process of attaching the meaning to each word. Type A.2 nonresponders should be given the colour-coding and visual approach to learning words. Should they be denied of their preferred way of learning words and are forced to use phonics, they will be unable to spell most words – even the CCVC words – save for a bunch of shorter words that they are regularly exposed to.

Type A.2 nonresponders seem resemble type A.1 nonresponders. They seem receptive to phonics and will dutifully construct words with the sounds in the presence of a teacher but they will never rely on phonics when they are left to their own devices. The issue is that they are mechanically constructing words with little awareness of what they are constructing. Unlike type A.1 nonresponders, there is little to no attempt at self-correction. This problem, while obvious, is not immediately crippling during the initial stages of literacy acquisition of learning CVC and CCVC words. This group of A.2 nonresponders will have low levels of reading and, in particular, spelling accuracy. You may teach such nonresponders for years – moving on to more advanced concepts – only to realise that they are still struggling with many simpler CVC and CCVC words. Such nonresponders remember the phonics sounds but do not find much meaning in using them to construct words. One of the type A.2 nonresponders who had been receiving phonics intervention for 4 years struggled with many spelling issues. The following examples are words that he constantly struggled with:

o   'spit' as 'sped' or 'spet'

o   'brag' as 'bet'

o   'pat' as 'pet'

o   'wine' as 'wne'

o   'flag' as ''fab'

o   'hurt' as 'hurn'

The lack of phonics application in the spelling of this group of type A.2 nonresponders – despite their ability to remember the phonics sounds – underscores the fact that type A.2 students should be taught using their visual memory and colour-coding.

- **High-frequency words**

Type A.2 students can read most words on the list. However, they have considerable difficulty with the spelling of some of the words in the list.

Type B

- **Receptivity to phonics**

Like type A.2 nonresponders, type B nonresponders rely entirely on their visual memory and colour-coding for all words. They are also unable to observe the trend among words in the same word family. Like type A.2 nonresponders. they do not use phonics in their independent reading and spelling of words as they rely on their visual memory to remember each word in isolation. However, they have slightly elevated understanding of the concept of blends. Like type A.1 nonresponders, type B nonresponders are receptive to onset and rime instruction – with a catch.

Type B nonresponders are unable to accept rimes that are not real words. They are only able to remember words with real-word rimes even with colour-coding. This means that the tolerance level towards abstract concepts is much lower for type B nonresponders as compared to type A.2 nonresponders.

To recap what is the rime, please take a look at the following example.

Let's use the word 'plan'. By segmenting the word before the vowel, you will get words that are split into 2 parts like these:

Pl   an

(onset)   (rime)

To demonstrate the difference between type A.2 and B students, do analyse the rimes of the following words 'plan', 'spat', 'flag' and 'trip':

Pl	an	Fl	ag
Sp	at	Tr	ip

(real word rime) (non-word rime)

Type B nonresponders are unable to remember words with non-word rimes. In their opinion, there are no such words as an 'ip' or 'ag'. Since these rimes are abstract, it does not make sense to them, which in turn translates to the inability to remember such words *even with* colour-coding. On the other hand, they are able to learn words with real-word rimes easily with the colour-coding method. Some type B nonresponders can see word patterns but cannot tell that the words are from the same word family.

Their inability to remember words with non-word rimes is detrimental to their literacy acquisition as there is an incredible amount of words with non-word rimes or parts. As such, type B nonresponders have limited literacy abilities as they are only able to learn words with real-word rimes or memorise words with much effort.

It is important to note that type B nonresponders may resemble type A nonresponders but their low receptivity to abstract concepts impedes their ability in gaining access to type A only instructional methods. In view of their learning behaviour, the intervention for type B nonresponders has to encompass interventions from type X and Y.

Type Y

Type Y nonresponders exhibit the slowest progress in literacy acquisition and/or the most atypical of learning styles. They seem to be resistant to any sort of instruction and progress may be abysmally slow. Phonics or whole word instruction is definitely ineffective. Even though it may seem as if the phonics or whole word instruction is initially effective (usually at the CVC word level), teachers and therapists will eventually realise that no further progress can be made. It seems as if these students are only able to effortlessly read or spell highly-selective words of their choice. (Such choices are important clues in determining the nonresponders' state of neurological functioning.)

These nonresponders who struggle with high-frequency words on the list are likely to be reading and spelling at grade 1 or 2 levels even if they are in their late teens. They may be most likely diagnosed with other co-morbidities like Specific Language Impairment (SLI). They will also have plenty of issues with executive functioning, visual processing, orthographic processing, extremely low working memory etc. Basically, they have immense struggles with the language, sensorial (perceptual) and sensorial (storage) domains.

To be clear, phonics responders, type A and B nonresponder may have similar diagnoses too but the degree of co-morbidity severity that type Y nonresponders have to grapple with often places them at the bottom one percentile of the nation. Instruction that does not include all the aforementioned comorbidities into account will not be effective and will not yield results.

Due to the severity of their co-morbidities, type Y nonresponders have an initial phase of inertia. The initial act of information acquisition taxes their cognitive facilities so quickly that fatigue from information overload sets in. There will be more confusion in this phase as they grapple with 'pruning' – meaning making and reorganisation of how they perceive concepts and information. In other words, through this process of uncluttering and alleviating confusion, the type Y nonresponders react negatively first by exhibiting more confusion and draining their mental reserves further.

Granted, type Y nonresponders will still face a lot of difficulties with literacy competency even with effective instruction. However, effective instruction ensures that type Y nonresponders will demonstrate slow receptivity and retention, instead of the previous state of absolutely no literacy receptivity and retention. More importantly, effective instruction for type Y nonresponders determines the line between illiteracy and basic literacy for daily functioning.

o   **Note**

In my opinion, Attention Deficit Hyperactive Disorder (ADHD) is not included in the list of co-morbidities that affect learning. Students with ADHD do not fare any better or worse than their counterparts of similar literacy profiles, be it phonics responding or nonresponders. During the period of exploration, I made sure that whatever method that I could eventually find was effective enough for students with even the shortest of attention spans to retain information. In other words, instruction had to be short and direct in order for the student to understand and internalise the information instantly.

Type X

Type X nonresponders are basically students who have the same atypical learning style as the type Y nonresponders with a greater learning progress. This learning progress stems from the dramatically reduced levels of inertia. Upon being presented with effective instruction, type X nonresponders show heightened receptivity towards instruction almost immediately without requiring long periods of 'pruning'. As such, their capacity for information acquisition is much greater than type Ys – though fatigue also sets in when type X nonresponders reach the point of information overload.

While both type X and Y nonresponders require reinforcement, the frequency of reinforcement needed for type X nonresponders is much lower as compared to type Y nonresponders due to their ability to retain information for longer periods of time. Some type X nonresponders are also more aware of their lack of receptivity towards phonics instruction. As such, these type X nonresponders would express their frustration towards ineffective instruction.

Like type B, X and Y nonresponders, their receptivity to abstract concepts is low. Most are likely to reject blends too. However, type B nonresponders may have just enough receptivity to abstract concepts to accept blends (but not non-real word rimes). Type X – and Y – nonresponders reject any mode of phonics instruction completely. There are exceptions but even if there are some signs of phonics receptivity, they are largely not meaningful to the nonresponders.

CHAPTER 2C

MAIN PRINCIPLES AND CONSIDERATIONS TO APPROACH NONRESPONDERS

Regardless of being a phonics responder or nonresponder, a dyslexic or typically-developing individual, the visualisation of words still remains as the only way for any of these individuals to be fluent readers and spellers. Almost all nonresponders rely on their sight – not their sense of hearing – to remember how words are read or spelt. If they do not do so, effective literacy acquisition is impossible. Segmenting a word into sounds is nonsensical to them. It is just like looking at a photograph - you look at the entire picture as a whole and not as shredded pieces.

Nonresponders do not like to segment words as segmentation do not make sense.
It is like shredding a picture into many pieces.

There may be claims about an auditory or kinaesthetic learning style, but those are merely preferred <u>means</u> to activate the mental visualisation of a word.

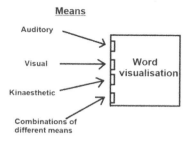

Means
Auditory
Visual
Kinaesthetic
Combinations of different means
Word visualisation

Regardless of the means, mental word representations are always visual.

Most nonresponders are ill-suited to use the auditory means to trigger the mental representations of the word in their head. In other words, the auditory and visual means are not integrated and synchronised together. Due to the limited time and resources that most teachers and therapists possess, a compensatory approach becomes necessary to guide the student to acquire literacy. An instruction pursuing word acquisition via visual means become necessary.

The more problems a student has with literacy, the more the student struggles with word visualisation. Period. Effortless reading and spelling are, after all, based on sight. [The only exception to this is when the student is unable to read or spell due to language impairment. Language impairment-based literacy problems are usually due to the inability to clearly define the meaning of words.]

As this approach capitalises on their visual processing, factoring the visual considerations of the student is of prime importance.

There is this misconception that an approach for nonresponders must be a whole-word approach. [A whole-word approach equates to the memorisation of an entire word by sight. Illustrations may be embedded in the words while stories may be told to provide the justification behind the embedded illustrations.]

I must correct this misconception. Many people perceive literacy intervention for dyslexics to be that of a dichotomy – the methods either fall into the phonics or whole-word camp. In reality, there are many more approaches apart from the two 'established' approaches.

Nonresponders utilise their 'sight' memory to remember words. However, their 'sight' memory is one that has variation. One psychologist that I spoke to many years ago termed it as "compromised sight memory".

A nonresponder with "compromised sight memory" has to account for many limitations before information can be retained. With regards with word acquisition, the words presented (1) must not be abstract in meaning, (2) must not trigger any visual or additional language confusion, and (3) have a word length that fits comfortably within their preferred visual span.

For nonresponders to have successful spelling attempts (depending on the type of nonresponders) , considerations and pre-requisites have to be met in order to ensure minimal abstractness, language and/or visual confusion.

The table below presents the typical 'sight' memory route for spelling and the additional pre-requisites/considerations for those with "compromised sight memory" (the nonresponders).

MECHANICAL DOMAIN - SPELLING USING THE SIGHT MEMORY ROUTE			
Typical sight memory route for spelling	**Step 1**	**Step 2**	**Step 3**
	Say the word	Recall meaning	Recall how the entire word is spelt

CONSIDERATIONS FOR THOSE WITH COMPROMISED SIGHT MEMORY			
Prerequisites for the different types of nonresponders		**LANGUAGE DOMAIN** *(for step 2)*	**VISUAL PERCEPTUAL + STORAGE DOMAIN** *(for step 3)*
Additional pre-requisites for type Xs and Ys	Pre-requisites for all types	1) No Jargon 2) Address homonyms immediately (words of the same sound with different spelling)	1) Fits within preferred visual span 2) Understand and demonstrate receptivity towards word segmentation (dependent on the level of abstractness) 3) Show all silent letters visually

		3) Clearly defined word meanings to avoid semantic substitution 4) Understand different categories according to the level of concreteness or abstractness	4) Understand the existence of all letters in a word (requires meaning making) 5) Accommodate chronic problems of visual perception or storage

Important note: All pre-requisites have to be met in order for nonresponders to be receptive towards the literacy intervention of sight words.

LANGUAGE CONSIDERATIONS

- **Pre-requisites for all types of nonresponders**

1. No Jargon

Jargons are abstract. Period. Jargons do not provide a direct description of the concept (e.g. How does an acute angle look 'acute' anyway?). It impedes understanding and aggravates existing levels of confusion.

This is not to say that all nonresponders will have difficulty accepting jargons. Afterall, it depends on the levels of receptivity that nonresponders have towards abstractness.

However, it is good to exclude jargons in your instruction as there is *a high possibility* of the nonresponding student having language difficulties. (If the student demonstrates little difficulty in handling jargon, you may go ahead and include jargons in your instruction.)

2. Address homonyms immediately (words of the same sound with different spelling)

Offer all possible forms of the word – that are high in frequency – with the same sound. In addition, a picture for each word has to be included to ensure that the students are able to make meaning of the word instantly.

P**ale**   p**ail**

B**i**t   b**ea**t

o *Justification*

If you do not address the homonym immediately, you will incur confusion among the kids. According to the phonics scope and sequence, 'a-e' (from '-ale') and 'ai' (from '-ail') are not taught together. '-ale' is a magic-e concept that is taught in the earlier stages of the literacy curriculum while the vowel team 'ai' is taught in the later stages in order to prevent phonics-responding students from being confused.

The same applies to the second example of 'bit' and 'beat'. According to phonics logic, the student should only be taught the word 'bit' as the vowel 'i' is an elementary concept. The word 'beat', on the other hand, should be taught much later in the student's learning as the phonogram 'ea' is essentially an advanced phonics concept called vowel teams.

However, by teaching only the word 'bit' and delaying the instruction of the word 'beat' till much later, it violates the logic of language understanding. The common meanings of the sound /bit/ are as such:

- A little bit
- The past tense of 'bite'
- Beat someone up
- Beat you (to win)
- Move to the beat

Should a nonresponder be taught the phonics scope and sequence and only learn the concept 'i' instead of 'ea', they will only be taught that the sound /bit/ only has two meanings:

- A little bit
- The past tense of 'bite' *

*If the nonresponder has language difficulty or impairment, the concept of past tense is likely to be too abstract for them as they have a poor concept of time.

Overtime, they may only remember that the word 'bit' only has one meaning. They will assume that the sound /bit/ will definitely be spelt as 'bit'. Then, they stumble onto the word 'beat' one day and are told that the word has the same sound as the word 'bit'. The students may be confused as they were only taught the word 'bit' and have accepted that all words that have the sound /bit/ will be spelt as 'bit'. Confusion ensues. For students who have poor sight memory, it is chaotic.

To make matters worse, they learn that despite being told that the short vowel 'i' (as in 'bit') and long vowel 'e' (as in 'Peter') make a different sound, in reality, both vowels sound the same. It increases the levels of confusion exponentially. In the worst case scenario, every /e/ sound becomes interchangeable like 'beat', 'bete', 'bet' and 'bit'.

o **Counter argument**

Phonics purist will have reservations. Even if the student knows how to spell the two words by heart, what if they get confused and generalise the /i/ or /ea/ sounds interchangeably? Students may spell a seemingly simple word 'bin' into 'bean' (or 'tin' as 'tean') because they are confused with the multiple sounds. **/i/ and /ea/ have to be taught separately to phonics responders because they will get confused if the sounds are taught together.**

Their reservations are indeed valid for students who are phonics responders. They have to be given ample time to learn each concept and recognise the words that fall under each phonogram. Only then would there be a reduced possibility for confusion.

[Therein lies the shortfall of phonics – ultimately, the students still need to visualise the mental representations of the words to achieve spelling accuracy.]

If a student is a nonresponder, however, he or she does not care about the individual sounds or the fact that /i/ sounds like /ea/. Nonresponders, unlike the phonics responders, do not generalise across words with the same phonogram. They do not see typical phonics patterns among words. Often, they do not see or hear the rhymes among the words. Each word is distinct to them as they remember words in isolation.

As such, including words with 'i' or 'ea' together during instruction is definitely feasible.

- ### Additional pre-requisites for type Xs and Ys

3. Clearly defined word meanings to avoid semantic substitution

In some cases, language impairment is the main obstacle to a student's literacy acquisition. Language impairment is bewildering to many due to its 'limitless' scope. Literally any breakdown in thinking and communication (verbal or non-verbal) that is not due to a speech production problem may be considered as a language impairment. For this point, I am specifically looking at language impaired students who cannot accept overlaps in meaning before any literacy receptivity and retention is able to take place. For instance, a student may read both words 'city' and 'town' as /town/.

This is because he or she does not have a distinct understanding between the definition of both words. Recall that earlier on in the chapter, we talked about the need for clear definitions of the words in order to ensure that there is no confusion over the word meanings. In extreme cases though, a language impaired student will only remember one meaning of the word even though there are multiple meanings – and that particular meaning will be the one that is most relatable to his or her reality. A lack of confusion will aid in the retention of meaning and increase the chances of word recognition.

Back to the example again, the student is confused with the difference between the words. From his or her point of view, both words give the impression of a place or huge area populated with buildings. There is no difference in the meaning. As such, he or she will just remember the word that is most familiar to him or her. When the student sees the word 'city', the student may recall an image of a place filled with buildings which automatically links to the word 'town'. Therefore, the student will read the word 'city' as 'town'. Perhaps the student knows the word 'town' due to the repeated exposure of that word via a frequented channel (e.g. The word 'town' is constantly repeated in the student's favourite computer game that requires players to construct buildings).

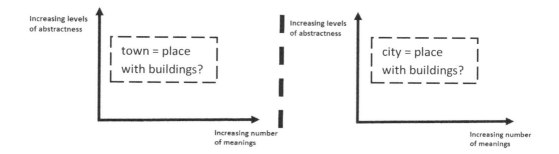

One of the proposed solutions is to establish a very clear definition between the words. Armed with pictures for each word, the student may be taught that a city consists of skyscrapers and office buildings while a town consists of residential buildings and houses.

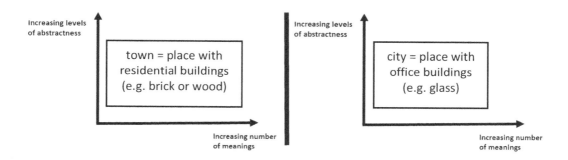

You may argue that those are not the actual definitions. A city can consist of residential buildings. An entire country can be a city. Certain countries house inner cities that, unlike the Central Business District, certainly do not consist of skyscrapers. Moreover, residential buildings can be found in cities and office buildings can be found in towns. Residential buildings can be made of glass while office buildings can be made of brick or wood.

These arguments are indeed valid if you are looking from the point of view of a typically-developing individual. For type X and Y nonresponders, however, it is better to prioritise distinction of meaning over accuracy. Or rather, the child only has the capacity to remember words with distinct meanings rather than the actual meaning that blurs the distinction. Remember, each word must have a clear and distinct meaning. In the most extreme of cases, the student only has the capacity to remember one word for each distinct meaning. There is no room for synonyms. For instance, if the student remembers the word 'student' to be a school-going kid, there is no way he will remember the word pupil. (Or he remembers 'pupil' but not 'student' – it depends on which word he is more exposed to). But then again, this is for the most extreme of cases.

○ **Note**

There are times when the type X or Y nonresponders cannot read the words at all but keeps insisting that they know the meaning. They will look at the words 'city' or 'town' and say "the place with a lot of buildings". This is because they are either (1) confused over which word to use as both words trigger the same mental image or (2) cannot seem to recall the word due to memory problems .

4. **Understand different categories according to the level of concreteness or abstractness**

There are different categories of words in the English vocabulary that differ across degree of abstractness. Some words are easier to understand because their meanings are literal and easily represented in reality.

○ **Nouns [Things/Animals/People] and Action words (present tense)**

These are the most concrete of word categories as the students can find a physical and literal representation in reality. They may demonstrate confusion when these words start to overlap in meaning.

○ **Action words (Past tense)**

Some students have poor concept of time. They feel that everything happens in the present and cannot understand an event that has occurred in the past. Often, they are forced to remember that it is just another way of saying the word.

In order to understand how it is like to have no concept of time, I read the accounts by stroke patients. In my opinion, Jill Bolte Taylor, a neurologist who documented her experience of succumbing to a stroke, gave a brilliant description of having no concept of time:

" Instead of a continuous flow of experience that could be divided into past, present, and future, every moment seemed to exist in perfect isolation.

Devoid of language and linear processing, I felt disconnected from the life I had lived, and in the absence of my cognitive pictures and expansive ideas, time escaped me.

Time stood still because that clock that would sit and tick in the back of my left brain, that clock that helped me establish linearity between my thoughts, was now silent.

Without the internal concept of relativity or the complementary brain activity that helped me navigate myself linearly, I found myself floating from isolated moment to isolated moment. "A" no longer had any relationship to "B" and "one" was no longer relative to "two."

I stopped thinking in language and shifted to taking new pictures of what was going on in the present moment. I was not capable of deliberating about past or future-related ideas because those cells were incapacitated. All I could perceive was right here, right now, and it was beautiful."

Source: My Stroke of Insight: A Brain Scientist's Personal Journey by Jill Bolte Taylor

---

DISCLAIMER

I am going to state again that in no way am I out to make any parent upset by stating that their child has a stroke etc. This is just how I understand the experiences of some of my students and discover new approaches. I take the most severe examples and moderate them drastically to fit my students' predicament. This is the only way you can actually understand what is going on in that world of theirs – especially when they are unable to express themselves. Only when you do not pass judgement quickly will you free yourself from preconceived notions of stereotypes or negative bias. You will be able to look at anything with an analytical view and gain new insights. A person that is affected by societal judgement and norms will just be perpetually stuck in that inertia.

Of course, the students do not have that kind of intense feeling in their heads. It is just that they cannot understand why there is a need for the concept of past tense. Everything is in the present. Everything seems like it is happening right now. Even the act of recalling a past experience seems like it is occurring right now as they are reliving that experience in the present time.

- o **Abstract words [no direct or physical representation in reality]**

  Some examples of abstract words are 'at', 'the', 'will', 'is', 'then' and 'than'. Students who do not have this particular strand of language impairment have enough abstract knowledge to accept such words and not be concerned about it. Those who have such severe language impairment to qualify a type Y nonresponder will be impervious towards such abstract words. These seemingly 'easy' high-frequency words are the bane of their lives as the lack of direct representation in reality messes up their understanding, hindering word retention in the process. (A more in-depth explanation of the detrimental effect of such abstract words can be found in chapter 5.)

- o **Note**

  I believe that this is the basis of the Ron Davis trigger word list. Some students will be so confused by the lack of meaning conveyed by the words that it triggers that perpetual confusion – assuming that the student has visual perceptual issues to begin with. Otherwise, the student will merely remain extremely confused without the visual perceptual distortion.

VISUAL CONSIDERATIONS

- **Pre-requisites for all types of nonresponders**

1. Fits within the preferred visual span

Nonresponders have poor spelling accuracy. One of the main reasons is because they are heavily dependent on their 'sight' memory to remember how the word is spelt but their visual span does not support their attempt at remembering words via 'sight' in a typical manner.

What I consider to be an optimal visual span of a student equates to the student's ability to look at a word and reproduce the word with ease. For instance, if you can look at the word 'grump', remember and reproduce it with ease. But if you are unable to segment words into syllables and struggle with reproducing the word 'rabbit', then in a very, *very* simplistic way, you probably have the visual span of 5 letters. This means that – in a very, very simplistic way – you can largely remember most words that are made up of 5 letters or less with ease and reproduce it with high levels of accuracy.

(There are other considerations involved in word retention but I am keeping the concept simple in order to focus on what is really important.)

According to my observations, when nonresponders attempt to remember words, the following behavioural patterns can be observed:

○ Most nonresponders are able to remember three-letter words with ease (e.g. pat, hit, hut).

○ Some are able to go one step further and remember four-letter words with ease. However, save for certain words that the nonresponders are frequently exposed to, this ability usually does not extend to four-letter words with two vowels attached together (e.g. bean, ploy, boil).

○ A handful of students can only spell two-letter words with high levels of accuracy (e.g. at, up). They largely struggle with the accuracy of three-letter words, much less words with more letters.

○ That rare one or two outliers seem to remember random words. They can spell a very long word (e.g. rabbit, sword) with no issues but cannot spell – or read – some two or three letter words (e.g. so, the, pit, jet) regardless of intervention or reinforcement. These students most likely have a strand of language impairment that directly affects literacy acquisition.

Certainly, nonresponders will be able to remember and spell a small pool of difficult words with accuracy. Those words are committed to memory using much time, effort and exposure. However, it is simply not efficient to learn like that. Thus, they are only able to remember a small pool of words by heart.

Based on the observations, a nonresponder approach should possess an instructional method that accommodates the widest range of nonresponders in order to even benefit a nonresponder with the shortest visual span. The instructional method, for most part, should be one that presents words that fit the visual span of two letters or, as you will realise later in chapter 4, two parts.

2. Understand and demonstrate receptivity towards word segmentation (dependent on the level of abstractness)

When you teach nonresponders long enough, you will realise that many nonresponders are able to spell multisyllabic words with greater ease as compared to single-syllable words. When nonresponders segment the word auditorily, a good number of nonresponders are able to segment a multisyllabic word into syllables effortlessly. It is way more difficult for them to segment the sounds in a single-syllable word. In other words, breaking down a single-syllable word (e.g. brag = /b/ /r/ /a/ /g/) is more difficult than breaking down a multisyllabic word into syllables (e.g. computer = /com/ /pu/ /ter/). Breaking down multisyllabic words into each syllable is reflective of reality.

Certainly, it is not that easy to break each syllable into its individual sounds too. That being said, some nonresponders are able to cope with spelling most two or three letter syllables with phonics. Others just use their visual strengths to remember many two or three-letter syllables that fall within their preferred visual span.

There are, of course, nonresponders who struggle with multisyllabic words due to various reasons. (One of the main reasons is the perceived abstractness of the syllables.) Please refer to chapter 6 for more information on multisyllabic word instruction for nonresponders.

o   **Different ways of perceiving single-syllable words**

Most may react negatively towards phonics instruction but the degree of rejection varies. The different ways that a nonresponder struggles with a single-syllable word reveals different ways of perceiving a single-syllable word.

Take the instruction of the word 'plan' for example. The nonresponders may exhibit one of the following behaviours:

a. Many of them will be unable to match the word 'plan' to a segmented sound /p/ /l/ /a/ /n/. If you ask them what is the first sound, some may be able to say /p/ as the first sound and then be unable to say the rest. Some are not even able to tell you the first sound. Phonemic awareness exercises are futile. They reject beginning blends readily. This group of nonresponders can be further categorised into further sub-groups:

- ***The need for real words parts***
    For instance, they may see the word 'an' in 'plan' but are unable to remember 'pl' because it is not a real word. Technically, 'lan' is an acronym but no one was familiar with it as they do not have previous exposure to it.

- ***No recognition of any real word parts***
    This group of nonresponder do not recognise the word 'an' because it was not 'real enough'. It does not have a direct representation in reality. They seem to have language difficulties and poorer sight word knowledge.

b. The nonresponders in this group seem to be the best spellers of the lot. They can accept beginning blends. In fact, they can spell 4 letter words with much ease. They seem to have higher levels of receptivity towards abstractness. However, anything beyond CCVC word level results in higher spelling inaccuracy.

c. This group of nonresponders are only able to spell the word according to onset and rime. This is to say that the teacher has to say the word as /pl/ /an/ instead of /plan/. These nonresponders seem to have a mix of possible traits:

- They seem like phonics responders who initially require the word to be broken into two parts before accustoming to the spelling of the word as a collective sound /plan/. However, they are not phonics responders because they have been in this state for a chronically long time. If they were phonics responders, the onset-rime instruction would have been highly effective for these students and they would eventually be able to spell without breaking the words into two parts. The fact that they are still in this persistent state means that phonics is not an effective method for them. After all, no one would speak to the nonresponders like this:

"Please write /pl/ /an/ in your book."

"I /pl/ /an/ to go on a holiday."

Regardless, this group of nonresponders demonstrates that they have some levels of receptivity towards abstractness as they are able to tolerate blends and segment a real word into two parts.

From these observations, it can be concluded that (1) for most part, blends should be eliminated from instruction for most nonresponders, (2) some nonresponders are comfortable with two word parts, and (3) all nonresponders have the tendency to locate smaller real words in a word (unless they have a strand of language impairment that affects their literacy acquisition).

3. Show all silent letters visually

All silent letters should just be shown visually. Words with silent letters have the tendency to be confusing. This is especially so when the word with the omitted letter 'e' is also a real word. For instance, the word 'tape' becomes 'tap' when the silent letter is removed. Phonics teachers try to actively play up this similarity and only use a phonics rule via auditory means to emphasise the difference (e.g. "The magic-e sits at the back of the word and makes the vowel say its name or the long vowel sound"). However, the words remain visually similar even though the sound between both words are different. This visual similarity confuses the students and results in random insertions of letter 'e's behind random words.

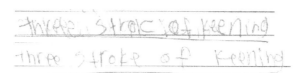

A student exhibits confusion over the word 'stroke' and proceeds to randomly include the letter 'e'. (He also spelt the word 'caning' as 'keening'.)

Phonics responders respond well to similarity between words as they are attempting to discover patterns between words. Nonresponders require each word to be distinct because they are attempting to establish a distinct meaning for each word. In research jargon, phonics responders are stimulating their sublexical processing while nonrepsonders are stimulating their lexical processing.

As a matter of fact, visually-similar words should be introduced together. Please refer to point 5 – "Chronic problems with visual perception or storage" – for more details.

- **Additional pre-requisites for type Xs and Ys**

4. **Understand the existence of each letter in a word (requires meaning making)**

Many store-bought manipulatives will attempt to embed a picture in the word.

An example of a manipulative that embeds a picture in sight word.

That may work for the typical dyslexics who would attach the meaning of the word together with the word itself.

However, type Ys want a justification for *every* letter in the word. Some of them even require the justification to be a relatable story that is linked to the meaning of the word. Other type Ys reject stories and require justifications to be a realistic explanation of the letter sequence in the word.

For instance, they want to know why the word 'eat' is spelt as such (and not 'eta').

From their point of view, it may be too abstract for them to just accept the choice of the letters or letter sequence in the word. The brain is unable to understand why the letter 'a' has to come before the letter 't'. As such, permutations of the word 'eat' arises. In order to reduce the abstractness and conceptualise the word in a more concrete (and relatable manner), they would like a reason for the letter sequence.

It is not appropriate to just dismiss their behaviour as just "merely reversals", "the usual vowel confusion", "the usual letter sequencing issue" or "the usual dyslexic symptoms that would abate with age". Indeed, there will be some students with severe visual perceptual issues who view almost every word with reversed sequence of letters – that would certainly require attention from the Behavioural Optometrist and Occupational Therapist (trained in vision therapy). Others with severe dyslexia will sequence the letters in almost every word incorrectly on paper but are able to spell them correctly verbally. Regardless, we must try our best to deliver when the student needs help. We are their teachers, after all.

Some teachers may claim that it is far too much work to create a story that is relatable to the student for every letter in a word that they are unable to remember.

The great news is that, often, the students will mercifully throw you a bone and say that they can remember the position of most letters in the word.

For instance, a student spells the word 'red' as 'rad'.

The teacher would just have to create a story to justify why was the letter 'e' used instead of the letter 'a'.

As I mentioned earlier, some teachers may claim that this is a usual problem of vowel confusion and students should grow out of it once they are older with greater exposure and a more developed 'sight' memory.

My students who spelt the word 'red' as 'rad' were twelve and fifteen respectively. Surely, there is a limit to such excuses. This is such an obvious sign that there is some other underlying problem that needs to be addressed immediately.

5. Accommodate chronic problems with visual perception or storage

Unlike the type A and B nonresponders, type X and Y nonresponders have problems with visual perception or storage that are atypical or serious enough to impede a student's learning and hinder basic literacy acquisition. This usually warrants a trip to the Behavioural Optometrist but many of these students are unable to receive such therapy due to financial constraints.

o *Perceptual problems*

Such problems are definitely not restricted to 'b', 'd', 'p' or 'q' reversals. It could be letters like 'm' where a student can never perceive it to be an 'm', but rather two 'n's. Or the letter 's' seems very difficult to distinguish from the letter 'c'. Putting the letters into a string of letters to form a word fuels further visual confusion of the word.

In general, the students grapple with visual perceptual problems when they deal with dots, lines and any other two-dimensional strokes on a flat surface (e.g. screen or paper).

They may experience a mild form of word animation. Not only may the letter position reverse into an incorrect letter order (e.g. eat, eta), the letters may also merge into the surrounding words and create different letters (e.g. 'clan' as 'dan') or just look overlapped.

Some experience more extreme word animation. Words shake, vibrate, fly or do some other form of literal word aerobics. Such word animation may be termed as visual stress or Irlen syndrome. One of the touted solutions seem to be coloured overlays. However, coloured overlays do not help if the visual perceptual issue stems from other neurological origins. Besides, coloured overlays are deemed as a crutch to an underlying problem. After all, to be truly functional in society, a person must be able to tolerate light of varying frequencies without a perpetual reliance on coloured overlays. Furthermore, coloured lenses are expensive and it is a huge financial investment that not many families are willing to undertake. Others tout vision therapy to be the solution to this problem that stems from probable causes like a lack of synchronisation between both eyeballs or the inability to shift between seeing into the distance and near effortlessly and repeatedly within a matter of seconds. While vision therapy is likely to be the solution, many families are again unable to afford that option due to financial constraints.

o   *Understanding*

The student needs to understand that the abstract symbol on paper represents letters that, in turn, represents sounds. The collection of individual sounds forms a group of sounds, which is essentially how the word is pronounced. Even if a student is unable to discern the individual sounds in a word, they should fundamentally accept that that the symbols form a word that makes a sound.

In rare cases, some type Y nonresponders do not deem the word to be formed by letters. They see it as a picture to sketch or draw.

o   *Storage problems*

-   Differentiating auditorily similar words

    The students tend to have difficulties with words that sound the same or have similar sounds (e.g. 'pale' vs 'pail', 'steel' vs 'steal', 'stab' vs 'step', 'clam' vs 'clan').

    This is due to two reasons:

    1. Their orthographic memory is not strong enough to remember how the word is spelt.

    2. They have difficulties linking the correct meaning to the correct word.

        ▪   Students who have severe difficulties in this area would often lament that they have no problems remembering the spelling and meaning of the word. The main problem lies with the perpetual confusion over matching the correct meaning to the correct word. Regardless of the frequency of repetition, the accurate matching the words and meanings largely remains as guesswork. Visuals, mnemonics or any other form of compensatory methods are usually used as a crutch but it unravels during stressful situations when their attention wavers (e.g. examinations).

-   Differentiating visually-similar words

It is very common for nonresponders to be confused with words that are visually similar. Usually, such words would be of the same length and would have first and last letters that are similar (eg. 'said' vs 'sold' vs 'seed' vs 'sped'). The degree of confusion depends on the degree of affinity that the nonresponder has with the printed word.

For nonresponders who have marginally higher word recognition capabilities, the shape of the word – the gestalt – matters. Such nonresponders would not be confused with 'said' and 'sped' as the outline of the words are different. 'Sped' has a protrusion at the bottom while 'said' does not.

Perhaps, they may be confused with 'said' and 'sold' instead and may proceed to spell 'said' as 'soid' or 'sold' as 'soid'. Perhaps the spelling of both words may be interchanged. It is evident that these nonresponders are not concerned that the letters have to represent an accurate sound. However, their orthographic memory, while rather compromised, exists.

On the other hand, nonresponders who have dramatically lower word recognition capabilities – a certain group of type Ys – but are still able to spell some words that are 3 to 4 letters in length may be confused with a wider range of words. This is because these nonresponders may not even recognise the last letter. All they remember in the above example is probably the initial letter 's' and the approximate word length of 4 to 5 letters. The overall shape of the word bears no relevance. The word 'said' may be confused with 'show', 'step', 'such' or any other word that fulfils their requirement. They may proceed to spell words that have variations of multiple words (e.g. 'stuch' or 'shep'). Assuming that the diagnosis of language impairment is not the main cause of their spelling difficulties, it is evident that these nonresponders have almost non-existent letter-sound representations nor orthographic memory.

Many type A and B nonresponders – even low-functioning phonics responders – exhibit mild difficulties in discerning auditorily and visually-similar words. For instance, students may have difficulties differentiating between 'when', 'went' and 'want'. Words like 'taught', 'thought', 'though' and 'through' have also proven to be challenging to such students.

For students with visual storage issues, it is futile to embed pictures in the letters or create stories out of it. Mnemonics helps but teaching too many mnemonics will be counterproductive as the students will be confused with the many mnemonics.

Even after years of exposure and practice, my sixteen-year-old student would write the following:

"I when home to slip."

The word 'home' was easier to remember as there are no visually-similar words to him nor are there any words with the same sound as 'home'. On the other hand, not only do the words 'sleep' and 'slip' sound the same, they are also visually similar as well with 'sl' as the beginning blends and the letter 'p' as the last letter.

This problem also affects type A and B nonresponders but the pervasiveness of this problem is evident among type X and Y nonresponders. The problem is the confusion over the visual similarity of the words. Another common problem is the visual confusion between words that contains '-nk', '-ck' and '-ke' endings. There are phonics sounds and rules that attempt to differentiate the words auditorily. However, the sounds and rules are not effective.

The type X and Y nonresponders are usually confused between words with '-ck' and '-ke' endings (e.g. 'tack' vs 'take'). The introduction of '-nk' makes it difficult to distinguish words ending with '-ck' (e.g. 'think' vs 'thick'). Taken together, the confused student proceeds to mix word ending with '-nk', '-ck' and '-ke'. Everything becomes a mess and it is difficult to wrangle this confusion. The only way to tackle this problem is to emphasise the visual difference between these words from the start using colours.

○ **Note**

Considering both language and visual considerations for nonresponders, type Ys will see the slowest progress due to all the extra language and visual considerations that a teacher must take into account.

If the information in this chapter seems overwhelming and you can feel that dread accumulating within you because teaching nonresponders seem like rocket science, do not fret. Chapters 3 and 4 serve to synthesize all this information and present a feasible solution it to you.

CHAPTER 3

SINGLE-SYLLABLE WORD INSTRUCTION FOR TYPE As

This chapter covers the basic techniques in **single-syllable** word instruction for type A nonresponders. The instructional approach is focused on **CVC to CCCVC words**. Please refer to the next chapter for instruction on high-frequency sight words.

There will be cases where a student seems to have characteristics across all types of nonresponders. Experience and a complete understanding of nonresponder logic should be able to tide you through such cases.

To aid in the understanding of this chapter, recall that type A nonresponders comprises of two subcategories with the following characteristics:

Type A.1	• Marginally receptive to phonics (till CCVC level)
	• Able to perform self-correction of CCVC errors
	• Seems to be receptive to blends but demonstrates much higher receptivity when dealing with single letters instead
	• Uses their visual span to remember words
Type A.2	• Extremely low / no receptivity to phonics
	• Uses their visual strength to remember words
	• Not receptive to blends
	• Only remembers the names – not sounds – of single letters

In planning how to teach type As, teachers or therapists should adopt two concepts from the phonics world – the 'onset-rime' and word families. Not only do these concepts facilitate the ease of planning, they usually help the phonics responding students by further easing their working memory and allowing greater retention of the concept. By incorporating these two concepts into nonresponder instruction, type A nonresponders will be able to greatly benefit as well.

- **Phonics instruction: Onset-rime**

In phonics instruction, there is a technique known as 'onset-rime'. It is used when a student does not have the phonological ability to segment the word into individual sounds. This technique is used to segment the word into two parts – instead of individual parts – to allow greater ease of reading and spelling. It is very similar to the concept of word families.

Skip = /s/ /k/ / i/ /p/ → It is difficult for some students to segment the word into individual sounds.

Skip = /sk/ /ip/ → Segmenting a word into two different groups of sounds allows for the ease of reading and spelling. It is easier for the student to segment a word into 2 parts (instead of multiple, individuals parts). The onset is segmented right before the first vowel in the word.
↓ ↓
Onset Rime
[Vowels = a, e, i, o, u ; Consonants = all the other letters]

The following words demonstrate other onset-rime examples:

- Cat   = /c/ /at/
- Kite   = /k/ /ite/
- Blink   = /bl/ /ink/
- Brown = /br/ /own/
- Freeze = /fr/ /eeze/
- Straight = /str/ /aight/

The phonics teacher will proceed to teach different types of onsets.

Different types of onsets		
Single letters		b, c, d, f, g, h, j, k, l, m, n, p, qu, r, s, t, v, w, x, y, z
Double blends	'l' blends	bl, cl, fl, pl, sl,
	'r' blends	br, cr, dr, fr, gr, pr, sr, tr
	Others	sm, sn, sp, sw, tw, st

Triple blends		spl, spr, scr, skr, str, squ
Diagraphs		sh, ch, th, wh

Like any other technique in the phonics toolbox, the different onsets are matched to the rime like puzzles. The phonics teacher attempts to show that by learning different onset and rime patterns, it is possible to create different combinations of words.

Onset	Rime	Word
m	ap	map
dr	um	drum
sp	it	spit
spl	at	splat

- **Phonics instruction: Word families**

Word families ensure that the rime stays constant while only the onset changes. Phonics responders benefit as it does not tax their working memory.

I chose word families because as a teacher, I would like to establish patterns in my wordlist for ease of introduction and planning. Word families were very conveniently categorised for me. It is not necessary to choose according to word families. You can go ahead and choose any other groups of words so long as they are grouped into very clear patterns. However, do be mindful that nonresponders do not recall words via rime patterns. They could be excellent at pattern recognition and are able to look like they are using a fixed pattern of rimes to spell, but they certainly do not rely on word family patterns as their primary mode of word recollection. If left to their own devices, the nonresponders still remember the entire word independently from other words.

When words from the same family are incorporated together with the onset and rime, only the onset changes while the rime stays the same. The following table shows an example from the '-ip' family.

Onset	Rime	Word
s	ip	sip
t	ip	tip
fl	ip	flip
dr	ip	drip
tr	ip	trip
sn	ip	snip
sh	ip	ship
str	ip	strip

To reiterate, the onset-rime technique – alongside with the word families – are considered to be the simplest word constructing techniques that are largely meant for students who have low literacy levels and/or are unable to respond to the usual phonics instruction.

The problem is that the onset-rime technique and word families do not work for the nonresponders. In order to teach the type As, you have to make changes to the onset-rime technique.

[These changes are simple. Many people may not understand the significance behind such simple changes. This demonstrates that all you need is a change in perspective. You do not need to spend a lot of money on another method that is touted to teach nonresponders when you actually understand the logic of nonresponders.]

This section will attempt to explain the teaching technique for type A and B nonresponders in the following order: (1) How to teach, (2) Planning the words, (3) Preparing the resources

1. How to teach

It is of paramount importance to observe three main principles when you teach the type A nonresponders:

1. Always show real words – no nonsense words or word parts

2. Introduce the (real) word in a word technique

3. Onsets must only consist of one letters. Double blends, triple blends and diagraphs have to be omitted.

There is no such thing as 'sk' or 'ip'. They are not real words. They are deemed as abstract, nonsensical word parts that serve to perpetuate confusion. The table below shows you just how many word parts are deemed to be nonsensical. The onsets and rimes that are shaded are word parts that are deemed to be nonsensical.

Onset	Rime
tw	in
fl	ap
st	op
wh	ip
k	ite
bl	ink
str	aight

With regards to the onset, the nonresponders are only largely receptive to a single letter onset. A single letter onset makes sense to the nonresponders as they have been made to sing single letters in the alphabet song or have been exposed to single letters in preschool. Some of the nonresponder may only know the letters by their names and not their sounds. For instance, they may look at the letter 'b' and say " 'b' for ball". They may not know that it makes the sound /b/.

Apparently, any onset that comprises of more than one letter does not make sense and are deemed as abstract. The only two letter onsets some students will probably accept are diagraphs 'sh' and 'ch'. 'Wh' and 'th' are deemed to be even more abstract as not only are they non-real word parts, they sound similar to letters 'w' and 't'.

For instance, many nonresponders will not remember how to spell the word 'twin' if they are taught /tw/ + /in/. They may remember letters 't' or 'w' as the letter names or they may know the individual sounds of each letter but are unable to put them together and make /tw/.

As such, their learning preference gives way to the **(real) word in a word** technique. This technique merely comprises of two steps.

Step 1: Locate the smallest real word(s) among the available words in the word families

In this example, I will use words from '-in', '-ip' and '-ipe' families.

Words with –in
in, bin, din, fin, gin, kin, pin, tin, win, sin, chin, shin, thin, skin, twin, grin, spin

The smallest real word would be 'in'.

Words with -ip
dip, hip, nip, lip, sip, tip, rip, zip, flip, skip, whip, chip, grip, slip, clip, ship, drip, trip

The smallest real words would be the following words: 'dip', 'lip' , 'hip', 'rip', 'sip', 'nip', 'tip', 'zip', 'skip'.

Words with -ipe
ripe, pipe, wipe, gripe, swipe, snipe, stripe

The smallest real words would be the following words: 'ripe', 'pipe', 'wipe', 'snipe'.

Step 2: Teach words by adding a single letter onset to a real word

You need to teach the smallest real word first. You must ensure that your student is familiar with the entire array of the smallest real words. Thereafter, you must ensure that only a single letter is placed in front of an existing real word each time.

Example	Teaching sequence	Verbal instruction
1	f + in = fin	When you add the letter 'f' to 'in', you will get 'fin'.
2	w + hip = whip	When you add the letter 'w' to 'hip', you will get 'whip'.
3	c + hip = chip	When you add the letter 'c' to 'hip', you will get 'chip'.
4	g + ripe = gripe	When you add the letter 'g' to 'ripe', you will get 'gripe'.

This way, you build upon the smallest real word and produce another real word each time. This allows the student to see a pattern not by rhymes nor word families but by the understanding that words are built upon other words. This understanding is exceedingly important. Should the students demonstrate thorough understanding of this concept, they will eventually be able to teach themselves and their literacy gains will become even more significant.

You will find that many words consist of multiple real words. You still have to start from the smallest real word and show how longer words are formed by placing a single letter in front of an existing real word each time.

Words taught	Teaching sequence	Verbal instruction
How to teach the word 'skin'?	k + in = kin	When you add the letter 'k' to 'in', it gives you 'kin'.
	s + kin = skin	When you add the letter 's' to 'kin', it gives you 'skin'.
How to teach the word 'twin'?	w + in = win	When you add the letter 'w' to 'in', it gives you 'win'.
	t + win = twin	When you add the letter 't' to 'win', it gives you 'twin'.

Prerequisites: The student must be aware of the meaning of the simplest word. For instance, if the student does not understand the meaning of the word 'hip', the student will be unable to remember the word 'chip' or 'whip'.

Some words like 'thin' have a real word embedded in it but do not allow a single letter onset in its instruction.

Word parts in the word 'thin'	Comments
in	Real word rime
hin	No such word
th + in	Students may perceive 'th' to be abstract as it is an onset that is made up of two letters.

Some words like 'skip' do not even have a simpler real word embedded in it.

Word parts in the word 'thin'	Comments
ip	Non-real word rime
kip	No such word
sk + ip	Students may perceive 'th' to be abstract as it is an onset that is made up of two letters.

Such words like 'thin' and 'skip' have to be learnt in its entirety like a sight word using other techniques. This means it is more time consuming to learn such words and retention rates are dramatically lower than the words with a real word in it.

o   **Differences between type A and B nonresponders**

It is at this juncture that I must justify why type B nonresponders are unsuited for instruction that is only meant for type A nonresponders.

The key difference between type A and B nonresponders lies in their receptivity towards abstract concepts in the form of non-word rimes.

Type A.1 and A.2 nonresponders	Type A nonresponders are able to tolerate rimes that are not real words.
Type B nonresponders	Type B nonresponders cannot tolerate non-real word rimes at all.

Type A nonresponders have enough receptivity towards abstract concepts to tolerate two letter non-real word rimes. As such, even if they are not taught the real word in the real word technique, they would still be able to remember four-letter CCVC words so long as the words are colour-coded according to onset and rime in order to fit their optimal visual span of two letters or two word chunks. (Type A.1 nonresponders use their scant knowledge of phonics to help them while type A.2 nonresponders just use their visual memory to remember the colour-coded word.) It is just that learning the (real) word in a word technique is even more effective for them as the brain definitely favours less abstract pieces of information for longer retention.

Type B nonresponders, like type X and Y nonresponders, have low tolerance for abstract concepts. They are, in fact, type X nonresponders that are masquerading as type A nonresponders. As such, non-real word rimes are entirely foreign to them. Aggravated by their very poor sight word knowledge, a lack of receptivity to words with non-word rimes means that there are way too many words that the teacher must omit in order for the type B nonresponders to be receptive to the (real) word in a word technique.

In addition, type B nonresponders, like type X and Y nonresponders, are intolerant of low-frequency words. It may be argued that a non-real word rime should not be a problem because the smallest unit of the word is always a real word (e.g. hip -> whip). However 'hip' is a low-frequency word and chances are, the student may not have been frequently exposed to the word nor find it useful enough to appropriate it into their vocabulary. As such, they do not recognise the word 'hip' and the word 'whip' will not be retained as a result.

Word parts in the word 'whip'	Comments
ip	Non-real word rime
hip	Unlikely to exist in their sight memory due to low frequency
whip	Unlikely to remember how the word is spelt due to prior low frequency of the word 'hip'.

Type B nonresponders require a high-frequency real word at every step of the way. Otherwise, there would be little retention of words that are built on top of each other. The table below shows another example.

Word parts in the word 'skin'	Comments
in	High-frequency word
kin	Low-frequency word
skin	Does not remember this word as a result

As such, type B nonresponders are not suited for type A instruction due to such restrictions. They are better off receiving instruction that is meant for type X and Y nonresponders instead.

2. Planning

It is of paramount importance to observe three main principles when you engage in lesson planning for type A nonresponders:

1. Always address words that sound the same together (this applies to both the entire word and rimes)

2. It is alright to tackle words with silent letters alongside with their visually-similar, non-silent letter counterparts (e.g. 'plan' VS 'plan<u>e</u>').

3. It is alright to tackle vowel teams with their non-vowel teams counterparts (e.g. plane VS plain).

The planning stage also comprises of two steps.

Step 1: Start from two letter vowel-consonant rimes (−VC rimes) and sort them according to real or non-real word rimes

Recall that vowels represent letters 'a', 'e', 'i', 'o' and 'u', while consonants represent all the other letters. (Depending on its position, the letter 'y' is both a vowel and consonant. However, it is not within the scope of this book to analyse more about its dual function.)

Also recall that words can be split into onsets and rimes.

$$skip = /sk/ \ /ip/$$
$$\downarrow \quad \downarrow$$
$$Onset \quad Rime$$

In the phonics world, words can be labelled according to vowels (V) and consonants (C).

$$skip = sk \quad ip$$
$$\downarrow \quad \downarrow$$
$$CC \quad VC$$

$$cat = \quad c \quad at$$
$$\downarrow \quad \downarrow$$
$$C \quad VC$$

$$drain = dr \quad ain$$
$$\downarrow \quad \downarrow$$
$$CC \quad VVC$$

Silent letters are also included in the labelling.

$$kite = \quad k \quad ite$$

$$\downarrow \quad \downarrow$$

$$C \quad VCe$$

$$scrape = scr \quad ape$$

$$\downarrow \quad \downarrow$$

$$CCC \quad VCe$$

The labelling of words is actually more complicated than what I have described. However, this level of labelling is enough for type A intervention.

You will start by sorting –VC rimes into two categories – real word rimes and non-real word rimes.

Real word rime
-am, -an, -at, -in, -it, -on
Non-real word rime
-ab, -ad, -ag, -ap, -ib, -id, -ig, -im, -ip, -ob, -od, -og, -om, -op, -ot, -ed, -eg, -em, -en, -et, -ub, -ud, -un, -um, -ug, -ut

[As a side note, the table above illustrates why a normal onset-rime instruction will not work for type B nonresponders. Recall that type B nonresponders are unable to tolerate non-real word rimes. Just look at the number of non-real word rimes in the table.]

For the purpose of illustration, I decide to teach words that contain the rime '-an'. As such, I have to teach the following words to the student: 'man', 'ban', 'ran', 'can', 'scan', 'van', 'fan', 'pan', 'span', 'clan', 'plan'.

Step 2: Decide on the words that should be taught alongside with –VC rimes

Now, I have to decide what other words I should teach alongside the words with '-an'. This is to ensure that confusion does not set in.

You always need to consider two things:

1. Rimes that look visually similar

    o The silent letter alternative (especially words with –VCe rimes)

2. Rimes that sound the same

It is exceedingly important to note that these two considerations that will result in massive confusion if they are not addressed properly. The table below offers two options for the instruction of the '-an' rime.

Option 1 Option 2	-VC rime	-VCe rimes *(Visually similar + silent letter)*	Rimes that sound the same as the –VCe rime
Those that sound the same as the -VC rime	-an	-ane	-ain
	-en		
	-and		
	-end		

You may choose option 1 and teach words with '-an' alongside with its magic-e counterpart '-ane'. Teaching words with their magic-e counterparts is a good way to avoid confusion as some students would randomly add the letter 'e' behind each word due to confusion over their visual similarities. The following words comprise of the rime '-ane': 'Jane', 'cane', 'sane', 'lane', 'plane', 'mane', 'crane'.

However, it is paramount to include words with '-ain' after you teach words with '-ane' as they make similar sounds.

The table below shows the spread of words that contain '-an', '-ane' and '-ain' rimes. The words that are underlined signal that there are other words that sound exactly the same as the underlined word (e.g. 'plane' VS 'plain'). These words run the risk of causing even more confusion among the nonresponders as they either look similar or sound exactly the same.

Real word rime	Non-real word rime	Non-real word rime
-an	-ane	-ain
ban	bane	gain
ran	pane	pain, Spain
can, scan	Jane	rain, brain, drain, grain, train
van	cane	
fan	sane	
pan, span	lane, plane	plain
clan	mane	main
plan	crane	vain
		stain

Alternatively, you may opt for option 2 and teach other common rimes that have similar sounds. The issue with rimes that sound similar is that it depends on the society that you are in. On paper, it would seem that the only similar rime to '-an' is '-en'. However, the people in my country do not enunciate the words properly. Often, they will omit the sounds at the back of the words. Thus, sounds after -VC tend to be omitted.

e.g. **stan**d

The sound /d/ is omitted.

As such, the lack of proper enunciation complicates matters exponentially as the number of rimes that sound the same increases dramatically to the following rimes: '-en', '-and' and '-end'.

In fact, the people in my country do not enunciate ending sounds of 'n' and 'm' as well. As such, I may have to include '-am' into the list as it sounds similar to '-an'. The list of potential similar-sounding rimes may extend. Not only does it depend of the society that you are embedded in, a lot also depends on whether the learner is able to discern the difference in sounds. If the learner has an auditory processing disorder and perceive many words to sound exactly the same, the number of rimes that you have to consider alongside with the rest of the similar-sounding rimes increases too.

Option 1 Option 2	-VC rime	-VCe rimes *(Visually similar + silent letter)*		Rimes that sound the same as the –VCe rime	
Those that sounds the same as the -VC rime	-an	-ane	-ame	-ain	-aim
	-en				
	-and				
	-end				
	-am				
	-amp *				
	-ant*				
	-ent*				

*This is assuming that a student with auditory processing disorder is unable to discern the ending sounds.

It gets really confusing if you include too many similar sounding rimes. Please exercise discretion and introduce high frequency words instead. The table below shows you the recommended words that contain similar sounding rimes.

Real word rime	Non-real word rime	Real word rime	Real word rime	Real word rime
-an	**-en**	**-and**	**-end**	**-am**
ban	ben	band	bend	ham
ran	den	sand	send	jam
can, scan	men	land, bland,	lend, blend	ram, cram, scram

man		grand, brand	mend	dam
van	hen	hand		yam
fan	pen	stand		slam, clam, glam
pan, span	ten			spam
clan			tend	scam
plan			spend	swam
			trend	
			friend	

If you are starting to get a bit overwhelmed, just remember to start teaching from the shortest words (CVC and CCVC words). In particular, you should choose to start with words that have two-letter rimes in order to plan for words that fit comfortably into their visual span. If the rime is a real word, the likelihood of word retention is even higher.

o   **Questions and Answers**

Question 1: Why is it okay to teach words with -VCe rimes alongside with the non-silent 'e' counterparts (-VC rimes)?

Answer: To facilitate my explanation, let us refer to the following examples of words with the vowel 'i'.

-VC words	-VCe words
bit	bite
pin	pine
win	wine
snip	snipe

In the phonics world, vowels make different sounds with and without the letter 'e' at the back of the word. In this case, the vowel 'i' in the –VC words makes the same sound as the letter 'i' in the word 'igloo'. The vowel 'i' in the -VCe word makes the same sound as the letter 'i' in the word 'nine'. In essence, when there is a -VCe formation, the letter 'e' – while silent – influences the vowel to make a sound that is actually the name of the vowel.

VCe words	Sound		-VC words	Sound
tape	'a' for 'able'		tap	'a' for 'apple'
theme	'e' for 'eject'		them	'e' for 'elephant'
ripe	'i' for 'idea'		rip	'i' for 'igloo'
hope	'o' for 'open'		hop	'o' for 'octopus'
cute	'u' for 'unit'		cut	'u' for 'umbrella'

Simply put, students are taught the following rule: When the letter 'e' is inserted at the back of non-magic-e words (that is at the end of –VC words), the vowel sound changes into the name of the vowel.

In case you are interested in jargons, phonics teachers give different terminology to label these different vowel sounds.

Category	Examples	Sound	Terminology
-VC word	win	Vowel makes the sound of /i/ in the word 'igloo'.	Such vowel sounds are known as "short vowel sounds".
-VCe word	wine	Vowel makes the sound of the letter name.	Such vowel sounds are known as "long vowel sounds".

Astute teachers may perceive that there are too many jargons and rules for some of the students to understand. As such, they may create stories that describe the -VCe rule. They may create any story and term this concept as 'magic-e', 'superhero-e' or 'sneaky –e'.

The fact of the matter is that the phonics curriculum tries to establish a **similarity** between the -VC and -VCe words. For instance, the words 'win' and 'wine' are visually similar. The word 'win' morphs into 'wine' just by inserting a silent letter 'e' at the back of the word and, as a result, manipulating the short vowel sound into a long vowel sound.

That in itself, if properly instructed, is very useful for phonics responders to understand the change between words like 'win' to 'wine'. Such students who are phonics inclined are receptive to phonics rules and able to manipulate the long and short vowel sounds instantly between words.

Nonresponders find all these talk about the short and long vowel sound, and phonics rules to be utterly pointless. In that split second of determining how the word 'win' or 'wine' is to be read, they do not think of all of these phonics sounds nor concepts. Should they be exposed to the phonics concept of –VCe words, the nonresponders who are more susceptible to confusion will start adding letter 'e's at the back of random words because they have little idea as to what the phonics concepts mean. From their perspective, it seems like the letter 'e's are randomly popping up behind words.

Frankly speaking, that is a nightmare. Should they exhibit such behaviour, it shows that the confusion of the silent letter 'e' has pervaded across their literacy bank. When such confusion crosses a certain threshold, no amount of instruction would be able to 'save' the student. [Refer to 'Chronic effect: Warren ' in chapter 5]

As mentioned in chapter 2c, this nonresponder attempted to write the same phrase "three strokes of caning" twice in the same essay. He did not know if the word 'stroke' had a letter 'e'. The confusion between words 'keen' and 'cane' will be addressed in chapter 5.
(This nonresponder received five years of phonics intervention.)

Instead of forming linkages and establishing similarities between the words (as seen in the phonics curriculum), nonresponder intervention **should focus on the**

difference between words with silent letters and their non-silent letter counterparts. Try as far as possible to ensure that there are no similarities between them. This way, the words form two separate word categories in their head and the separation allows the students to avoid mixing the spelling of the two words together.

Do refer to the section on "Material Preparation" for the emphasis on the difference between words with silent letters and their non-silent letter counterparts.

Question 2: Why should I introduce vowel teams together with single vowels?

Answer: You have to introduce rhymes that makes the 'it' sound in order to avoid confusion. In this case, it would be 'eat', 'eet' and 'it'.

In the phonics world, teachers are not supposed to introduce other phonograms like 'ea' and 'ee' as phonograms that consist of two vowels are advanced concepts that should not be introduced together with a basic concept like vowel 'i' for two reasons:

- *Vowel 'i' makes a different sound than 'ea' and 'ee'*

  For instance, 'beach' or 'feet' has a stretched 'ea' or 'ee' sound while the 'i' sound in 'bit' is not stretched.

- *To avoid confusion over which phonogram to use*

  In other words, they have valid concerns that should a student learn 'i', 'ea', 'ee' (and other /e/ sounds) together, the student will not be able to know which phonogram should be inserted into words with the /e/ sound. It will subsequently affect his or her spelling accuracy.

  E.g. 'sp___t'

  When asked to spell the word 'spit', the student may spell 'speat' or 'speet' instead.

  This is a valid concern if the student is phonics inclined. Time is needed to allow the student to build a bank of words relating to the vowel 'i' before teaching words with 'ea' or 'ee'.

On the other hand, nonresponders will not be confused by the introduction of these phonograms. In fact, they will be confused if you do not introduce them together.

They are not interested in the sounds that the different phonograms make. In fact, it does not make much sense to them. What is an 'ea' anyway? It is not even a word!

If they are taught phonics, some of them may humour the teacher by being able to recall the sounds for each phonogram but in no way will they apply the techniques into their spelling application. Some nonresponders will not be receptive to remembering the sound in the first place.

The entire word should be introduced together with the meaning, thereby alleviating confusion at that very instant. Should you only introduce the word 'it', nonrepsonders (who have poor spelling accuracy) will be confused as they would think that 'it' represents all the /it/ words they have come across. They may start spelling 'eat' as 'it' or 'eit'. Alternatively, they may get confused when they see the word 'eat' as they were not taught that version of /it/ and proceed to either perpetuate the confusion or forget whatever the teacher has taught. As a result, it gives the teacher the impression that the student has poor word retention and the teacher will proceed to reinforce the concept taught until they "get it".

Question 3: *Why do I have to go through so much trouble for words with the silent letter 'e' when you can just attach the letter 'e' at the back of a real word? (e.g. rip + e = ripe)*

This is indeed an easier method to introduce words with the letter 'e'. You can do this if you are 100% certain that the nonresponder will not be confused with when to include the letter 'e'. However, my experience tells me that the nonresponders are unable to recall when and where to insert the letter 'e' due to their limited working memory. In addition, this method of inserting the letter 'e' at the back of a real word promotes similarity – not difference – between the words 'rip' and 'ripe'. This similarity is likely to trigger confusion and the student may start inserting letter 'e's at the back of random words.

3. Material preparation

Let us assume that I have decided to go with option 1. I will compare words with '-an' with '-ane' and 'ain'. Each rime will have a dedicated colour. By default, I colour code two-letter rimes (e.g. '–ap', '-an', '-at') with red, three-letter magic-e rimes with purple and other rimes like '-and', '-end' and '-ain' get any available colour.

I colour code it like that in order to break the word into two parts, which falls perfectly into the preferred visual span of the nonresponders. In addition, this way of colour coding allows the teacher to kill two birds with one stone. I can use the card to teach students who actually respond to phonics by teaching the onset and rime (sc **an**) or I can use it for type A instruction.

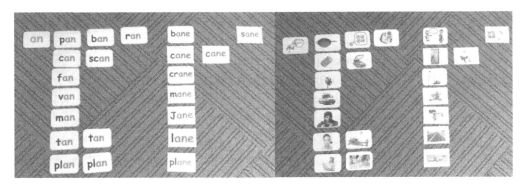

Front: Colour-coded '-an' and '-ane' cards   *Back: Visuals for each word*

I find it important to attach a visual behind each word to ensure immediate linking of the word to its meaning. It promotes retention and aids those with language difficulties. In addition, it is necessary to prevent confusion when I introduce homographs (e.g. 'plane' vs 'plain'). This is because the only way to allow students to achieve greater accuracy for visually or auditorily-similar words is to reinforce the difference through (1) colour coding, and (2) attaching a distinct meaning to each word.

To enhance the multi-functionality of the cards, I have also created the cards with grammar instruction in mind. I frame each card with a coloured border according to the grammar category of the word. Once again, I ensure that the colours between the different categories are distinct to promote difference. The colours of words within the same grammar category are shades of the same colour. Nouns are framed with a green border. Adjectives (describing words) are framed with a red border. Present and past tense verbs (action words) are framed with a yellow and orange border respectively. Abstract words are framed with a black border.

As a side note, I try to infuse as much meaning into everything that I design. This means that there is a rationale for the coloured borders as well. For instance, the reason why the present and past tense verbs are framed with a yellow and orange border respectively is due to my attempt at creating an 'aged' look. Logically speaking, time has passed from the present. Comparatively, the colour yellow has 'aged' into the colour orange.

Many teachers or parents simply do not have the time to prepare such an extensive array of materials. An easier alternative is to either write the colour-coded words on a piece of paper with the ipad or smart phone within arm's reach to show pictures that represents the meaning of the words. If you wish to teach each word individually, simply write and colour code it on a piece of scrap paper, organise the words accordingly (I use the old Kodak photo albums to keep them) and arm yourself with the ipad or smart phone to search for the meaning of the words anytime.

CHAPTER 4

HIGH-FREQUENCY WORD INSTRUCTION FOR TYPE Xs AND Ys

The difference between types A nonresponders and type X/Y nonresponders is the unusual lack of receptivity and automaticity towards what is perceived to be the simplest of words regardless of the frequency of exposure and practice. The "simplest of words" are high-frequency words that are found in the pre-primer and primer Dolch lists (e.g. 'it', 'about', 'was', 'then'). Despite its simplicity, type X and Y nonresponders are still unable to read or spell such words consistently. Even with constant exposure to such words in texts, the nonresponders are just simply unable to remember these words to read and, in particular, spell them accurately.

Even though there is much variation amongst the learning needs of type X and Y nonresponders, all of them struggle with what I term as the "three tracks of impairment". The three tracks of impairment forms the cornerstone of type X and Y instruction.

THE THREE TRACKS OF IMPAIRMENT		
Impairment of the language / comprehension track	Impairment of the auditory track	Impairment of the visual track

All type X and Y nonresponders face similar difficulties across all three tracks, which in turn affect their literacy acquisition of the simplest of words. In particular, the three tracks of impairment affect the following categories of words in each respective track:

THE THREE TRACKS OF IMPAIRMENT		
Impairment of the language / comprehension track	Impairment of the auditory track	Impairment of the visual track
• Words with multiple or similar meanings e.g. 'flat' [multiple meanings]	• Words that sound the same e.g. 'sun' vs 'son'	• Visually-similar words e.g. 'send' vs 'seed'*

e.g. 'get' vs 'receive' [similar meanings]		*What is deemed as visually-similar words varies among the nonresponders. For instance, some nonresponders who are only able to remember the first and the last letter may perceive the following words – 'said', 'sand', 'sized', 'sword', 'sound' etc. – to be visually-similar to 'send' and 'seed'. Nonresponders who are only able to remember the first letter may perceive an even wider range of words to be visually similar.
• Words with abstract meanings e.g. 'at', 'by', 'are' and 'upon'		
• Action words with tenses *(No concept of anything beyond present tense)* e.g. 'flew', 'drove', 'shown' and 'made'		

It may seem like there are similarities the planning of type A and type X/Y instruction. In particular, it seems like type X and Y instruction just has an added track for language and comprehension impairment. Please do not be lulled into this false assumption that the both types of instruction are similar. The difference between type A and type X/Y instruction greatly outweighs any perceived similarities that both types of instruction possess. While all types of nonresponders will have difficulties with auditory and visually-similar words, the degree of confusion that type X and Y nonresponders face upon dealing with words along the three tracks of impairment is vastly greater – and more severe – than the type A nonresponders.

This immense confusion translates into a perpetual block in their literacy acquisition. When they seem to be perpetually confused with the easiest of words, their word retention ability will be hindered. In many cases, such hindrance results in teenage illiteracy.

Another critical thing to note is that beyond this commonality of severe difficulties, each type X or Y nonresponder has a greater relative impairment affecting at least one or more tracks of impairment. In other words, while all type X and Y nonresponders struggle with difficulties across all tracks, each of them has a particular difficulty with at least one track of impairment.

Consequently, the track that they have particular difficulties with becomes the track that is (1) their least preferred track in learning and information acquisition, or (2) the very track that hinders the nonresponder from being receptive to literacy instruction. This is known as a 'disinclination'.

It is this disinclination that shapes a type X or, in particular, a type Y nonresponder's distinctively unique, yet extremely narrow, style of learning. Understanding their disinclination towards a particular track becomes **absolutely critical** in discerning and customising a method that facilitates their receptivity to learning.

As such, this chapter will be divided into two sections. The first section teaches you how to plan and teach the list of problematic high-frequency words that only seem to perpetuate confusion among the type X and Y nonresponders. The second section attempts to explain how the disinclination towards a particular track shapes a narrow and distinct learning style that is unique to each type X and Y nonresponder.

I have to emphasize again that this chapter is of paramount importance. The second section is generally the most mind-boggling part of the nonresponders instruction. Due to its complexity, many teachers fail to wrap their mind around it, thereby affecting their ability to even begin to understand how type X and Y nonresponders think. (There is a reason why many teachers are unable to teach the type X and Y nonresponders.) While I will attempt to simplify my explanation, I have to state a disclaimer that not everybody will be able to understand the second section.

Nevertheless, we have to try.

Part 1: Instruction for Type Xs and Ys

There are two reasons why type X and Y nonresponders, regardless of age, look like they are unable to spell the simplest of sight words that were taught since pre-school. One of the main reasons is language impairment.

(The other reason is due to a visual disinclination. This concept will be further elaborated in the second part of this chapter.)

Origin of problem	Resulted track impairment
Problems with conceptual understanding	• Impairment of the language / comprehension track
Problems with sensory processing	• Impairment of the auditory track • Impairment of the visual track

Planning for type X and Y instruction operates on the assumption that most type X and, especially, type Y nonresponders have problems with their conceptual understanding of the word (and the world in general). As such, planning for type X and Y instruction involves addressing their problems with conceptual understanding before tackling problems with sensory processing.

- *Explaining the impairment of the language / comprehension track*

Recall that students with language impairment have difficulty understanding abstract words or concepts that do not have a direct representation in reality. They only have tolerance for concrete words. An example was previously mentioned was about a language-impaired student who only understood the word 'race' as a running competition. He was not able to accept the other meaning – "ethnic group" – due to the abstract nature of the term.

Students with language impairment also have difficulty remembering anything beyond the present tense form of the word as their concept of time is not sound.

As such, words that are difficult to understand become meaningless and there will be extremely low rates of retention. In some cases, there will be absolutely no retention regardless of the frequency of word exposure.

This is known as the language or comprehension impairment track. Words of such nature are prevalent in high-frequency word lists that the kindergarteners and grade 1 students are expected to learn. In other words, the 'easiest' words in the English vocabulary turn out to be the most difficult words for type X and Y nonresponders to master.

1. Planning

Step 1: Account for the impairment of the language / comprehension track during planning

Before planning for type X and Y instruction, you have to mentally classify any word that you intend to teach into one of the three different categories (concrete, abstract or past tense). This is to accommodate the needs of type X and Y nonresponders who demonstrate an impairment along the language and comprehension track.

Often, type X and Y nonresponders who have impairments along the language and comprehension track bewilder their teachers and therapists. Feedback on their literacy performances usually revolve around the following comments:

- The student can read and spell words like 'sword' or 'chair' but not words like 'am' or 'us'.

- The student cannot recognise 'simple' words like 'now' or 'the' regardless of repeated exposure of the word just seconds ago.

- The student can read and write words like 'jump' and 'run'. However, his or her past tense is non-existent. The student cannot read and spell the word 'jumped' and 'ran' even though the student uses these past tense forms in their speech all the time.

Such puzzling literacy behaviour is readily explainable once the teacher or therapist reclassifies the word into one of the three categories.

In the following example, I will be using the following Pre-K and Kindergarten Dolch sight word list to explain the reason for such 'puzzling' behaviour.

Pre-K Dolch sight word list (40 words)
a, and, away, big, blue, can, come, down, find, for, funny, go, help, here, I, in, is, it, jump, little, look, make, me, my, not, one, play, red, run, said, see, the, three, to, two, up, we, where, yellow, you

Kindergarten Dolch sight word list (52 words)
all, am, are, at, ate, be, black, brown, but, came, did, do, eat, four, get, good, have, he, into, like, must, new, no, now, on, our, out, please, pretty, ran, ride, saw, say, she, so, soon, that, there, they, this, too, under, want, was, well, went, what, white, who, will, with, yes

I am going to sort these words into 3 categories – (1) abstract, (2) past tense, and (3) concrete.

Abstract (47 words)
a, am, and, are, at, be, but, can, did, do, for, have, in, into, is, it, must, not, now (here), on, out, please*, so, soon, that, the, there, this, to, too, under, was, well*, what, where, who, will, with I*, me, my, we, you, she, our, he, they *May not be deemed as an abstract word to some students

Past tense (6 words)
ate, came, ran, said, saw, went

Concrete (39 words)
all**, big, black, blue, brown, come, down, eat, four, find, funny, get, go, good, help, here, jump, like, little, look, make, new, no**, one, play, pretty, red, ride, run, say, see, three, two, up, want, white, yellow, yes** ** May not be deemed as a 'concrete' word to some students

Theoretically, type X and Y nonresponders will be able to remember concrete words more easily as compared to words in the other categories because concrete words are represented in reality. When they are taught the word 'eat', the word is validated because they see the act of consumption in reality. Abstract words trigger confusion because they have no direct representation in reality. Words in past tense (e.g. 'ran', 'cooked') are also more likely to spark confusion because type X and Y nonresponders are unable to understand the concept of time and, as a result, do not understand why a concrete representation is represented by more than one word (e.g. 'run' and 'ran').

This is not to say that type X and Y nonresponders will definitely spell every word in the concrete category correctly. Rather, it means that such students will demonstrate exponentially higher levels of receptivity towards concrete words as compared to words from the other two categories.

For instance, the word 'jump' is a concrete word. The word 'jumped', on the other hand, is not properly understood by type X and Y nonresponders. The words 'jump' and 'jumped' are represented by the same mental image of a person jumping. As such, it triggers confusion as the student is unable to understand the difference between both words. Hence, the past tense is deemed to be redundant and as a result, students often write in present tense and omit the other tenses altogether.

However, the most severe of type Y nonresponders with particularly dominant language impairment will have problems with some words in the concrete category. If a type Y nonresponder exhibits a particularly severe form of language impairment that affects the distinction of words due to the overlapping mental images, it is paramount that words with multiple or similar meanings should be factored in. Such type Y nonresponders have what I term as a "language disinclination". While I will be exploring more about disinclinations in the second part of this chapter, I would like to present an example right now to facilitate understanding of the additional language difficulties that this group of severe type Y nonresponders face.

For instance, these type Y nonresponders may read the word 'pretty' as 'beautiful' – or vice versa. This is because 'pretty' and 'beautiful' are likely to be represented by the same mental image. Since there is no visual distinction between the two words, these nonresponders get confused. Words that share the same mental image may cross grammar categories too. The word 'funny' shares the same mental image as 'laugh'. Both words may be represented by a picture of a person whose facial features express mirth. As such, the word 'funny' may be read as 'laugh' even though 'funny' is an adjective (describing word) while 'laugh' is a verb (action word). The student may read the sentence "The story is funny." as /The story is laugh./ and proceed to further undermine his or her compromised state of language development.

As seen in the recategorized Dolch word list, the high-frequency sight words that the students are exposed to at the pre-school level are predominantly abstract words. Type X and Y nonresponders who exhibit impairments in the language and comprehension track will undoubtedly be confused with abstract words and words in the past tense form. Such confusion will persist with age, resulting in a student's inability to recognise or spell seemingly 'easy' words even at an older age.

As such, the recategorization of words sets an expectation of the different intervention demands of each category of words. Each category of words requires a varied intervention approach, to which the intervention is further complicated by the different needs of each nonresponder. To simplify matters, the following example in step 2 will involve the planning of words in the concrete category.

Step 2: Including the three tracks of impairment in the vertical and horizontal planning

Once the teacher or therapist is able to recategorize the words into one of the three categories, the next step would be to select a word and engage in lesson planning.

For instance, a teacher or therapist would like to teach the word 'ear'. The teacher or therapist may wish to expand his or her planning by including words in the '-ear' word family. As such, the words 'year' and 'hear' are included.

However, words like 'bear' and 'wear' have to be included in the planning. Even though the rime '-ear' makes a different sound (short /e/ instead of /ear/), these words are still visually similar to the word 'ear' and confusion will pervade if the words are not addressed there and then.

For the record, it is important to note that the auditory patterns between words is rarely consequential to type X and Y nonresponders. Some type X and Y nonresponders may be able to identify patterns between the sound of the words while other type X and Y nonresponders will never find any meaning in distinguishing the sounds. Some type X and Y nonresponders will be able to replicate the onset and rime technique that is taught by the teacher or therapist to such a convincing degree that it seems like the nonresponder is a phonics responder. Regardless, when type X and Y nonresponders are left to their own devices, they will rarely – if ever – spell and read using the similarity of rimes among words. Often, they tend to remember the word in isolation, only demonstrating confusion when words along the three tracks of impairments are infringed.

With this, what I term as "vertical planning" is complete. Vertical planning means the planning of words within the word family even if the rime – in this case '-ear' – does not make the same sound.

The next step is to engage in "lateral planning". You have to incorporate the three tracks of impairment into your planning. For each word in the word family, you have to figure out if there are other words that fall into the three tracks of impairment. For instance, the word 'hear' sounds like 'here' and both words have to be taught together with the word 'hear' to avoid confusion.

The table below shows the entire vertical and lateral planning of the word family '-ear'.

| Three tracks of impairment

Word family	Words with multiple / abstract meanings	Words with the same sound	Visually-similar words
Ear			
Year			
Hear		Here	
Tear	Tear		
Bear		[Bare]	
Wear		Where	Were*

Vertical planning — Same pattern, same sound / Same pattern, different sound

Lateral planning

Things to note:

1. The word 'bare' is encapsulated by the symbol [ ] because it is a low-frequency word. You have to seriously consider if you wish to include low-frequency words into your instruction because the addition of another word with the same sound takes a lot more effort for the student to remember the meanings and spellings of the words 'bear' and 'bare'.

2. The inclusion of the word 'were' is a result of the inclusion of the word 'where' (not the word 'wear'). This is important because every word that you include into your planning, regardless of its origins from the word family or the three tracks of impairment, will be subjected to another round of scrutiny to determine if other words have to be included under the three tracks of impairment to avoid confusion. This means that, at times, the number of words planned for instruction will increase dramatically.Discretion is required to prevent yourself from covering too much ground.

Alternatively, you may wish to avoid words using the vertical planning axis and just plan to teach each word and its lateral planning counterparts on their own. That is perfectly fine as the use of words in the same word family is just a matter of convenience to the teacher.

2. How to teach

- **Approaches that only work for certain types of X and Y nonresponders**

1. **Targeted graphics for letters of confusion**
   (Note: Not just embedding a picture into the word)

If you look at publications or manipulatives available in the market, you will realise that embedding graphics into a word is usually one of the methods proposed for students who cannot respond to phonics. These students are identified to be the creative ones who are 'right-brained'. With the graphics, the 'right-brainers' can imprint the words in their minds. An additional benefit is that pictures provide meaning alongside with the shape of the wordform. As such, meaning is attached to the word and word retention is evident.

The picture below shows an example of such a resource.

Story: The butterfly was once a worm.

For struggling readers (and those with visual perceptual or storage issues), sight words without graphics are equivalent to blobs of ink. Sight words of the similar length and shape just looks the same to them. Initially, the only crutch that they have is to make sense of the graphic embedded in the word and guess how the word is read. It is only after much guessing and exposure to certain shapes of the word that a struggling reader be able to grudgingly recognise words without the use of graphics.

I support the inclusion of graphics in such words. Sight words without pictures are not effective tools for teaching. Graphics and stories allow abled-readers to read and recognise sight words faster than the non-graphic sight word cards as the combination of graphics and stories allows meaning making to occur, resulting in faster and longer periods of retention.

In other words, graphics are paramount.

However, a lot of the sight words with graphics only cater for meaning making.

Take a look at the word 'was' that is shown above.

Most students should be able to read the word when the card is shown to them. They would eventually be able to read the word without the aid of graphics. This is particularly effective for non-readers with dyslexia who are receptive to phonics.

Type X and Y nonresponders are unlikely to read the sight words even after being exposed to those sight word cards for a period of time. For those who are able to read the sight words, they tend to rely on guesswork. Regardless, both type X and Y nonresponders have great difficulties in spelling these sight words as spelling requires attention to detail and accuracy. They may spell it as 'wos' or 'wus'. They require an approach to remember the vowel 'a' in the word 'was'.

Sight word cards with graphics that are readily available in the market will not work for type X and Y nonresponders because the cards do not explain the existence of certain letters in the word. For instance, the sight word card above does not have a graphic and narrative to explain why the vowel 'a' exists in the word 'was'. This is because the primary objective of the sight word cards in the market is raise word recognition and not to ensure spelling accuracy. What type X and Y nonresponders require are targeted graphics for letters of confusion.

Story: The apple was eaten by the worm. (The worm was drawn such that the nonresponder can distinctively remember the letter 'a'.)

Different type X and Y nonresponders have difficulties with different letter(s) of the word. Perhaps, in the word 'always', one student may spell it as 'allway'. Others may spell it as 'awy', 'aw' or 'ay'. Some will not be able to spell at all.

Each student omits different letters, include wrong letters or reverse the order of certain letter sequences. As such, graphics and the associated stories have to be embedded in only these letters that were omitted or reversed. To make matters more complicated, type X and Y nonresponders fall into three subcategories with regards to their receptivity towards using graphics and stories for word retention.

Type X and Y subcategories	Receptivity towards graphics and stories	Reason
1	Those who can accept any graphic and story provided by the therapist.	- No language impairment
2	Those who can only accept their own graphics and stories according to their understanding.	- May have some degree of language difficulty - Only derives meaning from strong and relatable personal experiences
3	Those who reject graphics and stories entirely.	- Presence of language impairment

There are more type X and Y nonresponders who fall into the second category. It is no wonder that readily available graphic-embedded sight word cards are ineffective for them. Instead, you should just prepare many small pieces of scrap paper and embed graphics and stories into the targeted letters of confusion with magic pens or permanent markers.

In defence of the manufacturers of the sight word manipulatives in the market, it is impossible to produce targeted graphics and stories for each consumer as different nonresponders have different letters that they are confused with. The sight word cards target only the first subcategory of type X and Y nonresponders who can accept any story provided, leaving out the second and third category altogether. As such, the technique of targeted graphics and stories is a 'Do-It-Yourself' initiative for practical reasons.

However, not every type X and Y nonresponders will be receptive to this approach. The differences between type X and Y nonresponders who are receptive to stories and graphics, and those who are not are summarised in the following table:

Meaning making (for retention)	
The realist faction	**The story faction**

• Usually have language difficulties or impairment
 	
• Rejects the notion of forming stories or embedding graphics in the letters
 	
• Requires 'realistic' explanations for anything they do not understand (Otherwise, there will not be information retention.)
 	
• Receptivity to the other techniques (except the formation of stories or embedding graphics) depends on the nonresonders' degree of receptivity towards abstract concepts
 	
    a) Mild to moderate
 	
    They are accepting towards the following techniques:
 	
    ○ (Real) word in a word (RW)²
 	
    ○ Targeted graphics for letters of confusion
 	
    Should there be no 'realistic' explanation for the technique for "Removing, replacing or shifting letters from a combination of real words" (RRS), these students would rather remember the techniques as it is.
	• Receptive to all techniques
	
	• Requires the justification of the "Removing, replacing or shifting letters from a combination of real words" (RRS) technique using stories

b) Severe	
The most severe of cases rejects almost all of the techniques. They are only open to mnemonics.	

- **Approaches that work for most type Xs and Ys (only when the pre-requisites are met)**

1. (Real) word in a word

Completely identical to the techniques for type A nonresponders, type X and Y nonresponders are also receptive to the word in a word technique. Similar to type A.2 nonresponders, type X and Y nonresponders are not receptive to blends (e.g. fl + at = flat) and the effectiveness of this technique depends on the shorter real words that they are currently aware of.

For type X and – especially – Y nonresponders, however, their existing base of real word knowledge is abysmally small to the point that this technique is rendered useless. You have to drastically expand their recognition of sight words. If this pre-requisite is not met, this approach will not work for type X and Y nonresponders.

2. Changing the first letter of a (real) word into another word

Theoretically, type X and Y nonresponders are receptive to this technique. In fact, this technique is so common in the world of literacy acquisition that almost any student – dyslexic or not – have been instructed in the following way in one form or another:

"This is the word 'had'. Now, if you change 'h' to 'm', you will get 'mad'."

Type X and Y nonresponders have pre-requisites for this technique. Firstly, the words that are taught must fit within their preferred visual span. Usually, it is at most 4 letters but there are type Y nonresponders that have shorter visual spans. Secondly, the student needs to know how to spell the first word with great confidence. Many type X and Y nonresponders have exceedingly small pools of words that they can spell reliably and independently. Perhaps, they may confuse it with the word 'had' with 'hat' despite much reinforcement. In addition, 'had' is an abstract word and it is not easy to understand due to a lack of concrete representation in reality. So long as they are unable to spell the first word automatically and independently, it is safe to say that the subsequent word – in this case 'mad' – will never be learnt properly and confusion will persist.

3. Mnemonics

Mnemonics only works when prerequisites are met. As usual, the student must have an existing base of known sight words. However, they need not be able to spell the entire word. They just need to know what the first letter of the sight word is. For instance, the word 'does' may have the following mnemonic:

"Dogs only eat sausages." or "Dogs only eat sweets."

The student may not be able to spell 'sweets', 'sausages' or 'only' accurately but so long as they know that the word starts with the letters 's' or 'o' respectively, mnemonics remains as a possible option for literacy acquisition.

Type X and Y nonresponders have little problem remembering long mnemonics (unless they have a memory problem) but the chances of increasing retention of the mnemonic depends on the relatability of the story.

In addition, the problem with type Y nonresponders is that they are unaware of the first letter of many words (especially abstract words), rendering the technique ineffective. For instance, one of my type Y nonresponders was not able to spell the word 'because' using mnemonics as we were unable to find a suitable word that could represent the letter 'a'. The following sentence shows the conventional mnemonic for the word 'because':

"Big elephant can always understand small elephant."

While he was able to remember the mnemonic effortlessly, he struggled with the word 'always' as he could not remember that the world started with the letter 'a'. He thought that 'always' started with the letter 'u'. Even after changing 'always' to 'also', he was still unable to remember to spell the word accurately because he thought that 'also' started with the letter 'o'.

- **Approach that works for the majority of type X and Y nonresponders**

1. Removing, replacing or shifting letters from a combination of real words (RRS)

This seemingly unimpressive label lies a powerful method that is backed by the logic that we have discussed in this book – that type Y nonresponders (and some type X nonresponders) are only receptive to real words, period. Like type A.2 and B responders, their tolerance for abstract concepts only extends to single letters and not blends.

However, type X and Y nonresponders take it one step further. Every word that you teach them has to be a formation of a shorter real words. But it is not practical to do so as not all words have a shorter real word in it. For instance, there is no such thing as 'lat' in the word 'flat'. Does it mean that the word is inaccessible to nonresponders?

Not at all. This is what you do.

Step 1: Create a combination of shorter real words from the word 'flat'.

From the top of my head, I see the following short real words 'fly' and 'at'. I place these two words together – 'flyat'.

Step 2: Delete the offending letter

I delete the letter(s) that should not be in the word 'flat'.

fl̶y̶at

Step 3: Establish meaning making

To give meaning to these two shorter real words, it is highly recommended that you create a story to link the words 'fly', 'at' and 'flat'.

For instance, I may create the following story: "The drones will <u>fly</u> past that block of flats <u>at</u> nine o'clock."

As such, the nonresponders will demonstrate greater retention towards the shorter real words that are used to form the word 'flat'.

The realist faction does not need the story.

Looking at another example, you may wish to teach the words 'ear', 'hear' and 'year' that come from the same word family.

You may be tempted to use the "word in a word" technique. After all, 'ear' acts as a base word for the rest of the words. However, it only works if the student is aware of how to spell the word 'ear'. Often, they do not know how to spell it. My 16-year-old still struggled with it till the day of his graduation.

In cases like this, you have to use the RRS technique.

The word 'hear' is made up of two simpler sight words – 'he' and 'are' without the last letter 'e'

Demonstrate to the nonresponder that both words should be placed together before making a show of cancelling the last letter 'e' as shown below:

Hear~~e~~

The same applies to the word 'year'.

Year = 'Yes' + 'are' – 's' – the last 'e'   = **Ye~~s~~ ar~~e~~**

Note

There is a valid concern that using 'he' + 'are' – 'e' is not grammatically sound, and it will affect meaning making as 'he' is singular' while 'are' is plural. This is true if the student has severe language impairment and meaning making must be established. However, the student should assure you that using 'he' and 'are' to spell 'hear' is fine and that he is able to remember the two words without needing a story to establish connection. If the student needs a connection, then the words must be grammatically correct. I will change the words to 'the' and 'are' instead. The words will be a such:

Hear = 'The' + 'are' – 't' – the last 'e' = ~~T~~**hear**~~e~~

The following story will be conveyed: "Do you hear that? <u>The</u> children <u>are</u> very noisy."

How about the word 'ear'?

It is derived from the word 'are'. You can either shift the letter 'e' to the front or cancel the letter 'e' before adding it at the front.

However, in this case, this method only works if the student is aware of how to spell the word 'here'. Otherwise, the student will be confused between 'hear' and 'here' as the words sound the same.

In that case, they may prefer the 'RRS technique again. This time, introduce it laterally.

Hear = 'He' + 'are' – last 'e'   = **Hear** ~~e~~

Here = 'He' + 'are' – the 'a'   = **He** ~~a~~ **re**

If there are concerns that the student may be confused with the similarity of the RRS techniques for both words, you can change it accordingly to create a distinction between the words.

Hear = 'The' + 'are' – 't' – the last 'e'= ~~T~~ **hear** ~~e~~

Here = 'He' + 'are' – the 'a'   = **He** ~~a~~ **re**

It may be argued that the word 'here' has other combinations too.

Here = 'Her' + 'e' = Here

This may work too. However, the RRS technique is likely to be preferred due to two reasons:

1) The RRS technique uses two real words, which is less abstract and allows the student to recall the words quickly. The latter is made up of a word and a letter 'e'. The letter 'e' is not a real word and is considerably relatively more abstract as compared to a real word.

2) It has been informally observed to date that many students prefer to cancel letters than to insert letters. I suspect that it has to do with the problems of information retrieval that shapes the students' preference towards letter elimination instead.

As such, the RRS method is preferred due to its reduced abstractness and load on information retrieval.

(Of course, there are students who will prefer otherwise. It is a matter of what appeals to them. Perhaps those students have greater receptivity to abstract information or do not have much difficulty with information retrieval.)

o   **Question and Answer**

Question: I don't have much time to plan. In this case, should I prioritise lateral planning or vertical planning?

Do prioritise lateral planning. (Lateral planning stems from the confusion borne by words in the three tracks of impairment.) Without lateral planning, confusion will persists and word retention will be very low.

Vertical planning is mainly to show the pattern among words in the same word family. It was stated earlier on that vertical planning via word families is merely an option to facilitate planning. Conversely, it is not important for nonresponders as they usually do not use word family patterns to aid in their spelling. They may look like they are able to identify patterns very well but when you ask them to recall how certain words are spelt, they will not use the pattern recognition method to recall how words are spelt. For instance, they may not know how to spell 'ear' but may be able to spell 'year'. Word families are only largely useful for phonics responders. (Phonics responders will be able to spell 'ear' and plenty of words with 'ear' embedded in it.)

• **Case study – deciding on the techniques and style of meaning making**

An 11-year-old type Y nonresponder was unable to spell the word 'every'. He was also unable to spell the word 'very'. It was clear that I was not able to employ the (real) word in a word technique. While this student is highly receptive to the technique of embedding "graphics for targeted letters of confusion", he was not able to recall any letter in the word 'very' – thereby rendering this technique ineffective.

I was faced with a choice of creating a story of 'very' by using every letter in the word or using the RRS technique.

[I could have provided him with a mnemonic but I could not think of one at that point in time. In addition, I was concerned that he may be confused with too many mnemonics in his mind.]

I opted for the RRS technique as I perceived the creation of a story using every letter of the word to be more abstract. In addition, he has a history of spelling words inaccurately when the story is not impactful or relatable enough.

For the word 'very', I have to think of a simple sight word to represent 've-' and another to represent '-ry'.

Usually, I would use the word 'have' and cancel the letters 'h' and 'a' to produce 've'. The first few words that I could think of to represent '-ry' are 'cry' and 'try'. In this case, however, it is grammatically incorrect to get the student to remember the words 'have cry' or 'have try'. As such, I had to omit the word 'have'.

I listed all the simplest or shortest words that had an ending of '-ve' and '-ry' and ensured that those words are words that can be spelt effortlessly by the student. I omitted any word that was in past tense (e.g. gave) as the student struggled with the concept of past tense. The following table shows the shortest words that could be spelt by the student.

-ve	-ry
save	cry
give	dry
five	fry
	try

Note: The word 'live' was omitted as the student was confused between 'live' and 'life'.

The student and I decided on the words 'five' and 'cry'. The words were placed together:

fivecry

The following letters were eliminated:

Very = 'fivecry' – 'fi' – 'c' = ~~fi~~ ve ~~c~~ ry

137

If my student belonged to the realist faction, I would have left the instruction as it is. However, my student required stories and pictures to establish further meaning making.

As such, we set out to create a story to provide a reason why the words 'five' and 'cry' are related to the meaning of 'very'. After a minute, I created the following sentence:

"<u>Five</u> babies <u>cry</u> very loudly."

The student accepted the story and we could move on to other words that consisted of the word 'very'. In this case, it would be 'every'. As the student is now able to spell the word 'very' using the RRS technique, employing the technique of (real) word in a word for 'every' becomes a piece of cake as the student was able to see that the word 'every' comprised of the letter 'e' and the word 'very'.

Summary for part 1

- You must assume that a type X or Y nonresponder demonstrates severe difficulties across all three tracks of impairments.

- Along the auditory impairment track, different words of the same sound (e.g. 'pale' vs 'pail') trigger confusion. Type X and Y nonresponders are usually unable to use phonics to spell most, if not all, words accurately.

- Along the visual impairment track, type X and Y nonresponders have trouble with visually-similar words. This is particularly so when the visually-similar words are of the same length, usually comprising of the same starting and ending letters. They are also likely to have problems remembering how to spell seemingly short words – three or four letters – accurately despite the frequency of exposure. The most severe cases are unlikely to spell three letter words like 'hen', 'it' or 'pat' accurately. It leads the teacher to think that the student has a visual processing problem – more specifically, an extreme difficulty in remembering how to spell a word by sight.

- Along the language impairment track, many type X and Y nonresponders face challenges with basic grammar (e.g. is / was / are / were) even at an age of 12 and beyond. Their lack of time concept or low levels of receptivity towards abstractness affects literacy acquisition of words with greater abstractness (e.g. 'it') or those that are not in its present tense form (e.g. 'ran', 'bought').

Part 2: How the disinclination towards a particular track shapes a type Y nonresponder's learning style

Knowing how to integrate the three tracks of impairment into the intervention is a pre-requisite to teaching type X and Y nonresponders. However, that knowledge itself is not enough to yield intervention effectiveness for type Y nonresponders (some type X nonresponders). This is because type Y instruction needs to factor in the nonresponder's disinclination towards a particular track of impairment.

While the nonresponder will experience numerous difficulties across all three tracks of impairments, a type Y nonresponder will demonstrate further difficulties in a particular track. It is this disinclination that is the deciding obstacle in a type Y nonresponder's literacy acquisition. Disinclination affects the type Y nonresponders' approach towards literacy acquisition as their supposedly accurate perception of the word is marred by issues along the track that they are disinclined with.

Categorised according to the three tracks of impairment, disinclination can surface as a (1) visual disinclination, (2) language disinclination or (3) auditory disinclination.

(1) Visual disinclination

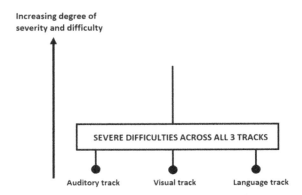

Most type X nonresponders will complain about visually-similar words of the same length (e.g. 'house' vs 'horse', 'take' vs 'talk' vs 'took' vs 'tank') and they may start to combine words together (e.g. 'tanke', 'talke', 'toke'). They may lament that too many letters may look like a mess of ink. Type Y nonresponders of the visual disclination route, however, face even more difficulty than that.

1. Visual sequencing issues

They may have visual sequencing issues of *extremely* simple words (i.e. three letter concrete words). They are aware of the letters that make up the words but for the life of them, the position of the letters (or any string of symbols) are not fixed. For instance, a 12-year-old student of mine spelt the word 'cat' as 'cta', 'girl' as 'gril', 'birds' as 'brids'. His visual sequencing issues persisted throughout his teenage life.

After instruction, the penchant for writing words with incorrect sequencing remains high when the students' attention wavers. In general, when students with visual sequencing issues copy words or number strings, the sequence would be incorrect.

o *Justification*

They – or rather, their brains – find the concept of sequencing too abstract. They do not understand why the letters must be sequenced in a certain position. They do not understand, for instance, why the letter 't' in the word 'cat' must be in the third position. They may question why the letter 'a' cannot be in the third position instead. There is no meaning to the position of letters and letter sequencing is deemed as too abstract. As such, their brains scramble the positions of the letters in the words. [In a neurological sense, their visual sequential memory is impaired.]

○ ***Very important note***

Sometimes, the student may spell the words correctly verbally but write the words incorrectly. For instance, the student may verbally spell a word as 'walk' while writing 'wlak' or 'wkal'. It is literally a situation where the student spells a word in one way while he or she writes in another. This means that the student is aware of how the letters are supposed to be positioned. However, the fidelity of information gets distorted when it reaches the hand and the hand proceeds to write the letters in different positions. In other words, the incorrect spelling may be due to a problem of the neurological pathways from the brain to the hand. The students may complain that "their hands have another brain" as their hands keep writing something different from what the students intend to write. As such, do get the student to spell the word verbally when letter sequencing problems surface on paper to check if it is an issue with confusion or distortion of information along the neurological pathways to the hand.

2. Visual perception issues (i.e. letter perception disorder)

They may perceive letters, numbers and any other symbol differently. They are unable to tell apart visually-similar letters. While many responders or nonresponders have problems with the word formation of certain letters (e.g. reversing certain letters like 'b' and 'd'), they are ultimately aware of the letter formation of letters. Type Y nonresponders who have a letter perception disorder have an innate confusion about how a letter should be shaped, much less the formation of most letters. This is actually an even more fundamental problem as compared to the orthography processing disorder.

3. Visual storage issues

Of all the subcategories among the disinclinations, visual storage issues – and visual perception issues – happen to be in a league of its own. In my opinion, both visual storage – and processing – issues assume the unenviable position of being the most detrimental of disinclinations to literacy acquisition.

a. Word-meaning connection problem

Such type Y nonresponders keep repeating the same mistake for what is perceived by others to be the simplest of words (e.g. 'sit'). Such repetition occurs over months or years regardless of age. No amount of stories or pictures will work for them as they belong to the realist faction. After all, nonresponders who have word-meaning connection problem often have language impairment. Deceptively, some of these type Y nonresponders may even be able to break down a word into phonic sounds but they have no idea what they are spelling – even if the word is spelt accurately by coincidence.

The problem arises when they are attributing the meaning of the words with the same sound (e.g. 'pale' vs 'pail', 'heal' vs 'heel'). Nonresponders who struggle with the word-meaning connection problem do not have issues with the visual sequence of the word. They perceive the words 'pale' and 'pale' accurately but for the life of them, they are unable to form a solid connection between the word form and the meaning of the word. You can tell the nonresponder to point to the word that means "a container that holds liquids", and the nonresponder – regardless of the frequency of exposure or instruction – will not have any confidence in pointing to the right word. At the end of the day, it is still guesswork for them.

b. Orthographic processing disorder

Nonresponders with orthographic processing disorder have an inability to discern real and nonsense words. As such, phonics instruction is an utterly awful choice for them. Phonics is ambiguous as it produces a lot of word parts that are not real words (e.g. 'step' vs 'stap'). Once the student is shown the different spelling possibilities, including the incorrect spelling, their inability to discern the difference is further aggravated and perpetual confusion ensues. As a result, they may produce different permutations of a word due to confusion. For instance, the word 'sit' may also be spelt as 'set', 'seet' or 'seat' – just to name a few.

c. Exceedingly poor orthographic memory

Recall that type A nonresponders are usually able to spell mostly four-letter words with relatively high levels of accuracy (with the exception of words with vowel teams). The ability to spell up to four letters accurately is, in itself, considered rather low ability by the larger part of society as there are much more words beyond four-letter words. Usually, type X and Y nonresponders spelling three to four-letter words inaccurately. The word 'bed' may be spelt as 'bad'. The word 'walk' may be spelt as 'wk'.

A type Y nonresponder with a visual disinclination involving poor orthographic memory are only able to remember the first letter of the word regardless of length. They usually struggle with three-letter words as their orthographic memory cannot seem to remember three-letter words. Often, they are only able to remember the first letter.

It can rightfully be argued that these type Y nonresponders may be struggling with an impaired visual span rather than poor orthographic memory. That being said, the problem will be considered an impaired visual span if the nonresponder consistently spells only the first letter for majority of the words that they are aware of. I have never witnessed such an extreme impairment of the visual span. What I have witnessed are type Y nonresponders who exhibit poor orthographic memory by only being able to spell the first letter for certain types of words.The nature of such types of words varies from nonresponder to nonresponder and it definitely requires further investigation by the teacher or therapist.

(2) Language disinclination

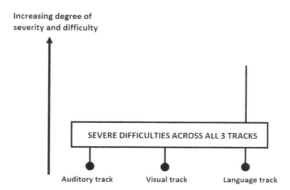

It is a whole new discipline to describe the ways to teach a student with severe language impairment. As such, this section only addresses language impairment that affects word acquisition. This is also known as language disinclination.

Recall that all type Y nonresponders will struggle greatly with sight words on the pre-primer list. Most type Y nonresponders will experience the same language problems where they are unable to understand words – no matter how simple it is perceived to be (e.g. 'it') – due to its abstract nature.

However, type Y nonresponders with language disinclination exhibit at least one of the following problems:

1. Mixing up words of similar meaning with the same mental representation

Depending on the severity of the nonresponders' language impairment, words (like concrete representations or actions) will be mixed up with associated words. For instance, they might look at the word 'ship' and read it as 'boat'. This is because the two words share the same mental image in their minds. They are confused because their black and white world states that each word must have a distinct meaning. In an example, the nonresponder may be confused with 'give', 'get', 'carry', 'hold', 'bring' or any other word with the same mental image of having something in a person's hand.

I have to emphasise that not all students with language impairment will have a language disinclination. Many of them are indeed able to spell and read with ease but are confused over the overlaps in meaning. This means that the intact orthographic processing in such students outweighs the language confusion during the literacy acquisition stage of word reading and spelling, and the confusion only takes precedence during the meaning making stage (which comes after the reading and spelling stage).

The type Y nonresponders who have a language disinclination read words wrongly and have an inability to spell the words due to such confusion. The confusion stems from two probable reasons:

a. The type Y nonresponder's language confusion takes precedence over his or her relatively intact orthographic processing. Even though the student has the ability to spell and read the words using their 'sight' memory or phonics knowledge, the student simply cannot force themselves to read nor spell because the confusion is way too overwhelming. They cannot move on without addressing the confusion. We can draw parallels with the examples that were presented in chapter 1, of which my student and I experienced a momentary paralysis in decision making when there was confusion over the function of plates and bowls, and the time needed to heat the test tube. Recall that I could not even force myself to grab a random bowl or plate due to such confusion. (Also recall that my student could not force herself to stop heating the test tube even though she knew that it was dangerous to carry on.)

b. Type Y nonresponders with severe language impairment have such poor word-sound connection that it fuels the their confusion towards the meaning making of the words. Such nonresponders do not understand how a letter makes a sound. Neither do they understand the concept of syllables nor any word part that does not represent the entire word. It can be said that such students do not know that words communicate meaning. They probably deem words as illustrations. The confusion over the word-sound connection serves as an additional obstacle in the nonresponder's attempt at making meaning of the word.

o **Note**
There are students with severe language impairment who have issues with words of similar meaning but are still able to spell those words. The emphasis of this section, however, is to highlight the type Y nonresponders who are unable to spell such words due to the confusion over words with similar meaning.

o **Note**
Noting the existence of an orthographic processing disorder alongside with language disinclination is important as it determines the approach towards literacy instruction. Assuming that the language disinclination is accounted for, the presence of orthographic processing disorder means that the student will still demonstrate very slow literacy progress.

o **Confusion over pronouns**
Usually, students with pronoun confusion demonstrate the inability to establish a distinct mental representation between pronouns and possessive pronouns. For instance, my 14-year-old student would say the following erroneous sentence:

"Teacher, this is she thing."

The concept of possession or ownership was abstract to him. In addition, 'she' and 'her' shared the same mental representation of a girl.

However, I have heard of a case where the student addressed males and females as 'it' instead of 'he' and 'she respectively. This means that the student did not seem to register the obvious differences between such distinct concrete representations in society – that a male, a female, a thing and an animal seem to have more overlapping similarities than there are discernible differences. This particular case of language disinclination is exceedingly severe as the student was unable to distinguish differences between obviously distinct mental representations. It is likely that the student needed to thoroughly understand the perceived abstractness between one category (people) and the other category (non-living thing or an animal).

2. State of confusion – receptivity, pruning and retention

a. Receptivity

When it comes to language disinclination, it is also very important to understand their state of confusion among the type Y nonresponders.

For nonresponders with auditory or visual disinclinations, they will be able to read or spell words even though their attempts may be riddled with errors. For nonresponders who have language disinclination, their receptivity towards ineffective literacy instruction is so low that they would most likely reject all attempts of instruction from the start. Unlike the type A/B nonresponders or students with auditory or visual disinclination, type Y nonresponders with language disinclination do not let the teacher or therapist harbour any delusion that ineffective instruction is marginally effective.

You may repeat one word continuously for the last 15 minutes, half an hour or an hour, with that word plastered all over your classroom, with that word in every conceivable example that you can think of, with all the activities involving just that word, and in the final 10 seconds of class, you repeat that word while pointing to it again. Then, upon asking the nonresponder to read the word, the nonresponder will respond something along the lines of "I have never seen it in my life" or something less dramatic but equally crushing for the teacher or therapist.

o **Note**

There are some students who have such severe language impairment that they are unable to comprehend what is happening around them. Alongside with issues involving vocabulary, grammar and syntax, these students are unable to infer and understand what others expect of them. As these students view the world to be such a confusing place, the information that they produce will not make sense to both themselves and others. As such, it is paramount that such students do not provide their own examples or stories during literacy acquisition. Instead, the teacher or therapist should find an example or any medium that is impressionable enough to plough through that thick haze of utter confusion in their heads, all while controlling every other factor that will trigger their language disinclination and stemming any secondary confusion brought about by the auditory and visual impairment track. It is not an easy task. Should anyone master this ability to control all possible confusion triggers while ensuring effective instruction with retention, the person should rightfully be deemed as an exceedingly skilled practitioner.

a. Pruning

Please note that for this group of nonresponders, their 'pruning' spans over a longer time as compared to others. Everyone goes through 'pruning' when they learn new information. For instance, most people will be somewhat confused for a few hours or days as they learn to make sense of the new information. Now, take 1% of the same information and assume that all possible confusion trigger factors are accounted for as this 1% is taught to type Y nonresponders with language disinclination. Their 'pruning' is pretty 'destructive' and pervasive. Immediately after the instruction of a new concept, every associated concept that is linked to the new concept will be adversely affected to the point where the nonresponders may not be able to attempt the simplest of questions that were previously of no problem to the nonresponder.

For instance, my 12-year-old math student was able to add, subtract, multiply and divide proper fractions. (The reason why I am using a math example instead of a literacy one is because it is easier to demonstrate my point using a math example.)

e.g.

$$\frac{3}{7} + \frac{5}{21} \quad , \quad \frac{3}{4} - \frac{2}{5} \quad , \quad \frac{2}{8} \times \frac{5}{6} \quad , \quad \frac{2}{5} \div \frac{7}{3}$$

As such, the new concept of the day was the addition and subtraction of mixed numbers.

e.g.
$$6\frac{3}{4} - 3\frac{1}{4} \ , \ 4\frac{4}{6} - 2\frac{1}{3}$$

The student understood it and was able to attempt the above questions independently. However, he started to stare blankly at the paper and was not able to attempt the following question:

e.g.
$$\frac{1}{5} + \frac{2}{5}$$

That is how destructive and pervasive their 'pruning' is. The same applies to literacy. During pruning, all previous words that were taught may be forgotten or be read and spelt inaccurately. While the nonresponder can understand the latest concept that was taught, he or she is unable to understand how the concept is related to all the previous concepts. This confusion will be resolved when the teacher or therapist goes through the previous concepts again and shows how the previous concepts relate to the latest concept that was taught.

b. Retention

When the type Y nonresponder with language disinclination initiates 'pruning', the teacher or therapist should proceed to address every confusion in the associated concept before repeating the instruction of the new concept. Thereafter, the nonresponder will likely be able to internalise the concept.

Then the real test begins.

If he or she understands what has been taught for that moment, the nonresponder will be able to remember for that hour or the day. However, the concept may seem entirely alien to them after a day. If this happens, it means that the nonresponder does not understand the concept despite his or her positive reaction to instruction the day before. As such, it is futile to continue instructing the nonresponder using the same method. It means that the instruction was not impressionable – i.e. 'powerful' – enough and it was only able to partially penetrate the thick fog of confusion. It is back to the drawing board and another highly impressionable method has to be developed to plough through that fog of confusion entirely.

For the type Y nonresponders who are able to understand the new concept even after a day, the 'pruning' may still take weeks before the nonresponders internalises everything. They will partially remember the concept during the weeks of pruning before demonstrating competence in the concept once 'pruning' is over.

The only way to determine a nonresponder's conceptual understanding is through the accuracy – not speed – of responses that is provided by the nonresponder. If the nonresponder is unable to provide accurate responses – or at least significantly improve the accuracy of his or her responses – after the 'pruning' period, it means that the nonresponder is still confused and the intervention approach has to change.

(Do note that only when the nonresponder is able to consistently produce a string of accurate – or significantly accurate – answers overtime is the teacher or therapist able to factor in response speed as an added measure of competence.)

o   **Special note on teaching nonresponders with language disinclination**

In general, the emphasis for nonresponders with language disinclination is on meaning making. This means that the priority is not word formation. There is no need to use the techniques like the (real) word in the word technique or the RRS technique. The words can also be written normally on its own without any added illustrations. The idea is to create a distinct and relatable mental image for each word regardless of how similar the words are in terms of their mental representations.

For instance, the words 'get', 'receive', 'give', 'hold' and 'carry' maybe easily confused because they share the same mental representation of a person holding something in his or her hands. As such, I would attempt to provide visuals that establish distinctions in meaning between the words.

Word	Distinct visual representation
Get	A person holding a thing in his or her two hands.
Receive	A present in 2 hands. An arrow indicates the movement of the present towards the body. (The thing in the hands is specifically established to be a present and nothing else.)
Give	A thing in two hands with an arrow indicating movement away from the body.
Hold	A ball in two hands. (No direction)
Carry	A person with one hand by his or her side while the other carries a bag. Both hands wrapped around a baby.

o   **Notes**

(1)

Many language-impaired students get confused by the many words that are represented by the same mental image. To them, the words 'get', 'receive', 'give', 'hold' and 'carry' is represented by the same image of a person holding something. As such, the confused student begins to read words interchangeably or experience massive difficulties in word recognition.

The solution to this problem is to create crucial differences in each mental image that represents each picture – and that is what I did. (Usually, these differences seem inconsequential to individuals without language impairment.)

The differences manifest in the form of conceptual variables. In this case, I ensured that there are only two main variables and one sub-variable to prevent confusion.

<u>The variables and sub-variable</u>

- The way the hands are grasping the object

    o   I ensured that in most illustrations, both hands are grasping onto the object/baby (except for the word 'carry'). This is to ensure consistency. What differed between the illustrations is the way the hands are grasping the object or baby.

    For instance, the hands in the word 'give' are fully outstretched while the hands in the words 'get' and 'receive' are slightly bent. In another example, the object in the word 'hold' is held in a different way from how the baby is held in the word 'carry'.

- The direction of the handed object

    o   An arrow will be drawn to indicate the direction of the handed object (if necessary).

If the both variables fail to create a difference between two illustrations (e.g. 'get' and 'receive'), the sub-variable, the object, is crucial in establishing a highly relatable example for the student to link each word to each distinct illustration.

- For instance, the words 'get' and 'receive' share the same mental representation – a person holding an item with his arms slightly bent in the direction towards himself. As such, I ensured that the illustration representing the word 'receive' was differentiated with a present (and the person wears a party hat as an added effort to differentiate).

  The illustration representing 'receive' would be accompanied with the sentence "I received a present on my birthday.". As such, the student will connect the word 'get' to the bottle and the word 'receive' to the present.

- In an exception, a vase of flowers is included in the illustration of the word 'give' even though the direction of the arrow is in the opposite direction as compared to the words 'get' and 'receive'. I was taking into account the possibility that some students do not understand how to interpret the direction of arrows. As such, the vase of flowers is included with the sentence "I give my mother a vase of flowers on Mother's Day." (A picture of the mother may be included.)

(2)

It is very important to note that the position of the man should remain fixed. I have received feedback from typically-developing, non-language impaired adults that the words 'get' and 'give' should be drawn according to the illustrations below to replicate the relationship between a receiver and a giver.

'Get'   'Give'

How a typically developing individual may illustrate

This is as compared to how I see it (as an individual with mild language impairment).

'Get'   'Give'

How a language impaired individual may illustrate

It is one thing to change the direction of the object in the person's hands. It is another thing entirely to change the position of the person in the illustration.

It is well known that many students have innate confusion with the concept of 'left' and 'right'. This translates into a problem of understanding their spatial relationship with other people.

When there is such an innate confusion, the students tend to eliminate the existence of "the other". In other words, these students perceive themselves to be the point of origin of any action in order to remove any lingering confusion that may threaten language and literacy acquisition.

However, severely language impaired type Y nonresponders are unaware of how to remove the source of confusion by mentally centering all language concepts around themselves as the point of origin and eliminating "the other". As such, these students tend to be unable to acquire literacy and language effectively. For instance, they will begin to read the word 'get' as 'receive' or 'give' (depending on the degree of their confusion) or will only know how to use words like 'he' or 'she' (and not 'him' or 'her').

The concept of the 'giver' and 'receiver' is a higher-level concept that is created with the assumption that students have a thorough understand of their spatial relations with others. This concept of the 'giver' and 'receiver' is subsequently used in grammar instruction – e.g. "The ball was given to me by Peter." – which further complicates an already bewildering concept for students with severe language impairment.

As a disclaimer, it does not mean that all individuals with language impairment will have chronic problems with "the other". I am only mildly language impaired and I am able to fully understand the concept of the 'giver' and 'receiver'. But even for me, my first reaction was also to eliminate "the other" in my conceptual understanding of language and illustrate accordingly. Needless to say, individuals with severe language impairment will definitely struggle with the concept of the 'giver' and 'receiver'.

For nonresponders who have language disinclination with orthographic processing, their literacy acquisition will be steadily apparent. However, for those who have language disinclination, together with some form of orthographic processing or memory problem, addressing the problem of language disinclination does not mean that literacy acquisition becomes significantly easier. (Please refer to chapter 5 for more insight.)

Lesson planning for nonresponders with only language disinclination is slightly different from language-disinclined nonresponders with orthographic processing or memory problems. The example that I would like to talk about are the synonyms 'hear' and 'listen'. Both mental representations are exactly the same in most neurotypical individuals. In this case, even if the word has an identical mental representation, a distinct mental image for each word has to be established nonetheless as the similarity of mental representations creates confusion.

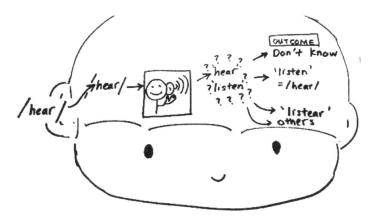

In this hypothetical scenario, a nonresponder with language disinclination becomes confused as the mental representation that is triggered by the sound /hear/ results in two different words in his mind.

The following table shows how the planning of words should be done.

Word family	Words with similar mental representations	Auditorily similar words	Visually similar words
hear	listen	here*	-
tear	tear pull	-	-
wear	-	where*	were*

*A nonresponder with visual or auditory disinclination will be confused and unable to discern the distinction between the spelling of 'where', 'were' and, at times, 'wear'. While, a nonresponder with language disinclination will not exhibit such confusion, he or she will nonetheless be unable to spell the words 'where' and 'were' due to an inability to represent each word with a concrete mental representation.

3. Auditory disinclination

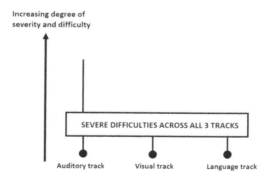

All type Xs and Ys have problems with words that have the same sound. Type Ys with auditory disinclination exhibit one or more of these additional problems:

1. The inability to discern blends

For instance, the words 'plan' and 'pan' sounds the same. 'Pram' and 'Pam' may sound the same.

2. Words or letters that do not sound similar appears to sound the same to them

This is severe for a disinclination. It is one thing to be unable to discern similar-sounding words or letters. It is another to perceive words that are not auditorily similar to sound the same. For instance, the student may perceive the words 'growing' and 'gummy' to sound the same.

Do note that due to auditory disinclination, the nonresponder will most like develop language problems. The nonresponder does not have a language disinclination as his or her language problems are caused by auditory disinclination. For instance, a nonresponder who is unable to hear the word 'is' accurately will have a high chance of being unable to understand and apply the words 'is', 'are', 'was' and 'were' in their verbal expression.

o **Questions and Answers**

Question 1: Do some nonresponders have more than one disinclination?

Answer: Yes, unfortunately. It means that progress will be excruciatingly slow. You will have to factor in the severe difficulties across all three tracks, alongside with shaping the intervention according to the multiple disinclinations. As mentioned earlier, a nonresponder's language disinclination may involve a disorder in orthographic processing. Orthographic processing disorder is a visual disinclination. As such, the nonresponder has both visual and language disinclinations.

In my opinion, there is a severity ranking among the disinclinations. An auditory disinclination is the least consequential of all disinclinations with regards to the student's literacy acquisition. In other words, nonresponders with only an auditory disinclination will progress much faster with effective literacy acquisition as compared to nonresponders with other disinclinations. This is followed by language and lastly, visual disinclinations. Nonresponders who have more than one disinclination, however, will always see exceedingly slow – or no – progress in literacy acquisition if one of the disinclination is a visual disinclination.

Question 2: *I am not very sure how to start. What if my student or child seems to show disinclination towards every track? I don't even know if it is a disinclination or just a common difficulty that spans across all three tracks.*

Answer: It is admittedly difficult and it takes a lot of experience and observation. Let me walk you through my thought processes regarding a recent case that just came on board.

Before I assess any case, I will have the following framework in my mind:

Step 1: Identify challenges		Step 2: Behavioural manifestation*
Identify 3 tracks of impairment • Difficulty with words that sound the same • Difficulty with words that that are visually similar • Difficulty with words that are abstract	**Determine disinclination** Primary disinclination Secondary disinclination (if any)	**Literacy problem (external)** Inability to read or spell words **Problem with real-world application (internal)** Unable to understand how the word is used in his or her speech

* I will determine the level of challenge that the nonresponder will face. If the nonresponder only struggles with the reading or spelling of a certain word but is otherwise able to incorporate the word effortlessly into his or her verbal expression, it is indicative that the nonresponder's understanding is not affected. I will proceed to customise a literacy intervention plan that accommodates the three tracks of impairment and the nonresponder's disinclination(s). If the nonresponder is unable to use the word correctly in his or her verbal expression, it usually signals a more pressing problem of conceptual confusion that requires urgent rectification before any form of literacy intervention.

Regardless, the nicely structured framework of analysis usually morphs into a complicated web when I am confronted with reality.

Let me use my student – let's call him Sam – as an example to illustrate the model above. Sam is a quiet 12-year-old boy who was unable to read what was perceived to be the simplest of words despite years of phonics intervention. I deduced that he was either a type X or Y. I asked him to spell a few words. The words were accompanied with examples of each word. For instance, when I asked Sam to spell the word 'and', I gave him the following example to allow him to understand the meaning of the word: "Tom and Jane went to the market to buy fruits."

Sam spelt the following words:

Words that Sam was told to spell	What Sam spelt
and	an
end	an
two	to tow two
after	aft
is	his
from	of for
before	bfor
also	os
hear	heer
about	abuot
buy	bey

o **Analysis of spelling errors**

His spelling errors seemed bewildering because it looked like he had problems across all three tracks. The more obvious problem seemed to be that he had a visual sequencing issue (e.g. 'abuot' and 'tow').

He seemed to be unable to tell apart the auditory-similar words using the meanings –

as evident from the words 'to', 'tow', 'two' ; 'an' for the words 'end' and 'and'. It may signal underlying language impairment too as some of the words like 'to' and 'too' are abstract words with no concrete representation in reality.

However, it is important to determine if language impairment is the primary cause of the confusion or that the confusion from auditory-similar words impaired his receptivity towards understanding of word meanings.

○ **Determining disinclination**

For now, it just seemed like the usual problems surfacing from the three tracks of impairment. However, I needed to determine his disinclination(s) – and subsequent inclinations (relative). The first thing that I noted was the possible auditory disinclination. He wrote the words 'of' and 'for' in response to the word 'from'. The words did not sound the same (though admittedly, the word 'for' and 'from' have some partial auditory similarities) but he perceived them to be auditorily similar. As to how extreme the disclination was is a matter of later concern. It may be argued that Sam had a language disinclination but Sam was able to verbally express himself accurately with 'of', 'for' and 'from'.

The next thing I noted was that relative to the auditory disinclination, he may have a visual inclination. The fact that he was able to remember the vague form of the single-syllable words (e.g. 'heer') and two-syllable words 'bfor', 'abuot' and 'aft' indicates a relative inclination. However, it also suggests that his visual span is about three letters and he was only able to prioritise one syllable over the other.

Essentially, I hypothesised that while Sam faced severe problems in both the visual and auditory tracks, the visual track seems to have lesser problems than the auditory track. Therefore, it is the "lesser of two evils" and hence it becomes a relative strength. While Sam omitted or reversed the sequences of the letters (with the latter manifesting because he was unable to understand the reason behind the letter sequences), his spelling was usually visually similar – albeit vaguely – to the original word. On the other hand, there were certain errors were wildly off the mark in terms of auditory similarity. For instance, he spelt the word 'from' as 'of' and 'for'. The word 'of' sounds very different from the word 'from'. The word 'for' sounds similar to the word 'from' if you imagine a student to be able to hear only two vague units of sound that are not blends(in this case, it would be /r/) or the last sound(in this case, it would be /m/) in the word. Either way, Sam's responses indicated severe problems with auditory processing – or what I deem as auditory disinclination.

He did not seem to be having a language disinclination. The fact that he could largely spell abstract words 'about' and 'before' without much hesitation seemed to signal that his language impairment was not the primary obstacle in acquiring literacy.

(Do note that language disinclination and language impairment are not the same. In this case, Sam was suspected to have language impairment but his suspected language impairment was not the main stumbling block in his literacy acquisition. As such, he does not have language disinclination.)

The words 'to' and 'too' were spelt incorrectly because they were sounded similar to the word 'two'. While both words were abstract, Sam's inability to spell them accurately was not due to their abstract nature This also lended more strength to my suspicion of auditory disinclination.

So just by looking at his pre-test, I began to have these thought processes.

o   **Analysis of response to initial instruction**

I started off by teaching him the difference between the words 'an', 'and' and 'end'.

He was receptive to stories and pictures that were embedded into letters. This meant that he most probably did not have a language disinclination. After all, he was okay with embedding stories so long as it made sense to him and he was able to offer his own stories upon prompting. However, I needed to give him a story first because he did not know how to form his own stories.

It was also more of a relief because any student that is receptive towards embedded pictures in a word will generally see greater progress in word acquisition (provided they do not have visual storage issues). More importantly, he was able to accept the stories that were formulated by me. That was a big thing because literacy acquisition among type Y nonresponders can be accelerated from what is perceived to be an excruciatingly slow pace if they are receptive to examples that are provided by others.

As I have previously mentioned, a lot of type Y nonresponders want examples of their own and reject the examples provided by others. This means that store-bought manipulatives (e.g. sight word cards with embedded pictures) will most likely be ineffective as the stories and examples are provided by the creators of the manipulatives. Apart from those with a visual disinclination, type Y nonresponders with the slowest rate of literacy acquisition are those who need but are unable to produce their own examples. The teacher has to analyse and deduce what will resonate with the student as such nonresponders are confused with their understanding of the world. This is what I term as "ploughing through the thick haze of confusion".

○ **Note**

There are reasons behind the location of the graphics. Recall that Sam spelt the words 'and' and 'end' as 'an'. This means that apart from confusion over the word meanings and an inability to discern the /d/ sound, Sam was also confused over the following letter position:

- Why should there be a letter 'd' in the word 'and'?

- Why should there be a letter 'd' in the word 'end'?

- Why does the word 'end' start with the letter 'e' instead of the letter 'a'?

Since Sam was receptive to stories and pictures, it mades my job much simpler. I had to embed pictures in letters 'a' and 'd' of each word, and form a story using those pictures that were related to the meaning of the word. I did not embed a picture into the letter 'n' because Sam was able to remember the position of the letter 'n' and thus, did not have any confusion over it.

If Sam did not have any confusion over the letters and was only confused about the meaning of the word (e.g. Sam understands the word 'and' as "the end"), I would not embed the pictures in the letters. Instead, I would just draw the meaning of the picture next to the word to differentiate the meaning of the words. This is because the embedded pictures are meant for students who exhibit spelling inaccuracies of certain letters. (Recall that embedded pictures are used as targeted graphics for letters of confusion.) In fact, nonresponders who only have a language disinclination would find the embedded pictures to be an unwelcomed distraction.

While Sam did not have a language disinclination, it was clear that he had language difficulties. His inability to use the words in a sentence was probably a result of what I assumed to be an auditory or visual confusion that was hindering his understanding of word meanings. He faced immense difficulties when I asked him to form a sentence with the word 'and'. Even though he understood the meaning of the word, he was unable to form a sentence. Usually, students can form examples even though there are syntax, grammar and vocabulary errors in their examples. This student, however, stared at me with his brow furrowed. After much prompting, he begrudgingly said, "... Mother and I..." The same happened for the word 'end'. He gave me another strained look. I had to prompt him, "When you finish reading a book or finish watching a movie, it's the ...."

"The end," he said begrudgingly again.

However, I repeat, while he had language difficulties, he did not have a language disinclination. His language was not the key factor in affecting his ability to spell and read. Rather, it might be an auditory or visual disinclination that aggravated his language difficulties.

o   **Presentation of words for maximum word retention: receptivity to abstract word parts**

When I taught him the words 'walk', 'talk' and 'take', Sam showed receptivity towards word retention when the words were colour-coded according to an onset and rime. What a bonus – there was a resemblance between Sam and a type A.1 nonresponder. That being said, he was also receptive to the real word in a (real) word in a word technique.

Onset-rime colour coding
▪ **W** alk
▪ **T** alk
▪ **T** ake

His receptivity towards onset-rime color coding further suggested that he did not have a visual disinclination nor a language disinclination. The fact that he was able to see the pattern of the abstract word parts '-alk' and '-ake' suggested that should the meanings of the words be stated clearly and the auditory disinclination addressed, Sam was actually able to remember more abstract patterns without getting confused.

As a side note, I had the following preliminary teaching strategies in mind before Sam demonstrated his receptivity towards words that were presented according to onset-rime:

Strategy 1: Changing a real word into another real word

- Cake -> Take   [Similar auditorily and visually]

- Tall -> Talk   [Similar visually]

- Wall -> Walk   [Similar visually]

Note: Obtaining the word 'talk' from 'tall' and 'walk' from 'wall' is effective if the student does not care about the auditory similarities between words.

Strategy 2: (1) RRS technique, and (2) changing a (real) word into another word

- Wallook -> W al~~look~~k -> Walk

    - Reinforced by the sentence: I walked over to the wall take a look at the painting.

- Walk -> Talk

o   **Degree of auditory disinclination**

Recall that Sam demonstrated an auditory disinclination. This problem was usually resolved when I drew a picture next to – or onto – the respective words and colour code according to how Sam was most comfortable with. In this case, Sam seemed to be comfortable with an onset-rime colour coding or (real) word in a word technique.

Confusion is easily triggered when a nonresponder receives input that they do not understand. The trigger for auditory or language-related confusion is often different. Regardless, information must be presented in a specific sequence in order to avoid triggering auditory or language-related confusion.

If a nonresponder hears the very first thing that sounds foreign or does not make sense, the nonresponder will experience a cognitive "shut down" immediately and will not be able to comprehend anything that has been said right after that.

For instance, if a nonresponder with auditory or language disinclination has always reacted poorly to the word 'bend' and is unable to understand its meaning, explaining this jargon the following manner does not work out:

"Bend means this." *Shows a bending action*
 [Word]   *[Explanation]*

OR

"This word is /bend/. /Bend/ means this." *Shows a bending action*
 [Word]   *[Explanation]*

Such manner of explanation risks triggering pervasive confusion in students who simply cannot accept the 'foreign' sound of /bend/ and proceed to 'shut down', denying their opportunity to understand the meaning of the word that is presented thereafter.

Instead, I will point to the word and explain to the nonresponder the meaning of the word *first* before reading the word.

"This word means this." *Shows many different bending actions* "Okay? This what is

/bend/."

I will also actively try to limit the number words that I say in order to reduce the risk off triggering confusion with the sound of any word that I speak.

(The difference in the sequence of presented information is that minute and very often, non-language impaired individuals will not be able to detect the difference. Even when they do notice the difference, non-language impaired individuals will not find such a minute difference consequential.)

Eventually, the nonresponder gets comfortable with how the word sounds. At that point in time, I will be able to read the word first before stating the meaning.

However, there are times when a word causes so much confusion, it is better to avoid saying the word entirely.

The word 'were' was like a nuclear bomb of confusion for Sam. He looked beyond strained – more like distressed. He physically looked as if he had a mind-crashing moment.

Not only did the word 'were' sound so utterly foreign to Sam that it did not even sound like an English word, his confusion was further compounded by (1) the abstract nature of the word, that resulted in the inability to understand all associated words – 'is', 'are', 'was' – that were linked to the word 'were', and (2) the visual similarity to the word 'where', that compounded the confusion as it sounded exactly like 'wear', which in turn affected the associated words 'ear', 'here', 'there', 'hear' …

You get the drift. It was an explosive chain reaction of confusion. There were far too many words that sounded or looked similar to the associated words that were affected in this ever widening sphere of confusion. That, in turn, affected even more words and Sam became even more confused.

As the repercussion of merely saying this word was far too great, I avoided saying this word to the best of my abilities. I just merely pointed to the word 'were' and explained the meaning.

o **Extreme auditory disinclination**

I deduced that Sam had auditory disinclination as his primary disinclination. He also experienced some visual confusion and both his auditory disinclination and visual confusion were affecting his language development. I thought I had him largely figured out in the first two sessions together-

-until I told him to spell the word 'funny'(without an example). He wrote the word 'flying'. That made me pay even more attention. Was it because he could not really remember how the word looked like and proceeded to confuse 'flying' and 'funny' together? That both words looked like they were of similar length and they started with the letter 'f'? That would be a visual disinclination.

Was it a language disinclination? Even for a disinclination, this was starting to infringe into extreme disinclination. It was one thing for a student to mix up words in the same category like 'jog' as 'run' (that's classic language impairment) but it was another thing entirely to be confuse with two unrelated words from different categories ('flying' is an action word while 'funny' is a describing word).

Was it an auditory disinclination? If so, his auditory disinclination would also be extreme. It was one thing to be unable to discern similar-sounding words and it was already a pretty extreme disinclination if a nonresponder coule not tell apart two single-syllable words that sounded different. This was a level higher. 'Flying' and 'funny' are two-syllable words that sound different. The longer the word, the more it should sound different to a student. Unless, the very first letter 'f' in both words led Sam to assume that both words sound the same.

Basically, it would be one of these three outcomes:

-   Visual disinclination

-   Extreme language disinclination

-   Extreme auditory disinclination

I proceeded to ask Sam, "You know when your friend tells you a joke and you laugh? You use this word to describe the joke. Which word tells you that the joke made you laugh?"

He pointed to the word 'flying'.

Then I asked him if the words 'flying' and 'funny' sounded the same to him. He replied, "Yes."

So extreme auditory disinclination it is.

He probably saw the word 'flying' when someone mentioned the word /funny/ and used it in the context of telling a joke. It shows that the student disregarded letter-sound logic despite receiving prior instruction in phonics. This was another evidence of auditory disinclination.

As mentioned earlier, for nonresponders with auditory disinclination, you avoid saying the word if you aim to teach the nonresponder how to spell the word or the meaning of the word. You only say the word when your objective is to teach the student how to discern sounds (e.g. "/faaaan/ vs /fuuuun/. What's the difference?"). Otherwise, you will run an extremely high risk of triggering immediate confusion the moment the nonresponder hears what they perceive to be an incomprehensible sound.

You will notice that in my initial question to him, I did not ask him the following:

"You know when your friend tells you a joke and you laugh? It means that the word is 'funny'. Can you point to me which word is 'funny'?"

I deliberately left out the sound of the word to take into the account the possibility of auditory disinclination. It just would not do if Sam got confused upon hearing the sound and gave me an answer that was not a true reflection of his abilities.

- ○ **Retention**

He did not turn up for two lessons – which meant that he did not receive intervention for two weeks. When he came back, he wrote those words that have been reinforced four weeks ago. He spelt the word 'friend' as 'firend'. There were many similar errors. This means to say that without practice, he would experience visual sequencing problems.

From my initial assessment, I constructed a working profile of this student:

- Type Y student

  - ▪ Severe auditory disinclination

  - ▪ Prone to visual sequencing issues of a word if he forgots the story/example

- Language issues are a subset of primarily an auditory disinclination

- Receptive to stories and other people's examples

- Is able to take a phonics pattern of visual presentation (onset and rime), alongside with the (real) word in a word technique

[I stood corrected. My initial assessment of Sam was open to any change once I got to know him better.]

It was obvious that Sam had a severe auditory processing disorder and an urgent follow up with the Audiologist was necessary. However, many cases that I handle were on bursary and they did not have the finances nor the logistics to see another specialist. The same applied to Sam. This means that I usually have to double up as my student's Educational Therapist, Audiologist, Speech and Language Therapist etc. Given the limited resources that I had, I needed to prioritise his understanding and settle the confusion over his auditory processing issues. I only had time to deal with his literacy issues - and not his auditory processing issues. If the opportunity arose, I would definitely refer him to see either a Speech and Language Therapist or Audiologist.

CHAPTER 5

TYPE Y CASE STUDIES: THE 4 (PLUS 3) HEAVENLY KINGS

This chapter provides detailed accounts of 4 (plus 3) nonresponders who are considered the most severe of nonresponders that I have taught to date. They were type Y nonresponders who have different ways of learning as compared to their type A and B counterparts. While there were commonalities in the approach to teaching them, their co-morbidities and other needs required extensive customisation. Group instruction was never effective for them.

Zeak joined the centre as the most severe case at that point in time. He was also the student who allowed me to finally gain the last piece of the nonresponder puzzle. Teaching him was largely experimental due to the fledging development of my approach to nonresponders. Zeak's section is termed as 'Discovery'.

Sean had the most severe case of language disinclination that I have ever seen in my career to date. He was also the biggest beneficiary of my newfound understanding of how to teach the nonresponders. As such, Sean's section is termed as 'Intervention'.

Truthfully, Xian's literacy woes did not qualify him to have the heavenly king status. However, his behaviour – due to his autism – was impeding his learning. As such, Xian's section is termed as 'Behaviour'.

Warren went beyond the point of no return. It was a little too late for him. The effectiveness of my newly developed solution was limited and did little to stem the confusion borne by years of ineffective phonics intervention by prior therapists. As such, Warren's section is termed as 'Chronic Effect'.

Nathan and Sophia had a serious issue – their eyes and ears were unreliable for literacy acquisition. The adverse impact on their literacy development was immense. They were the serious contenders for the positions as heavenly kings. In addition, Nathan was the only student who was directly affected by my initial inexperience. As such, Nathan's section is termed as 'Regret'. On the other hand, Sophia's section is termed as 'Pandora Box'.

Sam was the latest addition to the family of heavenly kings. His condition was so deceptive that it hid an unprecedented case in the guise of a typical type Y nonresponder. As such, Sam's section termed as "Dark Horse".

DISCOVERY: ZEAK

- **Profile**

Approximately one and a half years into my search for a solution, Zeak appeared. He spoke English as his second language. He was the most severe case the centre had seen at that time. He came to the centre at 12 years old and was subsequently transferred to me when he was 15.

He was the student who allowed me to discover the solution, the final piece of the entire puzzle. As mentioned in the first chapter, I did the Visual-Spatial Learner survey with Zeak after teaching him for three months. He maxed out the survey. He could spell long words backwards and locate any letter in the word accurately.

[Among all the nonresponders I had identified in the centre, only three students were that 'visual-spatial' to spell long words backwards at that point in time.]

- **Disclination**

Double disclination: Visual (perceptual) and language disclination

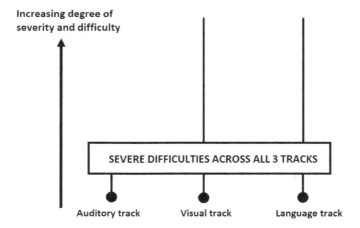

- **Literacy issues**

Zeak had extremely poor literacy. While he had visual processing issues, he was still extremely visual and approached his literacy with his unique brand of visual learning.

His phonics application was absolutely laborious. When he used phonics to sound out the word 'spit', he was trapped at the first sound /s/ for 17 seconds before I intervened and gave him the next sound /p/. In the end, he wrote 'speat'. If you recall, type Y nonresponders confuse similar-sounding words and they tend to gravitate towards words that are entrenched in reality as compared to their abstract counterparts. Zeak heard the /it/ sound and thought of 'eat' instead of 'it'.

He required instruction on the difference between 'eat' and 'it'. In addition, he needed a concrete representation of the word 'it' for him to include it as part of his vocabulary.

It took me another 10 months before I had a clearer and more structured approach to teaching type Y nonresponders. However, Zeak left the center within the year and I was unable to instruct him any further.

- **Co-morbidities / Accompanying problems**

  o   Epilepsy

  o   Specific Language Impairment

  He had immense problems with verbal expression, syntax and grammar. For instance, he was confused with the usage of 'he', 'she', 'his', 'her' or 'him' at the age of 15. He would say, "This is she thing."

  o   Dyscalculia (Suspected)

  o   Font consistency problems

  o   Issues with visual processing and perception

  There was one instance that served to emphasise the severity of his visual processing issues. One day, Zeak asked me, "Teacher, why is the 'plus' so funny?" (Why does the plus symbol look so strange?)

  I did not understand and asked him to elaborate. He wrote the symbol ÷ and reiterated that the 'plus' symbol looked 'funny'. I realised that (1) he kept thinking that the ÷ symbol was a + symbol, and (2) he had no conceptual understanding of division. The concept of division probably interfered with his understanding of addition.

  In addition, his handwriting and alignment showed obvious problems. As seen in the picture below. he also had a penchant for writing letters in dots and dashes. This led me to think that his perception of letters was not stable as writing in dots and lines suggested an inability or difficulty in viewing the printed symbol – in this case, letters – as a whole. It also suggested that his development of visual perception was very delayed. His writing became a lot more orderly when his previous teacher highlighted each space with a colour. It seemed that the many lines on the page created much visual confusion for him.

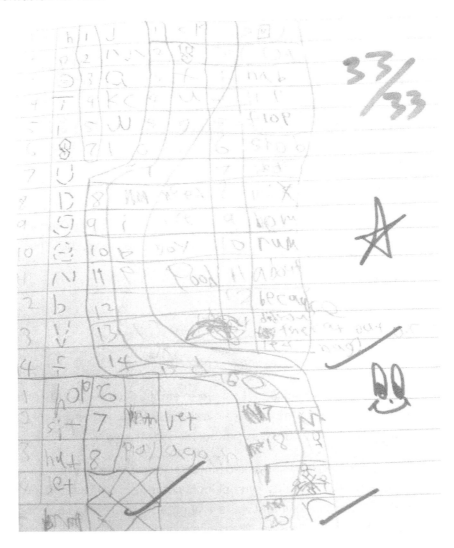

This is a picture of Zeak's spelling attempt with a prior therapist. He was 12 years old at that point in time. He was still stuck at CVC words for phonics and needed much reinforcement for very common sight words like 'because' and 'about'.

- **Intervention approach**

Instruction towards Zeak was largely experimental. While everything clicked into place three months after teaching him, I was still in the midst of uncovering and experimenting with what Zeak could and could not do. There was neither proper structure nor formal curriculum. It was rather freeform. I was trying to gain as much information from Zeak as possible in order to see how much of Zeak's experience could be generalised to the other students.

He stayed with me for another half a year before he left. One of the main things that I had learnt from Zeak during his brief stint as my student was how a type Y nonresponder of the "heavenly king" status viewed multisyllabic words. It allowed me to understand the difference between a phonics responder and the nonresponders' approach towards multisyllabic words, which in turn led me to understand how the degree of abstractness impacted a student's receptivity towards multisyllabic words. (Please refer to the next chapter for more details.)

INTERVENTION: SEAN

- **Profile & Co-morbidities**

Sean came shortly after Zeak left the centre. Sean was 11 years old then. He was, and still is, the most severe case of language disinclination that I have seen to date. Any more severe and I firmly believe that Sean would have been a clinical case. Unlike the other severe cases that the SLTs and I have seen, Sean's profile was one of the 'cleanest' – his difficulties stemmed largely from his receptive and expressive language impairment.

In his first year with me, I could hardly understand him. There were days when I could not understand him at all. Those days, I could only give him a blank look before asking him to repeat himself again.

It is pretty difficult for people who have not taught students with such an extreme expressive difficulty to imagine the Sean's verbal expression. While his speech was peppered with some grammatical errors, Sean seemed to speak rather fluently. In this case, fluency meant that the speed that he spoke was like the speech of a typically-developing individual. He did not pause nor experience any speech interruptions due to stammering or difficulty in word retrieval. Mechanically, his speech sounded okay. The structure was not his biggest problem. However, the meaning that he tried to convey was totally warped. It was either he spoke in extremely vague terms or there were incorrect usages of the words. The conversation would veer off topic or there seemed to be no logical connections made between his points. I mean no disrespect at all but it was as close to verbal nonsense as it could get. (His speech resembled individuals with Wernicke's aphasia.)

Recall the transcript in chapter 2:

"This one go to my neck and the smart one is in the neck. But I switch it. I can remember anything, but under here [below his neck] is nothing – no smart thing. It's all our lungs and here are say things one right? I got two things. Say …and play – watch movie over here and everything is here. Another one is do everything. The 'do' one is in my neck and play is in my brain. Test, I switch it [exchanging the places of 'doing' and 'playing'."

This was on a day when he was the most 'coherent'. In his case, 'coherent' meant that I could actually follow his train of thought and realise that his understanding was incorrect.

If I could, I would like to include a transcript of the days when his speech was totally incomprehensible. However, I simply could not remember how he had spoken then because it sounded too foreign.

[Comparatively, Zeak's expressive problems were the inverse. As mentioned earlier, his sentence structure and grammar was warped. Mechanically, it was a problem. In addition, Zeak spoke hesitantly and faltered at certain points. However, I could still understand what Zeak was saying. Meaning wise, he was largely accurate. Zeak resembled individuals with Broca's aphasia.]

Nearly half a year into teaching Sean, he approached me during Teachers' Day and asked me the following question:

"Teacher, you know who is Miss Amanda? My mother told me to give this present to her."

"Um, Sean," I replied after a brief pause. "I am your teacher, Miss Amanda."

The issue was not that he did not know my name. After all, many of my students are unable to remember my name. The issue was that even if he did not know my name, logic would have dictated that I was the only teacher who was teaching him all these months.

A conversation with his previous school-based Special Needs Officer enlightened me that Sean lived his lower primary life with no recognition of faces or awareness of what was going on around him.

At 13 years old, his expressive language had improved due to language intervention that allowed him to increase his accurate understanding of the world.

On certain days, Sean's first few sentences would sound rather coherent. Thereafter, it veered off into the direction of incoherence again. The following conversation with him – when he was 13 years old – accounted for one of his more coherent conversations with me:

Sean: I am not going to class tomorrow because I have got homework.

Me: Okay, so you are not coming for class tomorrow. What about your lesson next Saturday? Will you be staying at home to do your homework or study for your exams?

Cue puzzled look from Sean

Sean: No, I am coming for class tomorrow.

Me: You just told me you are not coming for class tomorrow.

Sean: No, I am coming tomorrow. Next week I am also coming. I have a lot of homework. Makes me tired.

This conversation led me to analyse it as such:

Assuming that Sean had misspoken, then Sean must have intended to say "I am coming for the lesson" instead of "I am not coming for lesson". However, it was illogical as he would mean that he was coming for class because there was a lot of homework and impending exams.

He might have been talking about two separate ideas that should originally have been separated by the following transition:

"I am coming for class. Oh, by the way, I have a lot of homework and upcoming exams."

He did not indicate a transition, which muddled his message – *"I am not coming for class. I have homework and exams."* To further solidify such confusion, he joined the two ideas with a word 'because'. In that split second, he probably misunderstood the meaning of 'because' or just added it in into his speech without realising.

It was also strange because Sean would never inform me that he was attending lessons. I still do not know why he told me that he was not turning up class when he did.

- **Disclination**

Disclination: Language disclination

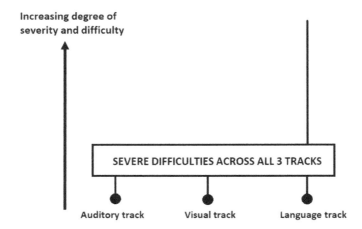

- **Literacy issues**

In Sean's case, his poor literacy levels were largely due to language impairment. In other words, Sean's language impairment resulted in his diagnosis of dyslexia. Of the 4 (plus 3) heavenly kings, Sean was the student who had benefitted the most from my new found understanding of nonresponders instruction. In fact, I would go as far to say that he would still be illiterate if I did not have that breakthrough in understanding.

He came in for literacy intervention at the age of 11. He had a Special Needs Officer who was in charge of his literacy education in his mainstream school. Sean did not give his previous educators any opportunity to think that he responded to phonics. If his inability to recall even the most basic of consonant sounds (he recited them by name instead), his perpetual confusion even between visually-dissimilar letters (he points to the letter 'm' and asks if it is 'f') or the fact that he did not spell any word using sounds to spell was not convincing enough, his pre-test was enough to thoroughly debunk the assumed efficacy of any pro-phonics approach.

○   **Pre-test**

I asked him to spell the word 'look' and he proceeded to *sketch* the following:

Bewildered, I proceeded to inform him that he left out the bottom of some letters.

"Oh," he replied. "I forgot."

Then, he proceeded to sketch the bottom of the letter 'O's.

The fact that he sketched it out told me that (1) he was a visual learner, (2) he did not view words as individual letters but as... art (that was why he was confused with the concept of letters), which meant that words had to be presented visually as a whole, and (3) it was absolutely ludicrous to approach his literacy with phonics.

It came as no surprise that he viewed every variation of a word as a new word. For instance, he could not see the similarities between the words 'come', 'comes' or 'coming'.

He knew how to read and spell a limited pool of words. These words comprised of largely single-syllable words that met the following conditions:

1. **A direct and physical representation in reality (things or actions) that were embedded in the present time**

    Any sight words that were abstract in nature or in the past tense form were totally non-existent to him. As usual, the word 'it', while innocuous, seemed to be the bane of his life. This meant to say that at 11 years old, he was unable to read books that were targeted at preschoolers as the books were packed with what was assumed to be the easiest, highest-frequency words that were known to English speakers.

2. **A clear and distinct meaning that did not overlap with other words that had similar meanings**

    He would frequently – still does, actually – look at the word and say a word that had a similar meaning. For instance, he would read the word 'pond' as 'sea' or 'river'. As long as there was no clear boundary between the words, all associated words would be thrown in the mix. He saw the word 'pond' and he knew that it was a body of water. The associated words – 'sea' and 'river'-also had a similar image of a body of water.

    Other examples of his confusion over similar words with overlapping meanings included 'drive' and 'ride', 'city' and 'town', 'pretty' and 'beautiful'.

3. **Visually dissimilar to other words**

    While not as problematic as the point 2, Sean tended to confuse words that looked visually similar. For instance, words like 'tail' might be spelt as the word 'tall'.

- **Inertia**

As long as Sean lacked understanding, he would **never** remember or retain anything that had been taught.

He was unable to remember a word – regardless of length and simplicity – even if he had seen it repeatedly a few words ago. I had a few students – phonics responders and nonresponders alike – who also exhibited the same behaviour. They were unable to read words that appeared multiple times in a passage or the previous sentence.

The difference between them and Sean was that they would eventually remember – with differing levels of ease – how to read those words (after months or even years) as their visual memory eventually developed. Sean's problem lay in the understanding of the words. As long as he was confused with the meaning or properties of the word, he would not remember.

The following example demonstrates the difference in Sean's receptivity to abstract concepts as compared to the other students. When Sean was 12, a Secondary school teacher from a mainstream Secondary school got permission to observe and teach some of the students at the centre in order to gain a greater understanding about how to help students with dyslexia and other co-morbidities. One of the classes that she was attached to was my class with two heavenly kings – Sean and Xian.

It was upon contact with Sean and Xian that she experienced the breadth of diversity within dyslexia.

She was drafting a lesson plan to teach Sean a new concept. She intended to introduce more sight words to him for an hour. I gave her a piece of advice in order to prevent her from overplanning and prove a point to her – it was not the amount of information taught or the frequency of word exposure that was important. It was his thorough understanding that mattered.

I told her that alongside with reviewing the words that was taught by me, she should just teach him the word 'or' for that one hour lesson. Her objective was to ensure that he was able to read that word by the end of the lesson.

I did not blame her for sporting that sceptical expression. It was probably the shortest lesson plan she had planned in her life.

An hour of effort later, with many activities revolving around the usage of 'or', the teacher showed Sean the word 'or' and asked him to read it.

Sean gave her a nonchalant shrug and said, "Don't know. Never seen it before."

It was comical to see that look of disbelief and exasperation as she spluttered, "I taught you and showed it to you many times!" [In response, Sean just replied, "Nope, never."]

Even if the same word was emphasized repeatedly for days, months or years, his lack of understanding resulted in an absolute rejection of the concept taught.

It was my job to ensure that there was a breakthrough.

- **Intervention approach (Primary school: 11 to 12 years old)**

My priority was to teach Sean as many abstract sight words as possible for him to be able to read sentences. He would be learning concrete words too but that was not my priority as he was able to learn those type of words much faster. Care would be taken to help him differentiate the different concrete words that overlapped in meanings.

The only way to ensure that a type Y retains the information taught was to establish a strong link between the word and the meaning. The meaning has to be shaped from his understanding of reality.

The problem was that Sean rejected all the usual recommendations for nonresponders. After experimentation, I realised that drawing pictures or using clay to mould a representation of abstract words did not work for him. While he was definitely visually oriented, a still image or figure was not impressionable nor relatable enough for Sean to establish meaning. He could create all the stories that he wanted but he would be unable to remember them. Tactile and physical movement of learning words also did not have any positive effect on his retention.

I realised that I had to reverse my tactics. I should not be depending on Sean to provide me with an experience or story that he could relate - not when he was unable to make sense of the world and when his confusion of the world around him changed everyday. He would never be able to understand an abstract word from his world view.

Instead, I should implant a relatable experience through a channel that he was most receptive towards. I was optimistic that I would be able to locate his channel of optimal learning. The fact that Sean was able to recognise a small pool of words and recall his life experiences meant that information was still trickling into his head via a very niche channel with many pre-requisites.

In order to maximise his learning, I aimed to teach multiple sight words at one go. This is in contrast to the mandated one-sight-word-per-week strategy.

After about one and a half of experimentation, I decided on nursery songs. I fervently hoped that he was receptive to music and rhythm (and that he was not belittled by something so 'elementary'). I introduced the song "She'll be coming round the mountain when she comes".

Fortunately, he took it like fish to water.

I took care not to include any contractions (e.g. 's', 'll) in the lyrics. It also had to be case-sensitive.

Among all the sentences in the song, I chose the following sentence to teach him.

We will all have cakes and ice-cream **when she comes**.

Sean did not know how to read the words that were bolded and underlined.

I would spend at least 15 to 20 minutes playing a video with that song repeatedly until he was familiar with how the song was sung. Thereafter, I would show him the sentence as that part of the song was played repeatedly.

It was exceedingly important for me to point to the words during the initial stages of instruction. Initially, I let him point to the words as he sang. However, two things happened that was absolutely detrimental to his word recognition:

1. His finger would move faster than the speed of his singing. As a result, he matched the word to the wrong sound.

What he was singing	We	will	all	have	cakes	and	ice-cream	when	she	comes.
What he was pointing and seeing	We	all	have	cakes	and		ice-cream	when	she	comes.

For instance, he would look at the word 'will' and say /all/. Look at the word 'all' and say /have/.

2. He assumed that each word was a single-syllable.

What he was singing	because		I	am	happy		clap	along	if	you	feel	that	...
What he was pointing and seeing	because	I	am	happy	clap	along	if	you	feel	that	...		

Had I allowed this to continue, he would have looked at the word 'if' and read it as 'feel'.

To overcome these problems, I placed a dot beneath each syllable, told Sean to point to each dot and look at the word above his fingers as he sang.

because I am happy, clap along if you feel that ...
• • • • • • • • • • • • •

This way, he would be able to sing and read the correct words at the same time.

After looking at the lyrics and singing – and pointing to – the words in that sentence dozens of times, I would proceed to isolate each word and ask him to read a random word. Such instructional method worked like a charm for him.

Now, it is time for a pop quiz. The word 'it' was usually the bane of many type Ys' lives. Which song did I use to embed the word 'it' into his head?

You guessed it. "Let it go" from 'Frozen'.

The retention was instantaneous.

The following table shows the list of songs and the associated abstract sight words (together with some verbs and concrete nouns) that were taught to Sean:

BOOK / SONG		WORDS TAUGHT		
Title	Sentence	Abstract	Verbs (Past/Present/etc.)	Concrete nouns
She will be coming round the mountain when she comes	"We will all have cakes and ice-cream when she comes."	we, will, all, have, when, she,	comes	cakes
Who took the cookie from the cookie jar?	"Who took the cookie from the cookie jar?	who, from, me, then	took	cookie jar

	Who, me? Yes, you. Not me. Then who?"			
Where are you going?	"Where are you going?"	where, are, you	going	-
Let it go	"Let it go. I am one with the wind and sky."	let, it, am, with		wind, sky
What does the fox say	"What does the fox say?"	what, does	say	-
Happy	"because I am happy – clap along, if you feel like happiness is the truth."	because, if	clap, feel, like	-
Do you want to build a snowman?	"Do you want to build a snowman?"	do	want, build	-
All I want to say is that they don't really care about us	"All I want to say is that they don't really care about us"	that, don't, really, about, us	care	-
Adventure times (Daddy, why did you eat my fries?)	"Daddy, why did you eat my fries?"	why, did, my	eat	fries
Bingo song	"There was a farmer, had a dog and 'Bingo' was his name. B.I.N.G.O (x3) And 'Bingo'was his name."	there, was, had, his	-	-

Leapfrog	"They were only playing leapfrog."	they, were, only	playing	-
Sugar	"Your sugar, yes please. Won't you come and put it down on me. I am right here, cause I need, little and little sympathy. Yeah you show me good loving... "	your, please, won't	here, need, show	-
He has done so much for me.	"He has done so much for me."	has, done, so, much	-	-

Eventually, Sean progressed to the point where he was able to recognise and read more words than he could spell. Such literacy behaviour was typical. His previous behaviour (what he could spell was what he could read) was not typical.

This strategy of using songs was not fool proof. I was well aware that there would be a tipping point. Unless the song was so relatable to his life experiences, he would have to screen through each song and the associated lyrics in his mind. Automaticity was not his strong point. The length of the lyrics mattered.

As such, the more songs that he learnt, the more 'rendering' time it took. Should he learn 10 songs and was asked to read or spell a word from the 7th song, he literally had to 'render' the lyrics from the very first song that was taught to him all the way to the 7th song.

As such, the longer the sentences, the longer he takes to render. It was a balancing act between:

- Introducing another song comprising of sentences with lesser lyrics for faster retrieval of words, in exchange for lesser abstract words taught alongside with increased number of songs with longer 'rendering' times to retrieve words

- Introducing another song comprising of sentences with more lyrics that encompasses more abstract words to control the number of songs introduced, in exchange for greater risk of inaccurate word recall due to the lengthy sentences

- The relatability of the song to Sean's reality

With reference to why his reading accuracy exceeded his spelling accuracy over time, you have to understand this uniquely Sean's problem.

- **Sean's reading process**

  - *Immediate recall of the word*

    Sean saw the word → immediate recall of the picture → immediate trigger of the associated song in his mind → immediate 'rendering' of the lyrics that he could recall from that song → read the word

  - *Did not have immediate recall*

    I had to source for a representative illustration of each song or nursery rhyme. It could appear in the form of a screenshot from the youtube video or a picture of the nursery rhyme. All the illustrations were consolidated into a prompt sheet.

    Sean saw the word → unable to read the word due to the inability to recall the representative illustration → went through every illustration in the prompt sheet and started singing from the very first song or rhyme → screened through the sheer volume of lyrics in his mind → located the correct song and the associated lyrics → read the correct word

  - *Required prompts from me*

    Sean saw the word → unable to read the word due to the inability to recall the representative illustration → required visual prompts using the prompt sheet → unable to remember the lyrics of one of the songs and the 'rendering' process was interrupted → required my assistance in providing the lyrics of the song → immediate screening of the lyrics of the remaining songs → located the correct song and the associated lyrics → read the correct word

- **Sean's spelling process**

  The independent recollection of words via auditory means was difficult for Sean.

This was because there were many more steps involved in the his word retrieval for spelling.

- *Assumption: Successful recollection of words to spell*

  Sear heard the word → required to successfully associate the word with the correct song → successfully locate the correct song among all the songs that he had learnt so far → recalled song → recalls the representative illustration of the song → recalls the associated lyrics → immediate screening of the lyrics in his mind → saw the correct word in his mind → proceeds to spell

  The spelling process was more challenging for Sean as he was supposed to use the *auditory* form of the word to recall the lyrics of the songs in an *auditory* fashion before attempting to trigger the *visual* representation of the song in his mind. Unlike his reading process, Sean's spelling process did not capitalise on his visual strength. As such, Sean found it more challenging to associate the word with the correct song, and it had repercussions for the rest of the spelling process.

- **Intervention approach (Secondary school: 13 to 14 years old)**

With much effort and hard work, Sean managed to clear his national exams and qualify for secondary school education. Between the transition from 12 to 13 years old, he had internalised most of the abstract sight words and seemed to be a bit more coherent in his thoughts. He no longer needed to take weeks to remember a new one or two syllable word. If the conditions were right (i.e word meanings do not overlap), Sean would be able to learn short words – preferably single-syllable words – with greater ease as compared to his previous attempts. On particularly successful days, he would be able to remember the words that were taught to him by the end of a two hour lesson and there would be retention!

Of course, the experiences that he had beyond the classroom meant that he might be confused by something that he saw, which in turn adversely affected a pre-existing mental concept. On other days, he might have seen or heard something that seemed to straighten out his thoughts and he would be able to read the words straight away – that was something that he could not do in the past.

However, our happiness was short-lived. The secondary school syllabus threw us another curve ball. What they demanded of him were multisyllabic words.

Historically, Sean had an acute problem with multisyllabic words. Whenever he tried to remember the entire words on its own, he confused it with visually-similar words. In addition, such long words went way beyond what his visual span could tolerate. His receptivity to abstract concepts was so low that nothing except the entire word was acceptable. As such, he was not even able to remember the syllables as each syllable usually lacked a direct representation in reality. The word 'present' for instance was problematic because there was no such thing as a 'pre' in this world. While 'sent' is a real word, the following issues would surface:

1. He had no concept of past tense and therefore retention of the word 'sent' was unlikely.

2. He did not know where to segment the word and would always attempt to read the word in its entirety. As such, it was unlikely that he would even segment and read it as 'pre / sent'.

It is important to note that even for most nonresponders, they are highly receptive to segmenting the word on the syllable level as it reflects how they speak. Zeak and Xian were also highly receptive to multisyllabic words so long as they fitted the nonresponder's requirements in remembering multisyllabic words. In fact, segmenting a word into syllables are as far as most nonresponders could do as they tend to struggle with segmenting a single-syllable word into individual sounds (e.g. 'spent' = /s/ /p/ /e/ /n/ /t/). As such, Sean's inability to segment words into syllables and his subsequent non-existent morphological knowledge was a rarity even in the nonresponder world. That being said, there was a small group of type Ys who struggled with the morphology of words. (Please refer to the next chapter for more information.)

Due to the expanding list of multisyllabic words that Sean needed to learn, I turned to a Speech and Language Therapist (SLT) to collaborate. Together, we ensured a consistent approach to his intervention. There was consensus that Sean could no longer rely on remembering the whole word due to the length of words. We had to teach him the many different types of syllables for him to have a chance of surviving the next four years in secondary school, regardless of how abstract Sean might perceive syllables to be.

We always started with a list of 10 to 15 words and only moved on when Sean largely demonstrated proficiency and automaticity in reading those words.

The first few lessons were very strange. The SLT reported that he would look at a multisyllabic word and be unable to divide it into syllables. However, when the SLT clapped according to the number of syllables, he was able to divide accurately them all of a sudden.

When it was my turn to instruct him, he would show evidence of dividing multisyllabic words into syllables but he would divide them in the wrong places. When I clapped according to the number of syllables, however, he could – all of a sudden – see the appropriate places to divide the words accordingly.

He was truly in tune with rhythm.

Things started to change just after a few weeks. Clapping no longer yielded such accuracy in segmentation. Suddenly, his brain no longer took to rhythm to segment the word. He was starting to look at patterns in words and that overrode the rhythmic part of his brain.

Sean required to link every syllable to an existing word that he knew in order to attach meaning to each syllable meaning and reduce Sean's perceived abstractness of each syllable. Fortunately, Sean only required prompting of the first two syllables in order to recall how the word was spoken. However, there were times that he required help for the entire word.

For instance, I taught Sean the word 'communicate'. While he was eventually able to segment the entire word into syllables 'com / mu / ni / cate', he could not remember how to read them as they were too abstract. As such, I had to associate each syllable with a word that Sean knew in order to create meaning for each syllable.

The table below shows the link of each syllable to an associated word:

Syllable	Associated word	Rationale
com	computer	-
mu	music	-
ni	-	Sean knew how to read this syllable after reading the first two syllables. It must be noted that if 'ni' was the first or second syllable, Sean would not know how to read 'ni'. It seems that reading the first two syllables triggered him to make an educated guess of the word.

		In this case, however, Sean read the word as 'community'. As a result, I had to proceed with the last syllable. I also told myself to introduce the word 'community' alongside with 'communicate' in order to allow Sean to distinguish the visual differences between both words.
cate	lo<u>cate</u> hel<u>lo</u>	Sean did not know the word 'locate' but I could not find any other word that he knew with the 'cate' syllable in it. In order for him to even read the syllable 'lo', I had to find another word that has the syllable 'lo' in it. The word was 'hello'. True to Sean's confusion with words of overlapping meaning, he would always read the word 'hello' as /hi/ and I had to prompt him to read it otherwise.

Taken together, this was an example of how Sean read the word 'communicate':

Sean: *Looks at the word 'communicate' and stares at the segmented syllable 'com'*

Sean: I don't know.

Me: *Shows him the word 'computer'*

Sean: Oh! Computer! Com... Com...This is so hard.

Me: *Shows him the word 'music'*

Sean: Music! Com.. mu... Community!

Me: *Gives him the pointed look and states that it is not read as 'community'*

Sean: Communi...

Me: *Shows him the word 'locate'*

Sean: I don't know.

Me: *Shows him the word 'hello'*

Sean: Hi.

Me: Another word for 'hi'?

S: Hello. Lo...cate. (Sometimes, I had to help him with this word.) Com...mu...ni...cate. Communicate!

Can you imagine how effortful it was for him to initially read multisyllabic words? Every abstract syllable had to be linked to a real word consciously. We had to repeat this whole laborious process of reading the word 'communicate' at the start of each lesson over a period of four weeks. In other words, it took him a month to finally read the word 'communicate' with semi-automaticity.

In another example, Sean had to learn the word 'construction'. In cases like this, there was a syllable – 'struc' – that was not commonly seen in Sean's world.

I covered the letter 's' and asked him which real word resembled 'truc'.

He said, "Truck."

Then in the next breath, he read, "Construction."

Effectively, he was reading it as /contrucktion/ without the letter 's' and with the letter 'k'. However, he got the meaning of the word and was able to read it with negligible difference from the original. I chalked it up as a win on our part.

- **Single-syllable words**

There were times when Sean was still unable to read single-syllable words. For instance, he was taught the words 'near' and 'far' but he could not, for the life of him, remember which word was read as /near/ and which word was read as /far/.

I fell back on the trusty strategy that tided Sean through his primary school years. I played the song "My heart will go on" by Celine Dion. The song contained the following line:

"Near, far, wherever you are..."

Sean never had problems identifying which was which after that.

- **Phonemic awareness**

While the SLT and I acknowledged that Sean was not a phonics responder, the SLT wanted to train him to just figure out the sounds of the first two letters of each syllable. While Sean found it laborious, the SLT reasoned that Sean had a history of guessing accurately after the first two sounds in each syllable as the sounds triggered Sean to make an accurate guess of the syllable. The SLT wanted to train Sean for the worst case scenario when he did not know how to read the word and his sudden inability to recall what was previously taught surfaced again. In addition, the SLT just wanted Sean to get the most basic understanding that letters actually represent sounds. That morsel of phonics instruction was like a measure of last resort.

The SLT focused on introducing the most basic of phonics sounds – the consonants and consonant diagraphs (e.g. 'sh', 'ch'). Sean just guessed the sound of the vowels due to the many different sounds that a vowel has. After two years of repeated reinforcement of basic consonants, vowels and diagraphs by the SLT, Sean still largely rejected the same set of phonograms that he saw every week. He still looked at the letter 'g', 'u' or 'c' and guessed wildly. He still read the same three letter words using phonics with such high levels of inaccuracy that he literally scored 1 / 180 for his phonics reading test year after year. However, that morsel of phonics really helped him to creak the gears of his typical word reading development – even though the effects may be microscopically tiny. For certain unknown syllables that I was unable to link to a real word due to Sean's limited store of words in his mind, that bit of phonemic awareness was indeed Sean's saving grace.

I was initially sceptical of introducing any type of phonics sound to Sean but the SLT proved it to me that a morsel of phonics was required to supplement a nonresponders instructional approach as a measure of last resort. Regardless, both of us agreed that Sean's affinity with phonics was nearly non-existent. It was illogical to expect phonics to chart Sean's route towards literacy acquisition.

The table below summarises the different modes of instruction used in Sean's literacy acquisition journey.

Primary school		Secondary school	
Focus: Single-syllable		Focus: Multisyllabic words	
Abstract words	Concrete words	All syllables	Unknown syllables
▪ Songs	▪ Draw pictures ▪ Songs	● Link to another known word with the same syllable	● Using real words ● Attempted phonics (laborious)
Others: Made accommodations for the three tracks of impairment		Others: Made accommodations for the three tracks of impairment	

On average, he took about a month to increase his automaticity in word recognition (though he still had occasional problems with the word 'communicate' in the first year of his secondary school life). He attended eight sessions in a month. There were days he would do very well and recalled most of the words on his own. The good progress would be reversed dramatically in a few days and he would be barely able to read most of the words. His progress was usually erratic for the first few weeks as his brain took a while to sort and categorise information through the process of pruning. Such transition would result in an erratic learning behaviour. Typically-developing individuals experience pruning over the course of hours or a few days. Sean's pruning attempts took weeks.

Fast forward another year and Sean was able to read and spell most multisyllabic words that were introduced to him. He was able to remember how to read new multisyllabic words within two lessons – a huge accomplishment in itself. Sean literacy acquisition remained a work in progress as he still struggled with multisyllabic words that he had never seen before or words that flouted the three tracks of impairment. Regardless, his literacy was slowly – but surely – improving at a pace that should be able to support his eventual objective of taking his national exams.

BEHAVIOUR: XIAN

- **Background**

Xian had a diagnosis of both dyslexia and mild autism. When he entered primary school, the teacher in-charge of Xian did not have an easy time with him as he lost interest or "shut down" in record time. While he did not have melt downs in my class, his typical behaviour disrupted anything that resembled group instruction. For just one task (e.g. verbally responding to a question), he needed half an hour of coaxing before he was willing to say something that was marginally answering the question.

I did not know why the teachers that I had met hold a certain 'timeless' stereotype – that individuals with dyslexia are more receptive to the big picture and not details (e.g. words) while individuals with autism love details and structure - and hence phonics - but they cannot see the big picture.

I presumed that they must have read it in books or attended lectures that covered the general difference between students with dyslexia and autism. Thereafter, they might have assumed such stereotypes without attempting to fully understand what dyslexia or autism really entailed.

When I knew about this stereotype, I had the following thought: If a child like Xian had both dyslexia and autism, did it mean that such children could neither think about the big picture nor focus on the details? That such children would be deemed as 'half-halfs'?.

What nonsense.

I took Xian in together with Sean. They were 11 years old then. They went to separate classes. Xian became my first student to have an official diagnosis of autism. Due to logistical constrains – and a lot of other constraints – Xian was in a class of five students. To make matters more extreme, this was a class of four nonresponders and one phonics responder. At that point, all of the nonresponders were type Xs or Ys and they required individualised instruction. In addition, some of them had extremely short attention spans. They would, at times, get into disputes and could not engage in independent work. For instance, I would try to get Xian to engage in computer work while attempting to teach the other students. However, he needed guidance in every aspect of the software and he did not like to operate the computer with a mouse. All in all, it was extremely trying during my first year with them and I was always drained at the end of their lesson. I would rant with exasperation that even if I found and understood the way to teach nonresponders, expecting me to perform miracles with such a large and diverse class for two hours per week was seriously pushing it.

Frankly speaking, Xian and I did not have any progress for a year. It was partly because everyone in the class needed my attention. In addition, I needed a lot of time to understand Xian's behaviour and engage him. I had his mother's support as she was facing a tough time with Xian's primary school teachers. She had an antagonistic relationship with special needs teacher and the form teacher as they did not seem to understand what autism – and of course, nonresponding dyslexia – entailed and proceeded with the usual phonics intervention approach. Xian was having melt downs in school to the point where the mother had to constantly stop her work to advocate for her child (more like fight for her child to be understood).

The special needs teacher insisted on carrying out phonics intervention for Xian even though he was not responding to it. The special needs teacher claimed that if Xian's literacy was not improving, it was because he was not being drilled enough of it. Phonics intervention seemed like the answer to all literacy problems. Xian's mother said that she was so stressed reinforcing phonics at home that she literally broke the leg of a table during her attempt at supporting Xian.

The special needs teacher only backed down when I became an unwitting participant in a 'showdown' that was spurred by desperation on the part of Xian's mother. The special needs teacher had been trying to teach Xian a list of 15 to 20 words (e.g. principal) for days to no avail. Her perception was that Xian was uncooperative and there was a lack of phonics reinforcement at home. As such, Xian shut down in spectacular fashion. Feeling exasperated, Xian's mother declared that I did not have problems teaching Xian. (I figured out how to teach Xian by then.) Xian's mother brought the spelling list to me to prove a point to the her – that if I could get Xian to remember the words and spell them accurately, it would mean that her teaching approach was wrong.

For those who were staunch in their belief of something flawed, the only way to rock their belief system was to provide such convincing results that there was no room for argument. I took the list, spent 15 minutes teaching him the words and another 10 minutes to test him. Thereafter, I sent him off his merry way to his iPad for rest and relaxation.

Xian responded beautifully and achieved complete spelling accuracy during the next spelling session with the special needs teacher. She was flabbergasted and acknowledged that my method – not phonics – worked for Xian. Xian's mother reported this to me with such immense satisfaction that I could not help but laugh.

- **Other notes**

While Xian was a type Y (and has since became a mix of type A and type X), his learning issues were not that severe to warrant a heavenly king status. However, his behaviour infringed into his learning attitude and at that point in time, he seemed like a heavenly king.

- **Disinclination**

None.

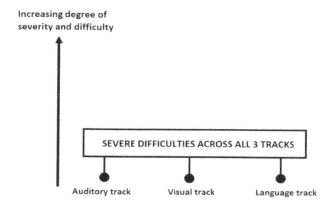

- **Intervention approach (Primary school: 11 to 12 years old)**

Initially, I used plasticine and clay to engage Xian. While he liked it, it seemed like it was not as efficient I hoped it would be. We would be shaping a few words with an embedded picture but it took way too much time and effort for just a few words. In addition, he would be playing with the clay and his classmates would join in the fun. The words that were learnt in 2 hours could have easily been learnt in 5 minutes if he was so willing.

Thereafter, I had a thought. Instead of parroting the stereotype that all individuals with autism are receptive to phonics because of their fixation towards details, I should teach them as if they have a video camera in their head. After all, they seem to remember stories and past events very well. As such, I just had to operate like how I always did with my other nonresponders with Attention Deficit Hyperactive Disorder (ADHD) – capitalise on their super short attention span by creating materials or resources that they could remember instantly with a single look (instead of forcing them to sit and attempting to drill it into them for as long as their patience can last – which was not very long to be honest).

Indeed, Xian's memory was fantastic.

Literacy instruction was carried out on three levels.

1. Single-syllable word instruction

   He favoured the (real) word in a word technique. At times, he infused a bit of phonics sounds into his spelling. His visual span was also at 4 letters. As such, Xian was able to remember single-syllable words without much effort.

2. Multisyllabic word instruction

   Each syllable was merely colour-coded in a different colour and he was able to remember effortlessly. (Please refer to chapter 6 for more information.)

3. Instruction of any single-syllable word that comprised of more than 4 letters

   In a uniquely Xian approach, he remembered how to spell words by embedding a story into the word. It was as simple and as low maintenance as it could get.

- **Behaviour**

During the initial spelling sessions, he would start drawing huge circles on the board or any other frenzied scribble on the board, books and test papers. Xian was either rejecting the notion of boring work or resisting to spell via paper and pen (or marker and board). As such, I modified it such that he spelt the words verbally, allowed him to write his words among the sea of scribbles (which I definitely could not read it and had him to spell it out verbally for me) or spell it using his fingers against the white board full of his scribbles. The ink in my markers depleted quickly but the spelling task became a lot less laborious.

Gradually, he would only stop doing his work if he did not understand the demands nor possess knowledge of how to attempt the task. Otherwise, Xian would do it in a jiffy.

At the end of the day, I suppose it was more challenging to figure out how to accommodate Xian's behaviour more than his lack of receptivity to phonics. He was both a type A and type X.

The secondary school teacher who taught Sean for a brief period during her attachment at the center also taught Xian when he was 12 years old. His frenzied scribble and other atypical behavior left her more than bewildered. Her attempt at teaching Xian obviously involved many 'shutdowns'. Getting him to erase the frenzied it scribble on the board was such an uphill task for that teacher that I was admittedly entertained. The teacher's exposure to both Sean and Xian was invaluable as it simultaneously exposed her to both extreme learning and behavioral issues.

- **Instruction approach (Secondary school: 13 to 14 years old)**

The transition into Secondary school was an awful time for Xian and his mother. There were melt downs, bullying incidents, more melt downs, continuous shutdowns and hospitalisation due to panic attacks. He seemed eager to seek solace at home and his iPad where he was safe from the outside world. We managed to get him to come to my class and he was gradually reminded that my class was another oasis of peace. However, his emotional state from school spilt over into my class and he would not be engaged with any work for about a year. As such, I continued to let the iPad and Youtube assume the role of his teacher. On days when he did not shut down in my class, work completion was a breeze. He was no longer of a heavenly king status in terms of literacy. The iPad did wonders for his language and literacy development. (This does not mean that the iPad benefitted other nonresponders that well. It was just that in Xian's case, it happened to be exceptionally effective.)

It would seem like I was fuelling Xian's iPad addiction. The other educators around him – with the best of intentions – really wanted to train him to be independent by weaning him off the iPad and instilling discipline into him. In addition, the newly acquainted special needs teacher in Xian's secondary school was adamant about using phonics to teach Xian as – quoted by the special needs teacher – "the book says that children with autism take to phonics". The special needs teacher professed that it was the first time he had encountered a student with autism. He got his supervisor – supposing to be more experienced in handling students with special needs – to assume temporary responsibility over Xian when he was unavailable.

It ended up in spectacular fashion. Xian "shut down" when he got yelled by the supervisor. The supervisor did not know how to engage Xian and suggested that it would be a good idea for Xian to stay at home – and miss school – until Xian felt like engaging with the world again. It was only when the special needs teacher returned to the school and realised that Xian was missing before Xian started to attend school again.

Looking at the perpetual "shut down" mode that he was having in school, the teachers and the special needs teacher's attempts to instil discipline into Xian seemed to be backfiring terribly. He deemed any attempt to wean him off his iPad as a reintroduction into the scary world of change and bullying. He was also not impressed by another round of phonics instruction.

His perpetual "shut down" mode caused great anxiety to his mother and Xian's emotional breakdown was constantly interrupting her ability to perform in her job, which was crucial as she was the sole bread winner of the family. Even after two years, Xian still refused to demonstrate his literacy abilities to his special needs teacher and language teacher. As a result, they seemed to have an impression that Xian's literacy skills left much to be desired.

If you are an educator, please note that being fixated on your ideals is not the way to go if you are dealing with financially-challenged, single-parent families whose children are not independent. In their situation, when survival and dealing with day-to-day problems take a toll on their sanity, their options are never clear between a good or bad decision. They are always choosing the lesser of two evils. While they are aware that addiction is not the way to go, they do not have extra help at home to look after the child. As such, they would rather the child be occupied with the iPad and be happy in order for the single parent to work with minimal disruptions and earn enough to pay the bills for survival.

CHRONIC EFFECT: WARREN

- **Disclination**

Disclination: Visual (perceptual) disclination

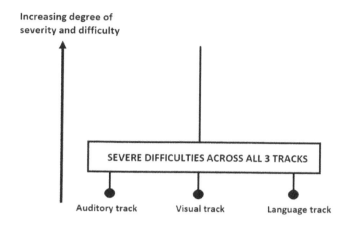

- **Profile**

Warren was the student who spurred me to look for a solution like a demon possessed.

He was flagged out to be at risk of dyslexia and language impairment in his 2nd year of kindergarten. He started phonics intervention in Primary 1. He was one of those outliers who not only failed to benefit from the programme but also experienced regression in his reading and spelling after 4 years of phonics intervention.

When his chronological age was 6 years 5 months, his word reading and spelling ages were 5 years 1 month and less than 5 years respectively. After 4 years of phonics intervention, when he was 10 years and 11 months, his word reading and spelling ages were 7 years 4 months and 6 years 4 months respectively.

Warren was passed around the other teachers for the first 4 years. I got Warren half a year into my teaching stint and his mother agreed to let me find a solution as she was aware that prior intervention was not working. It took me another 1 year 3 months before Zeak joined the centre and I found a solution. By then, it was his 6th year in the centre and the focus was to allow him to survive the national exams. Warren left the centre thereafter. As such, the nonresponder intervention that he received from me was limited. (At that point in time, I was only able to discover the type A intervention, begin to understand the characteristics of type Y nonresponders, formulate the notion of the three tracks of impairment and possess only a rudimentary (real) word in a word technique for nonresponders.)

The following essay was written by him in when he was 10 years old, after receiving 4 years of phonics intervention.

> One day, there was a marketing sale at aopen are spase suls, to bay think so popal boux finech tea plates. and ardor think so popaile bux some think.
>
> So there was tow prhsen one was wod man and ther was awamne there were a yong beggar how were asking lore money then there wore yong bck pocket so the box took away the walted form the man and the man should for help

When I showed his writing to the other teachers, they tended to think that Zeak or Sean's literacy woes seemed to be more problematic than Warren's.

"At least he is able to write something that resembles the word. It's just an inaccuracy or two," they said. "On the other hand, Zeak and Sean – especially Sean – do not know how to spell a ton of words! They even have difficulty with common three to four letter words! Surely their cases are more serious."

Therein lies the problem – and I think his previous therapists had the same assumption.

When Sean and Zeak learnt a new word, they would remember it and the word was consistently reproduced as such.

Warren's spelling changed repeatedly. Inconsistency was – and still is – the ultimate killer. This meant to say that at one moment, he spelt the word 'for' as 'for', the next moment, he would change the it to 'fore'. The word 'people' morphed from 'popal' to 'popale' interchangeably as if he did not know if an 'e' is needed. The word 'there' morphed from 'there' to 'ther' interchangeably. One of his habits was to add 'e' randomly at the end of words. This is one of the many signs of utter confusion – when the student is extremely confused with the magic-e concept in the phonics curriculum. Such utter confusion is what I term as "innate confusion". (This concept will be discussed at length later in the chapter.)

His spelling woes were further exacerbated by his (1) visual processing issues and (2) 'brain-hand' disconnect. For instance, he wrote 'tow' when asked to spell the word 'two' but he was able to verbally spell the word as 'two'. In another example, he wrotes 'lout' but verbally spells it as 'loud'. (Please refer to "Co-morbidities / Accompanying problems" for more details.)

Warren's spelling served as a stern warning to all teachers and therapists – if a nonresponder does not receive the appropriate intervention and the nonrepsonder just accepts the instruction that he or she does not understand, the nonresponder will produce an utterly disastrous display of unadulterated confusion. Witnessing such confusion as a newly minted therapist then was like watching a person being plagued with a disease that has no cure.

Furthermore, there were two incidents that made me very upset with my inability to help Warren:

    a.   When his mother handed me that writing piece that was featured earlier, I was at a loss of words – not at his writing but at what to say to his mother. The expression on her face was far from aggressive. Rather, she had this expression of calm acceptance, tinged with that bit of resignation, that his literacy standards would remain as it was regardless of the amount of time and intervention received.

b. One day, about a year since I assumed responsibility over Warren's literacy (and I still could not find a solution despite much experimentation), his mother approached me about his spelling. There was a change in his spelling results earlier that week.

"Warren spelt two words correctly. I was surprised. It seems like whatever you are teaching Warren must be working."

Again, I really did not know how to respond to the fact that she normalised his literacy ability to the point that any minute change seemed like an improvement, that those two words were spelt correctly probably due to luck. At that point, I was nowhere near finding a solution for Warren.

Thankfully, I was not plagued with questions of my self-worth as a teacher. It just made me even more determined to find a solution.

- **Co-morbidities / Accompanying problems**

Warren had a wide range of co-morbidities. His language impairment was detected when he was in preschool and recommendation for Speech and Language therapy was stated in his report. (He was also suspected of having autism but was never sent for an official assessment.) However, he did not receive language intervention as his parents were unaware of the recommendation. In addition, Warren was very resistant when it came to any additional therapies that dealt with academics and literacy. When he came to me, it was obvious that he seemed to have extensive executive functioning issues that should have been addressed by an Occupational Therapist (OT) – alongside with his SLT – before he came for educational therapy.

Aside from dyslexia, Warren had to grapple with the following co-morbidities:

- **Specific Language Impairment (Severe)**

  In order not to bore you with the specifics, let me cite an example that occurred when Warren was ten.

  I gave him a comprehension activity that spanned over two sentences.

  The question went something like this.

  "It was raining at night. Tom sighed and placed the telescope on the table

and went to sleep."

Question: Why was Tom disappointed?

Warren knew what a telescope was. He explained that it was a tool used to look at something that was far away. He knew that Tom sighed because he was disappointed. When Warren was asked for the reason for Tom's disappointment, Warren replied, "That's because he wanted to see the rain."

I told him that it was already raining outside and hence, Tom should not be disappointed. Warren explained, "That's because he wanted to see the rain in detail."

It was instances like this that admittedly made the inexperience me then panicked. I wrote an absurdly long referee report for him to have a long overdue psychological reassessment and language intervention.

○ **Difficulties with numeracy and math logic**

Warren was very bad at math and exhibited many symptoms of dyscalculia. In addition, he exhibited visual perceptual issues. For instance, he read the numbers off the screen of the calculator incorrectly. The font size of the numbers was approximately size 40. (The calculator was much bigger than the scientific calculators.). He kept seeing the decimal in the wrong place.

○ **Visual processing and directionality issues**

Warren had problems with letter sequencing and directionality (e.g. identifying left and right). He often counted the objects from right to left instead of left to right. As such, objects in the last position were seen to be in the first position.

○ **Figure ground problems**

Warren could not differentiate between foreground and background. There was an instance that highlighted his figure-ground problems clearly. He had an oral picture discussion practice with the SLT. The picture showed a lady in the kitchen. In the background, the doors to the lower cabinets were opened, revealing pots. The lady was standing in front of the lower cabinets (probably with a leg lifted off the ground), attempting to reach for something in the upper cabinets. When the SLT asked him what was the lady doing, he said that the lady was standing on the pot to reach for the things in the upper cabinet. It turned out that Warren was unable to discern that the pots in the lower cabinets were in the background. As such, Warren seemed to perceive that the lady was stepping on a pot in attempt to reach for things in the upper cabinets.

- o **Brain-hand disconnect**

A very common complaint that Warren had was that his hands seemed to write differently from whatever he was thinking. It was as if his hands had a warped mind of their own, operating independently from his brain. I have no other way of explaining it other than to describe it as the distortion of the information fidelity from his brain that was in the midst of being transferred to his hands. Often, Warren was able to verbally spell a word correctly. However, his hand would write the word incorrectly. As mentioned previously, he would verbally spell words like 'two' and 'loud' correctly but would write them as 'tow' and 'lout' instead.

I understand that this problem happens to students with learning disabilities occasionally when they are tired and their attention wavers. However, Warren's situation was a lot more alarming because his brain-hand disconnect seemed to be happening with every few words that he wrote.

Typing on the keyboard, on the other hand, does not seem to be affected by the disconnect. After all, the neural pathways for writing and typing are different.

[My colleague and I had students who had more distorted disconnection. These students had a brain-mouth-hand disconnect. What they said may be different from what they thought, and what they wrote would be different from the information in their brains or from their mouths. I had such a student three years after Warren graduated from my care.]

Similarly, these students did not seem to be affected by the disconnect when they were typing on the keyboard.]

- **Attempted intervention**

When I tried providing intervention with my newly minted intervention approach, Warren was the only nonresponder who did not demonstrate such a dramatic improvement. Sure, he achieved greater spelling accuracy but the improvements were inconsistent. Admittedly, I only developed intervention techniques for type As and was still unable to help him at that point in time. However, his prior confusion was extremely damaging as it kept interfering with the proposed solution, limiting its effectiveness in the process. This confusion – due to phonics instruction – was aggravated by his inability to determine between real words and nonsense words. It was paramount that Warren should have been exposed to real words from the start.

I learnt that confusion was a very damaging thing. If any special needs child, especially a non-responder, is fed information that adds on to the confusion (no understanding involved) and moves to the point of no return, it will take a herculean amount of effort – or perhaps even no amount of intervention – to right the wrong.

Some nonresponders have inertia that seems to prevent them from retaining anything that does not make sense. Such inertia becomes a blessing in disguise against damaging intervention approaches. On the other hand, some nonresponders are likely to just absorb everything regardless of their understanding and create a mess of confusion that would prove difficult to rectify. Warren is a prime example of such a student from the second group. (The concept on inertia will be elaborated later in the chapter.)

[Post-Warren reflection: A few years after Warren left my care, I found one of my most effective technique to date – the RRS. Thinking back, I realise that this technique would most likely have worked on Warren.]

HEAVENLY KING CONTENDERS

So far, I seem to have grouped students with dyslexia into two separate groups – phonics responders (who understand literacy concepts via their ears first) and the nonresponders (who understand literacy with their eyes). It is too simple a distinction as reality proves that there are many students who are hybrids (e.g. more phonics with some 'nonresponderness', 50-50, more 'nonresponderness' who are receptive to a hint of phonics). However, I will stick to this overly simplistic dichotomy for the sake of explaining the cases of Nathan and Sophia.

Over the years, I realised that there is small group of nonresponders who can neither depend on their eyes nor ears for literacy acquisition. Nathan and Sandra form this subgroup of nonresponders. Alongside with the heavenly kings (other than Xian), they form one of the groups who witnessed the slowest progress in their literacy acquisition.

Before I move on, I would like to say that there are two students whom I am apologetic to in my life. The first student is Warren, whom I was unable to find a solution in time to stave off the prior confusion that he had.

The second student is Nathan, whom I mistook him to be a phonics responder even after discovering how to teach nonresponders.

REGRET: NATHAN

- **Disclination**

  Disclination: Visual (storage) disclination

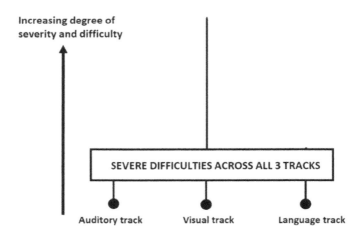

- **Profile**

Nathan came to me when he was 10 years old. At that time, I made a grave judgement of error and carried out the wrong intervention approach on Nathan. Nathan looked like he responded to phonics intervention. He could recall all of the sounds. He could blend and segment. He had the usual vowel confusion but he could recall the phonics rules without much effort. He encoded the sounds in a word slowly and steadily, but it was not laborious. Sure, he had issues with simple sight words and his vocabulary was limited. Nathan was from an English as a Second Language (ESL) background and his literacy performance was typical of students with an ESL background. Hence, his poor literacy abilities did not ring any alarm bells.

Nathan came to me one year after I discovered the nonresponder approach. At that time, I was able to sift out the nonresponders who looked like they were responding to the phonics programme. Those students were usually the type A nonresponders who are receptive to a bit of phonics before the rejection of a certain phonics concept surfaced through a series of errors that could not be rectified using the typical phonics approach. The type Y nonresponders usually crashed at the start, impervious to most attempts at phonics.

Nathan could use the phonics sounds to construct words but he made an error or two for some of the words that were constructed. It was a bit of a concern that he needed the sounds to construct 3 letter words too but there were other students who had similar struggles and they were receptive to phonics. He could not read fluently as well but he was proficient in using phonics to decode the words to read.

I classified him as part of the phonics camp, albeit one with poorer sight word memory. I deemed him to be an individual who was receptive to word construction via phonics but needed more time to gain automaticity in spelling. It was also probably an exposure issue as English was not his main language at home. He was suspected to be language impaired but he never went for a diagnosis.

During the first year, Nathan was placed in a class that had two type A nonresponders and one type Y nonresponder. Nathan was the only one who could apply the phonics sounds consistently. Initially, I was still on probation as a new therapist and teaching phonics to an entire class of nonresponders was exceedingly trying for both me and the students. Somewhere along the way, I discovered the approach to teach nonresponders and my attention was zeroed onto the other three in class. Nathan's performance was still consistent – a dedicated phonics responder who needed more time to develop reading and spelling automaticity. Then, Nathan was going to sit for his national exams came when he was 12 and we had to devote a year to ensuring that he passed. The dust settled when he was 13 and that was when I realised that something was horribly wrong.

He was still reading and spelling the simplest of words with phonics without gaining automaticity. At the age of 15, he still could not write words like 'sad' or 'that' with

100% accuracy. He was still guessing as he spelt them.

- **What went wrong**

I overlooked the most crucial of factors. It was not that Nathan had poor sight memory. Rather, he had close to no sight memory.

For the rest of the nonresponders, there would be varying improvements in word retention and spelling accuracy after receiving effective intervention.

Nathan seemed to have an orthographic processing disorder. Regardless of the amount or time invested in the intervention, he could not remember how the word looked like. Basically, Nathan had nearly zero ability to discern what were nonsense words and what were real words.

Period.

- **What were the types of words that Nathan struggled with?**

Recall the three tracks of impairment.

Words with multiple meanings	Words with the same sound	Visually similar words

Recall that nonresponders would get pretty confused with words along the three tracks of impairment.

Examples of easily confused words	
Reach	Rich
When	Went
Went	Want

At the age of 15, he did not read or copy a sentence word by word. He was still reading each word in a sentence letter by letter. He was unable to see the letters as a whole word immediately. He needed time to analyse that bunch of letters and conclude that they equated to a word. (He had many symptoms of surface dyslexia and alexia.)

Error analysis of Nathan's spelling errors demonstrated how different Nathan was from the rest of the students – phonics responders or nonresponders.

Usually, the students confuse words like 'their' and 'there' and they would write it interchangeably or spell other variations of the word.

At 15 years old, Nathan proceeded to write the following and self-corrected himself 4 times when he was asked to spell the word 'their':

der → dire → thear → theer → their

It was Nathan's formulaic approach to literacy. If you notice, he did not even write the word 'there', which was the usual word that would be mixed in the confusion. His first impression of how the word looked was 'der'. This meant that every word was just directly translated into one of the consonant sounds or letter names. In addition, it served to show that Nathan had absolutely no ability to discern what was a nonsense word and what was a real word.

Not only must the three tracks of impairment be taken into consideration, students like Nathan can only be exposed to real words and they are unable to handle multiple letters or phonograms of the same sound.

As such, phonics instruction are the utter nemesis of such students.

When Nathan was 13, he mentioned that phonics made him really confused and both his reading and spelling suffered even more as a result. (As his teacher cum therapist, it was absolutely the worst feeling to be responsible for the undoing of my student's literacy – even though I was technically complying with the system by teaching phonics.). His lack of understanding of what was a real word and a nonsense word was exacerbated by the nature of phonics instruction. For instance, the word 'step' can be spelt as 'stap' and they make the same sound! There are no rules to say which word is the correct spelling other than an ambiguous instruction from the teacher:

" 'Stap' also makes the same sound as 'step', but I want /e/ instead of /a/ (aaaaaaa)."

Such ambiguity essentially requires the students to use their orthographic memory. A student with very poor orthographic memory has no idea if 'step' and 'stap' are real words.

(Then, there is the word 'stab', which complicates matters due to its auditory similarity to the word 'step'. However, it is a low-frequency word and I usually do not introduce it.)

- **Other complaints**

  o Each time Nathan attempted to read, he was unable to read word by word. Instead, he read letter by letter. Basically, Nathan was unable to see words as a whole.

  o Nathan's spelling behaviour resulted in an unusual approach to the spelling of multisyllabic words. Such approach was different as compared to the spelling behaviour of the other students – phonics responder or nonresponder. (Please read the next chapter for more details.)

  o Nathan, for the life of him, could not remember how a word was spelt if there were words with similar sounds (homonyms). Nathan might look like he was able to do so after much practice but under times of stress, the word never materialised as the right one.

    "When I look at the words 'when' and 'went', I can never tell which is which. I know the meanings of the words, but I can never match the spelling of the word to the meaning of the word. I usually have to guess."

Nathan's experience taught me one important fact – the visual means of remembering words outweighs the auditory means in word acquisition, regardless of the severity of a student's dyslexia.

Phonics responders use phonics sounds to support their literacy learning but their orthographic memory ultimately takes over to remember how the words are formed.

Nonresponders capitalize on their altered visual route to remember how words are formed.

Nonresponders with visual recognition or storage issues will always struggle with literacy acquisition.

- **Attempted solution**

1) The only thing that works with nearly 100% accuracy is mnemonics. However, I was very careful about mnemonics because an overwhelming number of them would serve to confuse Nathan.

2) Nathan's formulaic approach to literacy did not yield high levels of accuracy. Under stress, Nathan's train of thought got distorted and the formula was adversely affected as a result.

3) The seemingly easier technique of (real) word in a word had extremely low rates of accuracy because Nathan did not recognise the smaller real words. His base of sight words was exceedingly small.

   For instance, we would usually say that the word 'hear' is made up of the letter 'h' and the word 'ear' because we use our ears to hear. However, Nathan could never remember the word 'ear' unless there was a mnemonic. As such, it was a constant battle for Nathan to distinguish between 'hear' vs 'here'.

4) Embedded pictures never worked for Nathan. He was the ultimate realist faction.

The following table shows Nathan's spelling attempt at the age of 15:

What Nathan was told to spell (with given examples)	What Nathan spelt (final word after corrections)
went	when
rich	reach
little	litter
their	there
think	thing
taking	takine
train	trine

hard	hade
father	fader
gone	gorn
where	ware
sit	set
tried	tride
hotel	hotal
dinner	dinire
toilet	toilit
follow	follo

PANDORA BOX: SOPHIA

- **Disclination**

  Double disclination: Visual (storage) and auditory disclination

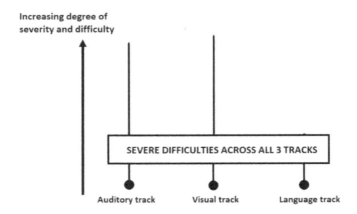

- **Profile**

Sophia came to me when she was 11 years old. She came in one year after Nathan. Nathan and Sophia were visually disinclined. However, Sophia was also auditorily disinclined.

Sophia had unreliable eyes and ears.

I harboured no intentions that Sophia responded to phonics. Unlike the other type Y nonresponders, however, her lack of receptivity to phonics manifested in different ways. The following table attempts to demonstrate the difference between Sophia and the rest of the students:

Phonics responders	Response to phonics
Type As	They seem to respond to phonics till CCVC. Anything beyond CCVC results in lower levels of accuracy. As such, they rely on the (real) word in word technique to remember longer words.
Type Ys – reliant on altered sight memory	The most severe ones do not even perceive letters as letters. They have no understanding of how individual sounds come together to form words. They perceive the entire word to be just one sound. e.g. Hot = / hot/ , not /h/ /o/ /t/ Literacy acquisition is based on typical type Y instruction. This is based on the assumption that type Y nonresponders rely on their altered sight memory abilities for literacy acquisition.
Type Ys – unreliable eyes and ears	Sophia's auditory processing was unreliable. She could not hear blends (e.g. bl, br). She could hear the letters 'l' and 'r' in isolation, but as a word, she could only hear the first letter of the blend. This meant to say the word 'plan' sounded like 'pan' to her. Essentially, she was only able to use phonics to help her spell three letter CVC words. That was very limiting. This was aggravated by Sophia's inability to process

sounds well. She could not hear properly in a noisy environment, especially when many people were talking all at one go. All symptoms pointed towards Central Auditory Processing Disorder (CAPD). The inability to differentiate individual sounds in the word meant that many words seemed to sound the same to her and that had a profound impact in the way it adversely affected her vocabulary acquisition. It was of no surprise that she has language impairment.

The hospital appointment to check her auditory processing proved to be disappointing as the audiologist merely did a general check on her hearing ability, despite receiving a long referral letter that explained my suspicions of Sophia having CAPD.

Usually, a visual approach would be used to offset the weakness in auditory processing. However, Sophia seemed to have major visual processing and storage issues.

Recall that nonresponders largely rely on their altered sight memory. Their visual spans allow them to comfortably remember three or four letter words – some nonresponders segment four letter words into two parts of two letters each to allow the word to fit comfortably into their visual spans.

Sophia could only comfortably remember two letter words like 'so' and 'at'. Three letter words like 'end' and was' were already a struggle. This was very severe even among nonresponders.

She attempted to commit words to memory by writing each word tens and hundreds of times over a span of a few days, only to break down in tears when her efforts were futile as she still could not remember how the words were spelt.

	Her visual woes were also aggravated by the fact that, similar to Nathan, Sophia, for the life of her, could not match the word to the sound regardless of the exposure.

Nathan and Sophia's visual pathways (storage) were unreliable. (Warren's visual pathways looked unreliable too but that was because phonics was the main reason that triggered his confusion.)

Both Nathan and Sophia attended the same secondary school and were exposed to the same curriculum. You may ask – between Nathan and Sophia, who was the student who had more severe literacy problems?

Nathan was the more severe of the two. While both struggled with literacy issues, Sophia began to pass her English exams at the end of her first year in secondary school. On the other hand, Nathan could not pass his English until the latter half of his third year. In fact, Nathan only started to recognise words on his paper at the age of 15. That was the year he no longer read laboriously as compared to the previous years when he needed help with almost every word in the sentence.

Both Sophia and Nathan continued to struggle immensely with spelling. Sophia could gradually spell some high-frequency four letter words by sight while Nathan continued to struggle with pervasive inaccurate spelling of words that did not meet his strict requirements till his graduation from the centre at the age of 16. With much concentration and effort, he was able to achieve greater spelling accuracy of some high-frequency words. However, his slight spelling accuracy always collapsed like a house of cards when he underwent periods of stress or distractions (e.g. exams). The word 'sit' is still spelt as 'set' to this day.

Nathan fell sick constantly. During his preliminary exams and national exams – partly due to his compensatory strategy to cope with his poor memory – he would wake up the night before any of his exams at 2:00 AM to cram information into his head, sleep for an hour or two till 5:00 AM before waking up again at 7:00 AM or 8:00 AM for his exams. Nathan claimed that if he tried to study the day before and slept without waking up to cram information, he would not be able to recall them.

Why was it the case that Sophia saw greater improvements as compared to Nathan? It may seem as if Sophia was the more severe case. While Nathan had 'unreliable' eyes (visual processing / storage), Sophia had both 'unreliable' eyes and ears. Surely Nathan would have seen greater improvements.

I would like to emphasise this crucial point – it is not the number of difficulties that has the most detrimental effect on literacy development. Rather, it is the degree of impairment of <u>what matters most</u> that has the greatest impact on a student's literacy acquisition.

Sophia's visual processing ability – while severely limited – was one tiny notch above Nathan's ability. At the very least, she was able to discern real words from nonsense words. As such, her orthographic memory was gradually able to retain simple high-frequency words after much practice over the years. On the other hand, Nathan could not reliably achieve spelling accuracy regardless of the amount of time or effort that he invested. This was regardless of the length of the word. As long as the word triggered confusion, Nathan would never be able to reproduce the words on paper with accuracy under times of stress.

DARK HORSE: SAM

This is the same Sam that was mentioned in chapter 4. I am writing about Sam in chapter 5 one year and three months after my initial pre-test with him in chapter 4.

To date, Sam is my most challenging case.

I assumed responsibility over Sam halfway into my sixth year of service. At that point in time, I was working with responders and nonresponders alike. The rest of the heavenly kings came in my first four years of service and since then, every student that came my way was diagnosed quickly and accurately before the appropriate intervention was given. Usually, I could figure a student out within a lesson or two. The more complicated cases took three to four lessons.

I took one year and three months to figure out this puzzle that came in the form of Sam.

Sam was a student from another teacher. That teacher transferred Sam to me after a period of ineffective phonics intervention in school and at the centre. He was 12 at the point in time. He was able to recognise enough words to understand what he was reading. On the other hand, his spelling ability was significantly lower than his reading ability. I carried out my pre-test that was stated in the previous chapter. If you recall, I deduced that he was a type Y nonresponder with disinclinations. Then, I carried out the intervention.

What I did not know was that Sam was an unprecedented case.

If Nathan's case was tricky because I could not tell him apart from a phonics responder, Sam's case was exceedingly deceptive because I could not tell him apart from a severe type Y nonresponder and a new category of type Y nonresponder.

Sam was such a tricky case because not only were his warning flags so subtle, nothing about his learning behavior or written output screamed "unprecedented type Y nonresponder". Rather, he looked like he fluctuated between a mix of type A and Y nonresponder.

- **Literacy levels and learning behavior (Primary school: 12 years old)**

Sam was in the same class with Sean, Xian and another type X nonresponder. Sam came to me during the year of his national exam. I spent my time providing literacy intervention and prepping him for the national exam. His attendance was not great and I saw him infrequently. He would turn up for a week before disappearing for another two weeks.

- ○ Sam could read the words in a sentence. Even if he did not know the word, he would be able to read it after a prompt or two. His single word reading accuracy level was noticeably reduced. However, this was the same for many of my nonresponders as they were able to accurately guess the word using the meaning of the sentence. This rightfully reinforced my initial suspicion that he did not have a language disinclination even though he had extensive problems with his language development.

- ○ Sam was a quiet boy. He had limited expressive vocabulary and was often unable to tell me what he was referring to. For instance, he would say "the dragon thing" or "What's that?". That being said, he was able to verbally express himself adequately using largely simple but proper syntax and grammar with little hesitation. When he spoke about topics of interest, his expressive vocabulary increases. His behavior was exactly the same as many of my other students. I have to emphasise once more that while he had plenty of language difficulties (and was probably at risk of language impairment), he did not have a language disinclination.

○ He liked to use phonics to spell whenever possible but the only possible words that he could spell accurately with phonics were '-ack' words (e.g. 'black'). The rest of his spelling was grossly inaccurate (e.g. 'ugly' as 'uglen').

○ His letter formation left room for improvement. For instance, his 'a' looked like a 'u' as he did not close the gap for 'a'. His 'n's looked like 'u' at times. Sam seemed like a lot of the students who had handwriting issues. It was not that his writing was ugly. Rather, different letters looked similar.

Upon investigation, Sam claimed that he was confused with the following similar looking letters:

- 'n' and 'r'
- 'a' and 'c'
- 'h' and 'n
- 'l' and 'i'
- 'z' and 'x'

○ **Example of instruction:** Based on one of his mini spelling pre-test, Sam spelt 'feel' as 'fell' and 'fall' as 'felt'. To clear the confusion, I had to teach him the words 'feel', 'felt', 'fall' and 'fell'. Usually, I do not include the past tense forms into my initial instruction. However, Sam seemed to have knowledge of the word forms 'fell' and 'felt'. I needed to address that to avoid more confusion. In addition, I felt that his relative language inclination should be able to tolerate instruction on past tense forms. He also used the words 'fell' and 'felt' in his verbal expression. (However, he might have been like Sean who was able to use words in his verbal expression but had no idea that he was using the words.)

I decided against introducing the words 'fill' and 'filled' into the mix even though they were auditorily similar to 'feel'. This was because I had a nagging suspicion that he could not cope with too many similar sounding words that had different meanings.

After using all sorts of methods that Sam was agreeable with, Sam started to produce a variation of words during the following lessons:

- Fett
- Fatt

- Felt
- Falt
- Fust
- Full
- Fall
- Fetl
- Fail

It was a disaster. Sam was experiencing what I term as "innate confusion". Not only did he produce variations of the four words that I taught him, other visually-similar words (e.g. 'fail' and – potentially – 'fast' that was written as 'fust') that existed in his word knowledge were being adversely affected in an expanding circle of corruption.

Did he have an orthographic processing disorder like Nathan? That he was unable to discern real words from nonsense words? It certainly felt different.

Nathan's errors were consistent. Sam's errors were always changing. However, Nathan was not able to read nor spell as phonics severely undermined his literacy. Sam was able to read significantly better than he could spell. He seemed to have a larger base of known words that he could spell as compared to Nathan.

Nathan's spelling was a direct representation of phonics sounds. Sam's spelling was usually grossly different from the phonics sounds.

Nathan tried to develop his formulaic approach to spelling, which worked during stress-free periods. Sam seemed aware that his spelling looked inaccurate but he still went ahead and just spelt in a jiffy.

It was during that period of time that I had this hypothesis about Sam's highly inconsistent spelling – and I did not like the conclusions that I was drawing from it.

In my first two years of service, I read a number of literature (including the approach proposed by Turner & Hope (2010)) that recommended outlining the shape of the words.

This is in line with the Gestalt theory. It was to facilitate word acquisition as this school of thought posits that learners perceive the overall shape of the words before they note the details. (Some approaches also claimed that learners would be able to know where the "boundaries of the words lie".)

I thought about it from another perspective. Sam only seemed to remember the first letter consistently. He was really inconsistent on letters beyond the first letter. It meant that his store of words looked something like the following:

Looking at the words that Sam had spelt for me over the many lessons, it really seemed like this was the case. He seemed to take the term "visually-similar word" to a whole new level.

Any word that seemed to fit the outline of the word was a potential contender to whatever sound that he heard.

This was shaping to be a huge problem but I did not realise the implications of how detrimental it was. One reason was – again – his highly inconsistent spelling behavior. There were words – regardless of length – that he could spell effortlessly with no issues. His words on the auditory and visual impairment tracks were merging with no clear pattern. Most importantly, as mentioned later in this section, Sam's auditory processing issues seemed like the most dominant problem at hand.

o   There were weeks that he could spell a word correctly while there were other weeks that he could not. Often, his errors were not consistent. The following table shows the transformation of Sam's spelling over a period of six weeks:

Transformation of his spelling over the lessons							
	Taught word	Week 1	Week 2	Week 3	Week 4	Week 5	Wk 6
1	sunny day	sunnday	saunnday suunnday	sunnday	sunny day	suning day	sunny day
2	shone	shoue shone	shoue	shoue shone	shoue	sho	shone (for three weeks)
3	shorts	shots	sht	shos	stong	shoet	shat shont
4	pants	pants	pants	pants	past	panest	paats punts paut
5.	tea teach	tec	tea teach	teach	teach	tcech	teach teqch

o   Sam had no idea when to use the words 'is', 'are', 'was', 'were', 'has', 'have' and 'had' in his writing. This was probably due to Sam's inability to deal with the sound 'were' that, in turn, affected his understanding of the word 'were' and the associated words. (It has to be noted that he was able to use these words in his speech without any problems.) I taught him how to use these words to construct grammatically-accurate sentences. Upon instruction, Sam was able to construct grammatically-accurate sentences with no problems.

- **Literacy levels and learning behavior (Secondary school: 13 years old)**

o   When Sam entered secondary school, his attendance became more regular. He was in a class of five. His classmates were all nonresponders – a type Y (Sean), a type Y turned A (Xian), a type X and a type A. It was the start of another hectic year in class as I had to struggle with Sean's 'pruning' and "mind wipe" in the midst of handling a class that was not independent in their learning. Moreover, at that point in time, Xian developed a coping mechanism of ending up in the hospital whenever he wanted to avoid something that was happening in school.

o   I did a massive pre-test again at the beginning of the year to evaluate his spelling abilities at the point where he was transiting into secondary school.

Many nonresponders experience an improvement in spelling abilities at the age of 13 and 15 respectively. Much to my delight, Sam was able to spell more words accurately and some of the words that he had difficulty spelling during his primary school years were also spelled correctly. I took it as a sign that we could move on with his learning and started to teach longer words that spanned five to six letters. The strange thing was that he would, like in his primary school days, make errors on sight words that he previously knew. In addition, his errors had no consistent pattern and each week presented a different variation of the errors of the same word. Within a few weeks, even his three and four letter word spelling experienced a regression.

o   There was only one lesson (in about 37 lessons) that he kept fussing over the way I wrote certain letters. As I sat opposite Sam, I had to write upside down. Sam kept insisting that many of my letters did not look like the letters that it was meant to be. He hated it when I wrote the letters 'h', 'r', 'a' and 't'. For instance, he complained that the horizontal stroke of the letter 't' was not at the right level that a 't' should be. Due to his insistence, I started to write letters the right side up. Even when I wrote it the right side up however, he did not seem satisfied with my penmanship. Admittedly, my penmanship left more to be desired and I usually compensated with my cursive handwriting when I was a student. However, I had never written in cursive when I taught the students. I always made sure that I printed the letters to the best of my abilities. Even then, he would argue with me. For instance, he insisted that the vertical line in 'h' should be higher. Otherwise it would look like a letter 'n'. Even after I extended the vertical line, he still insisted that it did not look like a 'h' when it clearly looked like one to me. Exasperated, I asked them exactly how high he wanted me to extend the vertical line until it looked like a letter 'h' to him.

Apart from that lesson, Sam did not voice any complaint about my handwriting or differing font styles. In fact, he would claim that my penmanship was 'okay' and he could distinguish the letters that I had written just 'fine'. This was proof that his feedback to me was also inconsistent.

o   Upon investigation, Sam claimed that he was confused with the following visually-similar letters:

-   'o' and 'e'

- 'o' and 'a'
- 'h' and 'm'
- 'b' and 'd'
- 'y' and 'g'

○ It must be noted that he was entirely accepting to stylistic features that I added to letters 'a' and 'n'.

○ At times, his 'a' still looked like a 'u'. Sam would also be unsure of some of the letters that he had written. It did not seem out of the norm as many of our students were also unable to read their handwriting or recognise the letters that they had written.

○ As observed in the previous year, I still could not teach him visually-similar words. For instance, I was not able to teach him the word 'house' as he knew the word 'horse'. Teaching him the word 'house' would destabilise his knowledge of the word 'horse'. As such, Sam always used the word 'home' instead of 'house'.

○ He was always entirely accepting to any method that I had proposed to tackle the spelling of his sight words. Regardless of the method, he would always respond with "Also can.", "Sure." or "That's fine." Then, he would proceed to demonstrate competence in the instructional method during that lesson. However, he would no longer demonstrate competence when I saw him the next lesson.

Three months into Sam's life as a secondary school student, his chronically inconsistent errors spurred me to give him a massive spelling test again. At this point, Sam was rightfully becoming more restless due to ineffective intervention. Through this spelling test, I hoped to uncover the reason behind his inconsistent errors.

The following table shows the words that Sam spelt:

	What Sam was told to spell	What Sam spelt		What Sam was told to spell	What Sam spelt
1	five	give -> five	11	wall	wall
2	fire	fian	12	tall	tall
3	find	find	13	talk	toke

4	find	fiend	14	wake	wyup
5	friend	fiend	15	well	will
6	train	trind	16	were	then -> they
7	say	san -> say	17	where	way
8	said (longer /a/ sound)	sade	18	wear	wey
9	said (shorter /a/ sound)	staed	19	are	are -> ar
10	walk	wand	20	are (emphasis on 'r')	awre

It was not easy to determine the cause of his inconsistent errors. When I asked Sam to spell the word 'are' however, I had a brain wave of a sudden and asked Sam if the word 'are' was a different word when I placed more emphasis on the 'r' sound. He said it was and proceeded to spell it differently. That was when I was struck with an understanding of the complexity and severity of Sam's auditory processing problems.

Sam had massive problems with auditory constancy. So long as a word was not delivered in the same tone, pitch or intonation, the same word would sound like a multitude of different words or sounds. (He also performed inconsistently on the word 'said'. I did not detect that at first as I erred on the safe side and assumed that he might not fancy past tense words during stressful periods.) His problem with auditory constancy had a profoundly adverse impact on his literacy and language development.

To confirm my suspicions, I went to dictionary.com and used the audio function to read the subsequent list of words that Sam had to spell. I wanted to see if the mechanical voice with a consistent pitch, tone and intonation resulted in any changes to Sam's spelling.

	What Sam was told to spell	What Sam spelt		What Sam was told to spell	What Sam spelt
1	is	is -> hes (claimed that he heard the /h/ sound)	18	always	awed
2	his	hes	19	cold	coold / could
3	were	were	20	cool	lcool -> cool
4	wear	ware	21	hold	hold
5	because	beca(q)urse	22	tell	tell
6	train	triad (claimed that 'n' sounded like a 'd')	23	again	aged
7	thank you	tan you	24	walk	wack
8	bent	abaut -> baut	25	walk	waak
9	out	out	26	talk	talk
10	after	afand	27	take	take
11	after	afantd	28	make	make
12	water	wate	29	cake	cake
13	eat	eta	30	happy	happey
14	eat	ete eta	31	very	vera -> very
15	eat	ate	32	every	ar -> urday
16	all	all	33	people	pepoly

17	also	also	

It confirmed my suspicions as Sam was able to spell with higher levels of accuracy. In particular, the words 'were' and 'also' were spelt correctly. As mentioned in the previous chapter, the word 'were' released a bomb of confusion in Sam's mind. Upon using the mechanical voice, I witnessed – for the first time – Sam's successful and effortless attempt at writing that word.

However, Sam voiced his complaints. The mechanical voice comprised of a male and a female voice. Sam produced more inconsistent spelling when the male voice was dictating the words. I deduced that he had even more difficulties with the lower pitch. It struck me again that Sam's difficulties with the lower pitch was probably the reason for Sam's inconsistent spelling errors over the past half a year. My voice is of the lower pitch and I was unable to produce a consistent intonation. Basically, he was allergic to my voice.

That being said, his spelling errors could not be entirely attributed to his issues with auditory constancy. He was spelling several words incorrectly regardless of the type of voice. It seemed like his existing base of sight words was very limited.

It was then that I started to ponder.

Usually, many nonresponders with auditory processing difficulties tended to develop strong visual abilities to remember the word by sight. However, this was not the case for Sam. The strange thing was that he kept favouring an auditory means of acquiring literacy even though his auditory processing ability was so unreliable. Then, it struck me for the third time. Any individual would use a sensory pathway that is the least confusing, least time consuming and most reliable to them. Supported by his language inclination, Sam deemed his highly unreliable auditory processing route to be more reliable than his visual processing. This meant to say that his visual processing issues were even more severe than his auditory processing issues.

At that point in time, I still did not thoroughly know the implications of his poor visual processing issues. Or rather, I just did not understand how severe his visual processing issue were. However, I hit the jackpot with his auditory processing issues and was able to thoroughly understand the implications behind his auditory processing issues.

I acted on the assumption that the moment Sam heard any sound that seemed just a tad too foreign to him, the confusion within him would be entrenched and linger long enough to affect his immediate class work. I assumed that his auditory nervous system was that fragile and I wished to avoid it at all cost. I made him wear sound cancelling earmuffs and provided written – instead of verbal – instructions. (If I could, I would type the question out.) He began to write without much hesitation and his spelling accuracy increased significantly. More importantly, Sam's errors became consistent. I made it a point to ensure that Sam wrote his response to a writing prompt during every lesson. This was so that I could analyse his error patterns that were finally becoming more consistent.

The following blocks of text were Sam's initial attempts at writing:

Why did you enjoy your horse-riding lesson? (30/3/19)

I like the horse it fan to play with the horse and can leason about the horse I on about the horse and how to riding the horse. My friend feli like ti fun to on a about the horse and there on how to riding horse lessan.

Why do you like Minecraft? (6/4/19)

I leans about Minecraft I can build Air Plane and I can fly an make my own city with mod and minecraft can make a home and a mod plane and a tack and a gun and a HDB and witmod minecraft and I can in inver my friend in to minecraft and can build a city with him and we can play war with Minecraft mod we have a gun an a tack and can and make [with my voice] AirPlane and dan We act more friend to buid a city with me and my friend. and we can play more of time.

Why do you like to go to school? (13/4/19)

Me and my frend go to school and play game and we play Xbox and gun game and Xbox game so we play the gun game it was fan me and my friend play more of gun game and my friend inve more of my friend so we play game like Xbox and gun OS we play xbox because got more peoled to play with game and so we play in the school and than we done with play in school game and than my friend sa than is lust to play game so my friend and I luft from school and we go out from school and we play phone game at my plast so we play Minecraft and PuG and than my friend sa the(i)n is time to go home.

227

The blocks of text also highlight how deceptive his writing was. While Sam's spelling problems were undoubtedly severe, it hid the fact that Sam had an unprecedented visual processing challenge. Any teacher would think that Sam had some basic level of sight word knowledge. This was compounded by fact that Sam, on one hand, complained about his auditory processing difficulties while, on the other hand, actively embracing his auditory capabilities – or lack thereof – and occasionally declaring that he loved phonics even as he spelt a string of highly warped words in successive fashion.

Sam was a walking contradiction.

Such emphasis on his auditory processing abilities or challenges further muted the presence of Sam's visual processing problems. Hence, I was not able to thoroughly understand the nature of Sam's problems at that point in time.

- **Attempted intervention**

I managed to largely diagnose Sam's problem but I was nowhere near finding a solution. I found myself at a loss and I started experimenting. I took out the Audiblox programme from cold storage and carried out a few cognitive exercises with Sam. I was largely testing his visual and auditory sequential memory of colours. I tweaked the programme by adding a component of recalling a sequence of random letters and letters in a real word. He was able to place up to four colour blocks in formation or sequence. Nothing set him apart from his nonresponding peers other than his ability to sequence letters – real word or not. He struggled with memory recall of certain letters in a three letter sequences, demonstrated dramatically lower rates of accuracy for four letter sequences and rejected five letter sequences entirely.

At that point in time, I did not see the complete picture. Sam's difficulties with the letter component seemed like he had a similar problem to many of my heavenly kings – orthographic processing disorder. However, the nature of Sam's word orthographic processing disorder seemed to have some subtle differences but I was not able to discern anything then.

After reading his written responses, I decided that I should attempt to teach him the words 'listen', 'lesson', 'learn' and 'invite' first. As the word 'learn' may be too long for Sam, the word ear' and 'earn' should be introduced before the word 'learnt'.

I tried two ways of colour coding. I colour-coded the real words in the word. I also colour-coded every letter differently in case he did not know how to spell the words and needed a distinct colour for every letter.

METHODS		ILLUSTRATION / WRITTEN EXAMPLE
Word in a word	Distinct colour for every letter	
e a r	e a r	Showed a picture of the ear
e a r n	e a r n	I earn lots of money by being a youtuber.
I ear n or I earn	I e a r n	I learn many things in school.

METHOD	ILLUSTRATION / WRITTEN EXAMPLE
Words taught using a "Word in a word" technique	
less on	The teacher is conducting a lesson.
I is ten	I listen to my teacher.
lis ten	

Upon getting Sam to put on the earmuffs, I gestured to him to read the examples on his own. Thereafter, I got him to spell by reading a few questions and filling in the blanks using only the words that were taught. (e.g. He had to choose to fill in the words 'listen' or 'lesson' in the blanks of the following question: "The teacher is teaching a _____. I _____ to my teacher in class.") I did not give him any verbal instructions as I was trying to prevent Sam from hearing my voice. He read the questions and was able to tell me the accurate answers for each question. Then, he proceeded to spell accordingly:

Words that Sam was supposed to spell	Words that Sam spelt
learn	lesing
	leson
lesson	lesoaar
listen	lessong
	liston
	lesson

Words that Sam was supposed to spell	Words that Sam spelt
ear	eam
	aen
	ear
earn	lean
	earn
learn	lean
invite	anvite

It was when he spelt the word 'invite' that I realised how unprecedented his visual processing issues were. Sam knew how to spell the word 'in'. I taught him the syllable 'vite' after determining that he should not have any other existing word in mind that had the outline of 'vite' with 'in' as the first syllable.

He was able to spell the syllable 'vite' but at the expense of the syllable 'in'.

He was **not** supposed to – regardless of how demanding the circumstances were –

forget how to spell the real word 'in'. It was a word that he knew through and through. He was the first student that was unable to spell two letter sight words reliably. Sam broke Sophia's record.

Spelling the syllable 'vite' accurately was enough to tax Sam's cognitive reserves to affect the word 'in'. It meant that every word that Sam knew – or thought he knew – was actually a mirage. Every word had the potential to change. In other words, he did not know how to spell anything reliably. He might have been guessing at every word. It was not only his auditory nervous system that was fragile. Both his auditory and visual nervous system were exceedingly fragile.

From the perspective of literacy acquisition, Sam was functionally blind and deaf.

- **Breakthrough**

After that, I did not teach Sam anything literacy related. I gained an almost complete understanding of Sam's deceptive literacy profile after nine months but I was at a loss again. How was I to teach a student who was functionally blind and deaf? His inclinations were not strong enough to compensate his extreme disinclinations. How was I supposed to teach a student with such serious innate confusion?

I stuck Sam's pre-test and the colour-coded words that I attempted to teach him on my wall. It acted as a daily reminder that there was another student that I could not help.

One day, nearing into my third month of literacy-less lessons for Sam, I thought that surely Sam had a cognitive inclination. Was there a component of Sam's memory that was intact and reliable? I remembered his performance on the Audiblox tasks and recalled that he performed decently for his sequential memory for colours.

I colour-coded the words like 'ear' and 'lesson' but he was unable to spell anything accurately even though I made sure that he wore earmuffs and prevented him from hearing my voice.

What was the difference? As I stared at the colour-coded words that were stuck on my wall, one word surfaced in my mind.

Interference.

That was when I had a complete understanding of Sam's profile.

Sam's visual nervous system was so fragile that the shape of the words distracted him from utilizing his inclination for colours. His confusion over visually-similar letters must have been so entrenched that his fragile nervous system was not able to use his inclination to override his perpetual letter confusion. I should not have included letters when I used colors for his literacy acquisition.

Sam was not like Nathan. Nathan had a word orthography disorder. Sam had a letter perception disorder. It was this letter perception disorder that led Sam to subsequently develop a word orthography disorder.

Most of my nonresponders did not have much letter formation problems. At the age of 15, Sean still did not know the names of the letters. (e.g. When Sean was told to write the letter 'k', Sean wrote 'h'.) However, he distinctively knew how each letter looked like. Nathan had intact letter formation knowledge but he was not able to see the letters as a whole to form words. Many students had issues with penmenship and not visual perception – they might write a letter incorrectly but were usually aware that it was another letter. For instance, the letter 'a' was written like a letter 'u' but they were aware that it was a letter 'a'.

Zeak and Warren's letter formation issues were visual perceptual in nature but they had enough letters to work with. In addition, their visual inclination towards whole words overrode any existing confusion over letters. Zeak and Warren had confusion over letters that even a typically-developing individual would have seen the similarities. More importantly, only 2 or 3 letters were confused together at one time. These letters included the following:

- 'b' and 'd'
- 'l' and 'i'
- 'h' and 'n'

Sam's letter confusion was pervasive. After combing through all of his writing and analysing his spelling behavior, I determined the letters that he was confused with.

- 'a', 'c', 'e', 'o' and 'u'
- 'a', 'q', 'u' and 'g'
- 'r', 'h', 'n', 'm' and 'u'
- 't', 'l' and 'i'
- 'g', 'y' and 'x'
- 'z' and 'x'

With such pervasive confusion, it was no wonder that Sam was unable to remember many words reliably. Everything made sense now. His attempt to compensate was admirable as his innate problems were not immediately apparent. In the following picture of an artist impression of Sam's written response [20/7/19], the innate problems that were hidden in his attempt to compensate became obvious once I knew what to look for.

I like the country because and the country
I like is usa I love the view and the city and
I can bring my friend to the country and
tell than is fun to have because is the bug
county and the usa is have a lla of city
Like Texas is the usa because it it good

Sam always wrote "It is" as 'is'. He probably heard the two words as the same word. In addition, the syllable 'cause' in the word 'because' was always plagued by letter formation issues and his four-letter visual span (for words that he was more familiar with). There were plenty of other problems that were embedded in his writing responses and spelling pre-tests. Hence, it is recommended that you reread every example of Sam's spelling and writing attempts to gain insight of how complicatedly deceptive Sam's learning profile was.

o **Sam's literacy profile and disinclination**

- Extreme visual disinclination (Visual perception issues: Letter perception disorder / Lack of letter constancy)

- Extreme auditory disinclination (Lack of auditory constancy)

- Slight language inclination – Not enough to compensate for the double disinclination

- Was accepting to almost any instruction and font style because the he was perpetually confused with the letter formation

- Functionally blind and deaf (literacy wise)

He was allergic to my voice and handwriting. I was the worst possible teacher for him.

- **Intervention**

I set off to equate each letter with a distinct colour. After analysing his latest writing attempt, I decided to teach him the word 'know'. It was within the visual span of four letters. He confused the word 'know' with 'on' and 'no' due to an expanding corruption of words along the visual and auditory tracks of impairment. The words 'now' and 'new' were probably thrown into the mix. I was wary of writing the letters in my handwriting but Sam's letter perception was even more unreliable than my handwriting. I went ahead and wrote them.

Deep yellow = k, Lime green = n, Sky blue = o, Pink = w

Letters should not be included when colours were used for his literacy acquisition. I only ensured that he knew which letter each colour represented before I flipped the pieces of paper around.

This is the crux of the technique. He was to learn every word like this from then on. If Sam's inclination for colours was strong enough, he would be able to effortlessly remember each colour that represented the letters and the sequence of colours for each word. His perception of the letter might be constantly changing but the colours would be able to ensure that Sam's verbal spelling was accurate.

I tried this technique on another 10-year-old type Y nonresponder who had similar –

albeit milder – issues than Sam. That nonresponder was able to remember the colour-letter representation and colour sequence for each word effortlessly. I was the one that had to keep referring to the letters written on the flip side as I could not remember the colour-letter representation!

When I used this technique to teach Sam, I merely introduced the sequence of colours as the word 'know'.

Me: This is the word 'know'. Like "I know this person. He is my classmate." *Pointing to each colour* K. N. O. W. Now if I remove the letter 'k' *removes the deep yellow paper*, I will get...

Sam: Now. N.O.W. Oh wow.

He saw a real word in another real word accurately for the first time – without physically seeing the letters.

As with all type Y nonresponders, the real stress test came when the pruning took place right after the lesson. I waited for 2 lessons before I asked him to sequence the slips of colored paper for the word 'know'. He did so successfully. Upon asking him to verbally spell the word, Sam proceeded to spell it as 'k u a w'. I was glad that he remembered the sequence of colors and then finally, I was able to tackle the root of his confusion. If his letter confusion was factored in, Sam was actually able to remember the letters. According to the principles of nonresponder instruction, visually-similar words should be presented together to alleviate the confusion. In Sam's case, however, visually-similar letters should be presented together.

He confused the letter 'n' with 'u', and the letter 'o' with 'a'. I made sure to find other colours that were very distinct from the colours that represented 'n' and 'o' and wrote the letters '' and 'a' on them.

Deep blue = u, Deep red = a, Pale yellow = e (just in case)

Note: I got Sam to write the letter 'a'. He wrote it like this – *. I added the 'tail' to the letter 'a' and Sam replied, "Also can."*

Then, I flipped the slips of coloured paper and proceeded to teach him accordingly.

Recall that there are sources that state the benefits of using gestalt or colour coding for literacy acquisition. However, when each technique was used in isolation, they were not be effective enough to override Sam's extreme disinclinations.

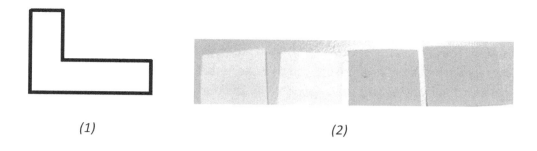

(1)   (2)

(1) The gestalt of the word merely promoted the recognition of the overall shape of the word. Sam would have been guessing wildly at the word.

(2) Colour-letter representation of the word using pieces of paper of equal dimensions would still be ineffective. While the slips of coloured paper would have provided a sequence of colour-letter representation for each word, it did not promote the overall shape of the word. In particular, it might potentially distort Sam's perception of the 'taller' or 'longer' letters (e.g. letters 'l' and 't') in relation to the 'shorter' letters (e.g. letter 'a' and 'v').

My newly minted technique for Sam was essentially a combination of both gestalt and colour-letter representation without the letters. It was not to say that Sam was completely agreeable to everything about this technique. For instance, he saw the deep yellow paper as an orange colour while the pale yellow paper was an unidentifiable colour to him. Regardless, it felt like a step in the right direction.

➢ SPECIAL TOPIC: WHEN 'EXTREME' CASES ARE EASIER TO TREAT THAN 'PARTIAL' CASES

The divide is very stark among the type Y – and X – nonresponders. There are those who reject phonics entirely (or any other incomprehensible instructional concept) and there are those who seem like they are responding to the most basic of phonics (e.g. blends, some consonant sounds – very similar to type A.1s).

• Superficial confusion

The former would not allow the therapists to harbour any delusion that their instruction is effective. Often, the work produced by these nonresponders is largely devoid of any resemblance to the instruction given by the therapist. Alternatively, the nonresponders would not write anything at all. While it may seem that these nonresponders are really 'problematic' and are really 'severe', their complete rejection to any perceived incomprehensible instruction is actually a blessing in disguise. These students are exhibiting what I term as "superficial confusion". Contrary to the name, I can assure you that these students are exceedingly confused. However, they have a very "thick layer" of inertia that rejects any incomprehensible input and protects the – admittedly – small part of their understanding that is still intact and crucial in making sense of his or her small slice of the world.

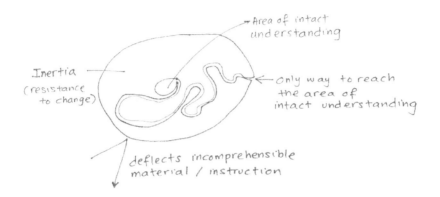

My artist impression of a mind with high levels of inertia.

(Note: The illustrations describing inertia are not based on any scientific understanding. Rather, they are graphic representation of 'extreme' and 'partial' cases.)

Let us just focus on the receptivity and understanding of literacy among such nonresponders. The fact that a type Y nonresponder is able to read or spell a few words consistently means that a small part of his or her intact – not confused – understanding has secured these words in an uninterruptable part of the memory. This intact part of the understanding is fortified by a very thick layer of inertia with only one complex pathway to reach the area of intact understanding. The layer of inertia effectively deflects any hint of abstract or incomprehensible material, and only an instructional method that fulfils the unique pre-requisites and needs of the nonresponder will be allowed to access the area of intact understanding. The deflected, incomprehensible information – which is at the periphery of the nonresponder's understanding – manifests as superficial confusion.

With a prolonged period of effective instruction, the level (or in this case – thickness) of inertia reduces while the area of intact understanding increases. The number of ways to access the area of intact understanding increase while the pathways become less complex due to a reduction of pre-requisites that is fuelled by a greater understanding of the world. Lesser inertia and more pathways yield greater receptivity to the input from the external environment. Regardless, the nonresponder will be confused by such external input unless guidance is received. In addition, the time that the nonresponder is stuck in his or her phase of confusion will be progressively reduced as the area of intact understanding increases. Among my heavenly kings, Sean is an example of a nonresponder with "superficial confusion".

- **Innate confusion**

Among my heavenly kings, the most severe cases were Warren, Nathan and Sam. They experienced the slowest rates of improvements even after receiving the intervention for nonresponders. The deciding factors that made these three students lag behind the rest of the type Y nonresponders were their "innate confusion" and orthographic processing disorder (or in the case of Sam – a letter perception disorder). Warren and Sam's innate confusion regularly surfaced as inconsistent errors.

Nonresponders like Warren, Nathan and Sam give educators or therapists the delusion that the instruction are effective so long as reinforcement is carried out over a longer period of time. They seem to be receptive to some basic phonics and look like they just require much more time for the rest of the phonics instruction to set in. These nonresponders have seemingly lower levels of inertia from the start and more direct pathways towards the area of understanding. As such, they are susceptible to confusion from abstract and incomprehensible information. Such information easily extends into their area of intact understanding and proceeds to corrupt it.

Area of intact understanding

- More openings to reach the area of intact understanding.

- Greater susceptibility to incomprehensible instruction

Inertia

These nonresponders may began to change and spell certain words inconsistently. A word may be spelt correctly on one day, only to be spelt incorrectly on another day. Their spelling mistakes keep changing – a sign that they are even confused about the consistency of their errors. The word 'walk' may change to 'wake' in the second week, then it changes into 'wawk', then 'wlak'...

The phonics concepts strike much confusion in their existing area of intact understanding and it starts to destabilise their understanding of literacy. Words that were spelt correctly initially will also be adversely affected. The word 'walk' would be 'wud', 'wude', 'work' or anything that looks like a word that starts with the letter 'w' of that length.

It is a disaster. This is what I term as "innate confusion".

What is the reason for such an out of control confusion? There are many students – be it partial phonics responders or nonresponders – who do not experience such immense confusion even if they do not understand the phonics concept that is being taught.

Perhaps, phonics responders may spell 'Paul' as 'Pawl'. Perhaps, nonresponders may consistently spell 'Paul' as 'Pall' or 'Pal' or 'Pl'. Regardless of the type of error, these students maintain a consistent error. The difference between them and this special bunch of type Y nonresponders is their orthographic memory. This is an area where word forms are stored. It tells you how to read and spell the word 'Paul', understand the meaning of the word 'Paul' and secure this particular area of intact understanding. It helps a student to distinguish between nonsense words and real words. Orthographic memory allows students to discern that there is no such thing as 'wlak' because it looks so foreign. Individuals who have strong orthographic memory are strong spellers even if they do not understand phonics. Many phonics responders may not have very strong orthographic memory and that is why they may spell 'Paul' as 'Pawl'.

Nonresponders may have significantly poorer orthographic memory to the point that they spell 'Paul' as 'Pl'. However, the avoidance of the phonics route by using a visual route provides them an opportunity to remember the accurate word using their unique – or rather, compromised – orthographic memory. While they do not have strong orthographic memory, they have, at the very least, some level of orthographic memory.

On the other hand, this special group of type Y nonresponders have nearly no orthographic memory. From their point of view, all nonsense words are words while all words are nonsense. There is no difference. Apart from inertia, the presence of an orthographic memory is the final line of defence to preserve – and expand – the area of intact understanding. Nonresponders with abysmally low orthographic memory can only learn when there are no nonsense words. Phonics instruction is their ultimate nemesis as it produces all sorts of nonsense words combination. To aggravate matters, nonresponders who get confused by phonics but are unable to abandon the sounds that were taught will not be able to unleash their visual talents due to the degree of interference from the phonics instruction. They would want to remember the word using an alternate method but the sounds have caused so much confusion that the sounds impede their ability to do so. The confusion prolongs and corrupts the area of intact understanding further, resulting in the persistent destabilisation of literacy.

This is why I termed Warren's section as "Chronic Effect". When such confusion pervades and affects the area of intact understanding, it is nearly impossible undo the damage to the point where these type Y nonresponders can achieve their potential by meeting their literacy milestones.

CHAPTER 6

MULTISYLLABIC WORD NONRESPONDERS

Some teachers and therapists seem to hold a linear view of literacy acquisition. They seem to think that single-syllable words are easier to spell or read than multisyllabic words. In particular, words that are shorter in length (lesser alphabets per word) are deemed to be easier to read and spell as compared to longer words (more alphabets per word). The following words are deemed to be sequenced in an increasing order of difficulty:

it, cat, that, spend, subject, computer, indestructible

However, as seen in earlier chapters, the degree of interference from language impairment, poor visual and auditory processing for nonresponders who have to grapple with both poor literacy and severe co-morbidities challenges this linear view of literacy acquisition. I proposed a different approach to the instruction and acquisition of single-syllable words in the earlier chapters. This chapter – albeit short – explores the different approaches to the instruction of multisyllabic words for nonresponders.

1. Typically-developing individuals' approach to acquiring multisyllabic words

For typically-developing individuals who have high tolerance levels for abstract information (alongside with well-developed visual and auditory facilities), multisyllabic word acquisition is done rather effortlessly by remembering the sound of the syllable types. Remembering words like 'stipulation' or 'anti-establishmentarianism' is simply a mix of two different processes that occur instantly upon the first contact of a word:

i.   Remember the sound of the difference syllables

E.g. 'sti' makes /sti/, 'la' makes /la/, 'tion' makes /tion/

Therefore, the knowledge of such syllables allows an individual to read words with such syllables (e.g. 'stimulation').

ii. Comparing similar words to understand the meaning of certain syllables

For typically-developing individuals with marginally lower levels of receptivity towards abstract knowledge, they may link a syllable to another known word. For instance, should the syllable '-del' in the word 'strudel' prove to be perplexing, the individual may remember it by linking it to the word 'model' and volià, the individual instantly remembers how to say the word 'strudel' now. This process is instantaneous and it requires one or two tries before the individual gains automaticity in reading the words.

At times, they may also be able to partially infer the meaning of a word. For instance, while an individual does not know the meaning of the syllable '-tract' explicitly, the individual quickly infers the meaning by comparing words with the same syllable (e.g. contract, attract, retract).

Looking at the meaning of these words, an individual can infer that '-tract' relates to pulling. Such inherent meaning making of the word parts is known as 'morphology'. Words comprise of different word parts – prefixes, roots/body and suffixes. Each part has its inherent meaning. For instance, consider the words 'construct', 'constructed' and 'constructing'.

Word	Associated parts and meanings
construct	Prefix: con (with/together) Root/Body: struct (to build)
constructed	Prefix: con (with/together) Root/Body: struct (to build) Suffix: ed (occurred in the past)
constructing	Prefix: con (with/together) Root/Body: struct (to build) Suffix: ing (currently occurring)

The embedded meanings into these word parts are of Latin origin. The Shakespearian era scholars pieced English words like jigsaw puzzles. Combined together, the individual meanings of each word part form the combined meaning of the word.

The mainstream approach to vocabulary acquisition is through morphological instruction. Unsurprisingly, morphological instruction is similarly used to teach dyslexics and other students with literacy needs. Morphological instruction for dyslexics is explicit. Ideally, the teacher teaches meaningful prefixes, roots/body and suffixes to the student. Each lesson focuses on a root/body or suffix, discusses the meanings of the root or suffix and explores the meaning of new words (with the same suffix) by inferring the meaning of the word through the word parts.

o *Example: Morphological instruction for mid-ability students*

The student may be taught the suffix '-ous'. The meaning of the suffix '-ous' generally means "full of". The following words may be presented to facilitate understanding of the suffix:

- Dangerous (full of danger)

- Generous (full of generosity)

- Joyous (full of joy)

- Mysterious (full of mystery)

- Zealous (full of zeal)

- Courteous (full of courtesy)

- Harmonious (full of harmony)

Alternatively, the teacher may also teach a root/body part like '-tract', which means "to pull". The following words may be presented to facilitate understanding of the root word:

- Contract (to pull inwards)

- Retract (to pull back)

- Attract (to pull towards)

- Subtract (to pull from under)

- Distract (to pull away the attention

For higher-ability students, understanding the meaning of certain advanced root words allows them to further appreciate the overall meaning of the words. For instance, the root 'ambi' means both sides or around. As such, the following words contain the inherent meaning:

- Ambidextrous (able to use both hands equally)

- Ambivalent (repelled and attracted at the same time)

- Ambiparous (both leaves and flowers)

- Ambiguity (uncertainty in meaning)

- Ambience (the surrounding atmosphere)

- Ambilateral (affecting both sides)

- **Problem**

The problem with the typical morphology approach is the level of abstractness. It requires students who have a higher level of receptivity towards abstract concepts to accept such morphological instruction. It is undoubtedly a very powerful tool to build a student's literacy and vocabulary abilities, but it is also not direct nor concrete.

Students who have serious language impairment, possess low levels of receptivity towards abstract concepts or do not speak English as his or her first language will face problems with typical morphological instruction.

Let us take the word 'contraction' for example. Recall that nonresponders are very particular about whole words. They tend to mix the root part 'tract' with the word 'track'. In addition, explaining that '-tract' means 'pull' does not make sense. In the worst-case scenario, the student will confuse the meanings of both '-tract' and 'track'.

As such, there is a group of students who are unable to tackle multisyllabic words according to the typical approach. While nonresponders usually struggle with multisyllabic words, some phonics responders (for single-syllable words) will also face challenges with typical multisyllabic word instruction.

The table below summarises the different types of multisyllabic nonresponders:

Typically developing individuals	Nonresponders				
	Decreasing levels of receptivity towards abstract concepts →				
		Only receptive to real words			6. Confusion between real and nonsense words
1. Receptivity to morphology or the ability to remember the composition of abstract syllables	2. Learns via patterns and colour-coded syllables (Each syllable should ideally fall within a certain length to fit the visual span.)	3. Able to segment multi-syllabic words into syllables	4. Able to segment multisyllabic words into syllables but does not have strong knowledge of word orthography	5. Cannot segment multi-syllabic words into syllables	
	|--------May be interlinked--------|				

2. Learn by patterns and colour-coded syllables (instead of meanings)

Many students usually dominate this group of nonresponders. They find multisyllabic words to be easier to spell as compared to single-syllable words. This is because each syllable in a multisyllabic word usually contains lesser sounds per syllable as compared to a single-syllable word. For instance, they feel that it is easier to spell words like 'computer' (com pu ter) and 'registration' (re gis tra tion) as compared to words like 'spend' and 'breath'. Regardless, they have certain limitations that must be considered by the teacher to ensure an effective multisyllabic word instruction.

You will see quite a diverse bunch of nonresponders in this group. Some will find multisyllabic words to be easier to tackle even though they are able to spell single-syllable words without much problems. Others will struggle with single-syllable words because these students are, at most, able to segment a word into syllables. They are not able to tell apart the sounds in a single-syllable word. This is especially so when there are far too many sounds in a word or when there is the existence of vowel teams (two vowels that are placed together). Multisyllabic words are easier for them because many syllables comprise of at most three letters, falling well within their preferred visual span.

Regardless, this group of nonresponders require visual segmentation of multisyllabic words to 'break' the multisyllabic word into smaller 'parts' for effective instruction.

Each syllable in the multisyllabic word should be colour-coded in different colours to allow the brain to visually discern each syllable easily.

If a multisyllabic word is presented in one colour (usually black), the accuracy rate among these students will be comparatively lower as these students will attempt to remember the entire word at one go as the colour dictates. These students will not be able to do so successfully as the long word exceeds their limited visual span.

For instance, if the word 'computer' is printed entirely in black and the student attempts to remember all eight letters at one go, the word may overwhelm the student. The student may only be able to remember the front and back parts of the word. Should each syllable of the word be segmented into different colours, they will be able to remember the word with greater ease and word retention increases dramatically.

o   **Syllable-pattern instruction for this group**

Bear in mind that these nonresponders deem the word according to syllables instead of morphological parts. An emphasis on syllable patterns is needed. The only thing that is adapted from the morphological approach is to plan the teaching list using suffixes.

The table below shows some examples of suffixes.

Examples of suffixes (or spelling patterns)			
-al, -el	-age	-less	-tion, -sion
-ant, -ent	-age	-ous	
-ance, -ence	-ful	-ness	
-able, -ible	-ly	-ment	

These suffixes are high-frequency patterns as compared to the other morphological word parts (e.g. 'tact', 'rupt'). The nonresponders do not care about the meaning of the word parts – just the reoccurring pattern.

Note: Some morphology purist will argue that spelling patterns and suffixes are not the same as suffixes have an inherent meanings (e.g. like '-ful' = full of). However, those are inconsequential details for nonresponders who do not care about the inherent meaning of suffixes as they are too abstract. If you were to tell them that suffixes '-tion' or '-sion' means "the state of something", they will just give you a blank stare and the explanation will sail over their heads.

However, a syllable-pattern instruction based on a teaching list that is comprised of suffixes will not be very effective and the nonresponders are not able to incorporate the taught suffixes easily into their spelling. This is because it does not reflect how the nonresponders say the words.

For instance, even though the suffix '-ous' has been taught, the student may still face difficulties spelling words like 'enormous', 'fabulous', 'jealous' or 'disastrous'. The students are unable to generalise the suffix '-ous' across all words because – as mentioned in the earlier chapters – nonresponders can only segment sounds to the syllable level.

An example would be the word 'enormous'. 'Enormous' is spoken as /e/ /nor/ /mous/. Not /e/ /norm/ /ous/. The following words with the '-ous' suffix are similarly segmented into syllables:

- Dangerous = /dan/ /ge/ /rous/
- Famous = /fa/ /mous/
- Fabulous = /fa/ /bu/ /lous/
- Nervous = /ner/ /vous/
- Jealous = /jea/ /lous/
- Fabulous = /fa/ /bu/ /lous/
- Disastrous = /di/ /sas/ /trous/
- Delicious = /de/ /li/ /cious/

As such, the last syllable of many words with the '-ous' suffix does not merely comprise of '-ous'. If you teach the suffix '-ous', you have to teach the syllable pattern that includes '-ous' in every conceivable high-frequency syllable.

Every conceivable high-frequency syllable with '-ous'		
-bous	-nous	-cious
-lous	-rous	-tious
-mous	-tuous	-duous

If you remember the three tracks of impairment, similar-sounding syllables that are shown in the following tables have to be addressed together to avoid confusion.

Syllables with '-ous-	Auditorily-similar syllables
-ous	-ess
-bous	-
-lous	-less
-mous	-
-nous	-ness

Syllables with '-ous-	Auditorily-similar syllables	
-rous	-ress	-rest
-tuous	-	-
-cious / -tious	-	-
-trous	-tress	-tres

Nonresponders with poorer orthographic memory may be confused with which ending syllable to use. Should they spell 'kindness' or 'kindnous'? Should they spell 'atrocious' or 'atrotious'? The challenge surfaces when the teacher or therapist has to justify the reason for such spelling (e.g. using stories, mnemonics, (real)word-in-word strategy, RRS etc).

In addition to the aforementioned point, this group of nonresponders:

- Is able to tolerate at most three to four letters in a syllable – though two to three letters are very much preferred

- Prefers no vowel teams – two vowels that are stuck together – in a word (e.g. caution, jealous)

- Abhors silent letters (e.g. correction, attraction, shape)

- Has a tendency to separate syllables containing a vowel and a letter 'r' as the nonresponders have low tolerance for 'ar', 'er', 'ir' and 'ur'

    E.g. generate → ge ne rate [not 'ge ner ate']

    inherent → in he rent [not 'in her ent']

    generous → ge ne rous [not 'ge ner ous']

    average → a ve rage [not 'a ver age']

    - *Examples of exceptions: 'Terminate' [Ter mi nate] , 'External' [Ex ter nal]*

3. Only receptive to real words: able to segment multisyllabic words

This group of nonresponders usually prefers single-syllable real words. They are so used to spelling real words that the syllables in multisyllabic words usually trigger a real word response. While this group of nonresponders are able to segment long words into syllables, they have low tolerance for any syllable that is not a real word. As a result, accuracy rates for abstract word parts will not be high.

For instance, the syllables in the word 'similar' are 'si', 'mi' and 'lar'. However, the inclination of such nonresponders to remember single-syllable real words is so strong that it interferes with the spelling of multisyllabic words. The syllable 'si' brings up the word 'see' in their mind. The syllables 'mi' and 'lar' may be perceived as ' me' and 'ler' (or 'learn' or whatever concrete word that sounds like that) respectively. As such, they may spell it as 'seemeler' or they will start to write 'see...' before stopping and asking for help instead as they are aware that their spelling attempts are inaccurate.

There are two ways to tackle this issue:

a. *Linking the syllable to other known multisyllabic words with the same syllable*

In an extreme way, you will have emulate what I did with Sean. Recall that Sean's multisyllabic intervention approach was to link every abstract syllable to the syllable of another known word. Thankfully, this group of nonresponders is not as extreme as Sean. You ill just need to do this whenever they have trouble with a specific syllable.

For instance, the nonresponder may spell the word 'similar' as 'similer'. As 'lar' is the only syllable that is a problem, the teacher or therapist just needs to tackle this problematic syllable (e.g 'lar' from 'dollar').

b. *RRS*

A type X nonresponder for single-syllable words – who was also a nonresponder for multisyllabic words – was taught the syllable pattern '-ous'. Instead of teaching him the suffix '-ous', he was taught according to syllable patterns (e.g. 'mous', 'rous', 'lous'). However, unlike the previous group of students, such degree of accommodation for his nonresponder tendencies was not enough and he was still unable to achieve higher levels of spelling accuracy.

While he was able to link certain syllables to the same syllable of another known word, he did not know enough multisyllabic words to allow him to link every unfamiliar syllable to his existing base of multisyllabic words. As such, he was unable to remember any syllable beyond those he could link to his existing base of known words because the syllables were too abstract and his bias for single-syllable real words was way too strong.

What I did in this case was to exploit his knowledge of single-syllable words by substituting or rearranging the letters of real words.

- ○ Examples (I have underlined the letters that he was unable to remember.)

  - ▪ cons<u>truc</u>tion , s<u>truc</u>ture [truck]

  - ▪ fa<u>mous</u> [mouse]

  - ▪ fabu<u>lous</u> [soul → lous]

251

Note: Switching the positions of letters 's' and 'l' in the word 'soul' – this can only be done if the nonresponder does not get confused with letter positioning.

Encouraging the type X nonresponder to take a lead in his learning, I worked with him to brainstorm many possible solutions. We went all out to cover a range of problematic syllables.

- fur<u>ni</u>ture [~~burning~~]

- s<u>pecta</u>cles [pe   t
                     c   a~~t~~]

RATIONALE									
Initial attempt at spelling 'spectacles'	s	_____					c	l	e	s
Include the word 'pet'		p	e		t				
Include the word 'cat' - the letter 't'				c		a	t		
End result	s	p	e	c	t	a	c	l	e	s

4. Only receptive to real words: Does not have strong knowledge of the word orthography

This group of nonresponders are able to segment multisyllabic words into syllables but colour coding is definitely not enough to ensure retention. Linking the syllable to other known multisyllabic words with the same syllable or employing the RRS technique only works to a certain extent due to his or her poor knowledge of single-syllable sight words. Often, they are uncertain of the spelling of single-syllable words that are visually or auditorily similar.

They may be even more uncertain of multisyllabic words as they are likely to only remember to first and last few letters of the word, all while being unable to remember the letters in the *middle portion of the word* due to its length. While the previous groups of nonresponders may have this problem, the difference is that the previous groups of nonresponders know how to accurately segment the middle portion of the word into syllables – they are just unable to recall the syllables. However, the nonresponders in this group are neither aware of how to accurately segment the middle portion of the word into syllables nor are they able to remember the syllables.

These nonresponders may have received phonics intervention but show little progress in phonics classes. They still regard letters by the letter names (as of most nonresponders) and not by the sound that the letters make. Fortunately, these nonresponders have enough inertia to reject most of the phonics intervention that they have received (if any). Thankfully, the dreaded confusion does not set in and their limited base of sight word knowledge, while lacking, is not undermined to the point where the nonresponders start making inconsistent errors of the same word over time.

However, their knowledge of syllables – while present – is not as strong nor as important to them as compared to the previous groups of nonresponders. As such, should the need arises, they have a penchant for segmenting each syllable into even smaller parts to fit into their preferred visual span of two letters. At times, the letters in the segmented word part correspond to the letter names instead of sound, promoting the ease of retention in the process.

Recall that most nonresponders in the earlier groups also favour segmenting the words up into their preferred visual span. However, they always segment the word according to syllables. For instance, many of them prefer to segment the word 'generous' into 'ge' 'ne' 'rous' and proceed to remember the words using strategies that were mentioned earlier.

On the other hand, this group of nonresponders do not like the syllable 'rous' and they are unable to (1) link this syllable to another word with the same syllable or (2) substitute/rearrange a real single-syllable word due to their poor knowledge of single-syllable words. In this case, they will prioritise fitting the syllable into their visual span and will proceed to segment the syllable 'rous' into 'ro' and 'us'. Subsequently, they may colour code and remember the word 'generous' into 'ge', 'ne', 'ro', 'us. They will be happy with this strategy as due to the following reasons:

- Each segmented word part fits into their preferred visual span of two letters.

- The last segmented word part 'us' is a very common sight word that the student can effortlessly remember.

- The first three word parts allow the nonresponder to remember the vowels according to their names instead of sound.

  As such, the nonresponders remember how to spell the words as /gee/ /nee/ /row/ /us/ even though it is not read as such.

The key difference between this group of nonresponders and the previous group of nonresponders is that this group does not require the number of parts to correspond to the number of syllables in a word. The earlier group has a lower tolerance for such mismatch as they have a more stable understanding of word orthography, which in turn translates to a lack of understanding of this mismatch that does not visually adhere to the number of syllables in the word.

In another example, the word 'nervous' will be 'broken' into 'ner', 'vo' and 'us'. The syllable 'ner' is a higher-frequency syllable as compared to 'vous'. It is likely that the nonresponder is able to find another word with the syllable 'ner' even if their sight word knowledge is limited.

The needs of this group of nonresponders represent the final threshold that a therapist or teacher can accommodate as an acceptable learning style of a nonresponder.

The needs of the next two groups of nonresponders should not be accommodated as their approach towards multisyllabic words proves to be detrimental to word acquisition (instead of providing a new, student-centric approach to learning multisyllabic words). Intervention for the next two groups of nonresponders should be directed at changing the way they perceive words.

5. **Only receptive to real words: Unable to segment multisyllabic words into syllables**

This group of nonresponders are unable to segment syllables from multisyllabic words on their own. While the previous group of nonresponders finds it a challenge to segment the middle portion of the multisyllabic word, this group of nonresponders is unable to segment the multisyllabic word entirely. From their point of view, multisyllabic words cannot be broken down as into syllables as every word is deemed as a whole and real word. The colour coding of syllables may spur different behavioural patterns but the underlying problem of an absolute lack of syllable understanding remains. Such nonresponders will ignore the colour coding and attempt to use their visual span to remember the entire word to no avail. Other nonresponders will remember the colour-coded syallbles with no idea what they are actually remembering.

Zeak and Sean took this to the extreme. Zeak, like Sean, found it extremely difficult to understand syllables as they were too abstract. In the word 'creation' for instance, there is no such thing as a 'cre' or 'tion' to them as these syllables are not real words. As such, they endeavour to remember the entire word in its entirety even when the syllables are colour-coded. In Sean's case, the SLT and I managed to train him to segment words into syllables (as mentioned in chapter 5). Zeak left the centre before any additional intervention was provided.

One special characteristic of this group of nonresponders is their extreme bias towards single-syllable real words. Their penchant for real words is so strong that the real word takes precedence in a multisyllabic word and the rest of the letters becomes secondary in nature.

Let me mention Zeak's case.

Zeak found it extremely challenging to spell single-syllable words. At the age of 15, he was still struggling to spell four letter words like 'spit' (he spelt it as 'speat').

When he was presented with multisyllabic words, he was unable to segment them into syllables.

However, he was able to remember colour-coded syllables effortlessly. He stared at eight long multisyllabic words on the board – with every syllable colour-coded – for less than a minute and he would be able to remember every word and replicate it on paper accurately. As a side note, he was one of the three students at the centre who was able to do what the book "Right-Brained Children in a Left-Brained World: Unlocking the Potential of Your ADD Child" mentioned – to remember a long word, spell it backwards and even locate the position of the letters upon enquiry. For instance, he was able to spell the word 'celebration' forward and backwards, and was able to tell me that the second 'e' in the word was in between letters 'l' and 'b'. His visual-spatial memory was just that powerful.

However, there were two main problems. Two huge problems.

His style of remembering multisyllabic words was simply unsustainable. He was unable to ensure continuity and remember more than 10 to 12 multisyllabic words before inaccuracies surfaced into due to two reasons: (1) the interruption of proper word segmentation due to his extreme bias towards real, single-syllable words, and (2) his difficulty in matching the sound and letters to the spelling.

He was taught the word 'creation' with each syllable colour-coded differently. He remembered the word easily. However, he remembered it because he saw the word 'eat' stand out prominently. By remembering the word 'eat', however, he effectively broke the word into very unnatural parts that was not based on syllable segmentation.

Creation → Cr   eat   ion

As he endeavoured to remember everything using real words, he probably segmented the word even further.

Creation → Cr   eat   i   on

Zeak's penchant for real words helped him remember the word effortlessly but it flouted the structure of multisyllabic words by a mile. More problematically, he did not know what he was reading.

He remembered that this word of such length that started with 'cr' and contained the real word 'eat' is called 'creation'. It was a problem because when I showed him the word 'creature' (a word of similar word length and pattern), Zeak also read it as 'creation'. This served to show that Zeak's approach towards multisyllabic words was simply unsustainable.

6. Confusion between real and nonsense words (Exception: The case of Nathan)

Recall that Nathan was a possible surface dyslexic who was suspected of orthographic processing disorder. He struggled with all the basic words that fell onto the three tracks of impairments. He could not tell the difference between real and nonsense words, which made phonics even more problematic for him.

However, Nathan was able to spell many multisyllabic words. He was largely able to spell words like 'delicious', 'annotation', 'communicate' (would spell 'cate' as 'cat') and 'relation. Nathan was largely able to remember the suffixes that were taught as each suffix had a distinct sound. So long as the word or syllable did not fall onto the three tracks of impairment, Nathan would be able to spell the words with relatively higher levels of accuracy.

List of suffixes or spelling patterns that Nathan was able to internalise and spell		
-ed	-tion (He confused it with '-sion'. I told him to prioritise '-tion'.)	-ous
-ing	-ture (He confused it '-tion'.)	-cious (I did not teach '-tious'.)
-ful	-sure	-able (He confused it with '-ible' even after being taught the rule.)
-less	-tive	
-ness	-sive	

Nathan's ability to spell some multisyllabic words may lead teachers and therapists to assume that his literacy problems were minor. Yet, his spelling behaviour just seemed to reinforce my observations of Nathan that he had a severe literacy problem.

Why was that so?

When Nath was 14 years old, he spelt the syllables in a multisyllabic word the exact way that he would spell a single-syllable word.

- 'Row' → 'Ro'

- 'Though' → 'Do' or ' To'

- 'High' → 'Hi'

- 'Leap' → 'Lep'

- 'Lie' → 'Li'

Literally, any sound that Nathan heard was represented by one letter. While this became a problem when it came to the spelling of single-syllable words, many syllables in multisyllabic words thrived on this one letter per sound representation. Nathan had an inverse problem as compared to the nonresponders whose real word bias interfered with the spelling of non-real word syllables in multisyllabic words.

In addition, Nathan's ability to spell multisyllabic words over single-syllable words was a cause for concern. It seemed to reinforce the fact that Nathan had no idea what a real word looked like even after so many years. Between a nonresponder who demonstrates real word bias at the expense of multisyllabic words and a nonresponder – like Nathan – who is able to spell multisyllabic words at the expense of real words, I can assure you that the former is very much preferred.

AFTERWORD

Now that you have reached the end of this book, you would have realised that the system that I have established is not such a lofty system that radically addresses the weakness of my students or to orientate them back onto the path of what is perceived to be typical functioning.

Instead, it is system of intervention based on the ruthless exploitation of my students' cognitive strengths and avoidance of their weaknesses.

It is an attempt at tackling a chronic problem within the constraints of an educational role.

It was based on the context where expectations of conformity is expected of a teacher – or as an Educational Therapist – in a large organisation, of which deviation from the mainstream is rarely permissible. Based on that environment, alternative methods like the Davis method, the Audiblox method, the Tomatis method, Brain Gym etc. were not given room to thrive. I had to work with what was permitted in the classroom and stretch the limits to deliver the most effective intervention within the given constraints.

However, I have long understood that it is not about bringing different forms of intervention into the classroom. Rather, it is a matter of thoroughly understanding the commonality among every bit of intervention out there, taking the bits that matter the most and reproducing it as my interpretation in the classroom.

After all, a breakthrough in understanding is often just a shift of perspective.

As such, not as a Neurologist, a Psychologist, a Neuro-Optometrist, an Occupational Therapist nor a Speech and Language Therapist, this is my take on how a teacher – or an Educational Therapist - is able to deliver to most effective and efficient form of literacy intervention purely from an educational point of view.

- **Moving forward**

After my third year, I continued to refine my phonics and nonresponders intervention for phonics responders and nonresponders respectively. I developed my writing and comprehension curriculum for primary and secondary students of all ability levels. Then, I started my foray into math, prioritising the severe cases that actually seem to be maths nonresponders – or dyscalculic.

At the start of my seventh year in service, I decided that it was time for a relook at my nonresponders system.

My system was based on the assumption that even the most severe of nonresponders have some type of visual strength – no matter how atypical or relative. However, there was a bunch of students – like Nathan and Sam – who did not have that visual strength for literacy acquisition and my ability to help them was (and still is) rather limited. This is the limitation of my system.

The societal context started to change after my fifth year of service. Due to a national shift towards inclusivity, public schools officially rolled out a dyslexia remediation programme for all primary school students. This was built on top of an existing reading support program that was extended to at-risk students in primary 1 and 2. The dyslexia remediation program is basically a phonics intervention program on steroids. The higher-functioning phonics responders with no cognitive lapses should be able to benefit immensely from the pace. On the other hand, the nonresponders and lower-functioning phonics responders would be getting the shorter end of the stick.

Unfortunately, more type X and Y nonresponders are streaming into the centre with a boatload of visual issues that are aggravated by confusion. Basically, their relative strengths are greatly compromised due to the national drive for phonics intervention for dyslexics in schools. More students are becoming like Warren. The relative strengths of more students are undermined due to phonics confusion. Their relative inclinations are no enough to counterbalance their disinclinations.

I am finally at the crossroads where there is probably not enough room left to further build upon a compensatory system based on the ruthless exploitation of my students' strength. It is time to directly address my students' cognitive weaknesses or lapses to ensure that at the very least, my students can develop some relative inclinations that would not be compromised by ineffective literacy instruction. While Sam has opened a new frontier for me to explore, it is also time to figure out a way to tackle the problem of orthographic processing disorder and search for a way to save future Nathans.

For a while now, my interest has been geared towards Neuropsychology, cognitive rehabilitation, Neuro-optometry, and sensorial integration. I read the book "Ghost in

My Brain: How a Concussion Stole My Life" by Clark Elliott. The phenomenal work done by Dr Zelinsky and Dr Donalee – a Neuro-optometrist and a Neuropsychologist respectively – that was described in the book would shape a new phase in my thinking for years to come. Padula (2012), Kaplan (2006) and Schuhmacher's (2017) books were also equally eye opening for me. I have been drawing many links between Traumatic Brain Injuries and Learning Difficulties. I have also been re-evaluating dyslexia and the associated learning difficulties in a new light. Of course, I am not going to foray into a realm that only a certified Neuro-optometrist can enter. The goal is to appropriate their ideas into a teaching or intervention setting.

It is the start of another project, alongside with countless of other projects.

REFERENCES

Arwood, E. L., & Kaulitz, C. (2007). *Learning with a Visual Brain in an Auditory World: Visual Language Strategies for Individuals with Autism Spectrum Disorders*. Shawnee Mission, Kan.: APC.

Bellis, T. J. (2003). *When the Brain Can't Hear: Unraveling the Mystery of Auditory Processing Disorder*. New York: Atria Books.

Cognitive Exercises for Learning Disabilities and Learning Difficulties. (n.d.). Retrieved from http://www.audiblox2000.com/audiblox-01.htm

Davis, D. R., & Braun, E. M. (1997). *The Gift of Dyslexia: Why Some of the Smartest People Can't Read, and How They Can Learn*. New York: Perigee.

DeGraaf, K. H. (n.d.). *14 Steps To Teach Dyslexics How To Spell & Read*. Dyslexia Victoria Online. doi:www.dyslexiavictoriaonline.com

Elliott, C. (2016). *The ghost in my brain: How a concussion stole my life and how the new science of brain plasticity helped me get it back.* London: Penguin Books.

Eide, B., & Eide, F. (2012). *The Dyslexic Advantage: Unlocking the Hidden Potential of the Dyslexic Brain*. London: Penguin Group.

Farah, M. J. (2004). *Visual Agnosia*. MIT Press.

Freed, J., & Parsons, L. (1998). *Right-brained children in a left-brained world: Unlocking the potential of your ADD child*. New York, NY: Simon & Schuster Paperbacks.

Golon, A. S. (2008). *Visual-spatial learners: Differentiation strategies for creating a successful classroom*. Waco, TX: Prufrock Press.

Grant, D. (2005). *That's the Way I Think: Dyslexia, dyspraxia, ADHD and dyscalculia explained (2nd ed.)*. Great Britain: David Fulton Publisher.

Irlen, H. (2005). *Reading by the Colors: Overcoming Dyslexia and Other Reading Disabilities through the Irlen Method*. New York, NY: Perigee.

Kaplan, M. (2006). *Seeing through new eyes: Changing the lives of children with autism, Asperger syndrome and other developmental disabilities through vision therapy*. London: Jessica Kingsley Pub.

Lane, K. A. (2005). *Developing ocular motor and visual perceptual skills: An Activity Workbook*. Thorofare, NJ: Slack.

Major, S. M. (2010). *The Illustrated Book of Sounds & Their Spelling Patterns: The right brained approach to teaching reading in 20 minutes a day*. Gastonia, NC: Child1st Publications.

McGuinness, C., & McGuinness, G. (1999). *Reading reflex: The foolproof Phono-Graphix method for teaching your child to read*. New York, NY: Simon & Schuster.

Meet Ron Davis. (n.d.). Retrieved from http://www.davisautism.com/meet-ron-davis.html

Padula, W. V., Munitz, R., & Magrun, W. M. (2012). *Neuro-visual processing rehabilitation: An interdisciplinary approach*. Santa Ana, CA: Optometric Extension Program Foundation.

Poole, J. (2008). *Decoding dyslexia: 14 programmes for helping dyslexia & the active ingredient they share.* Leicester: Matador.

Sacks, O. (1990). *The man who mistook his wife for a hat and other clinical tales.* New York: Quality Paperback Book Club.

Schuhmacher, H., M.D. (2017). *Vision and Learning: How Undiagnosed Vision Problems Cause Learning Difficulties and What You Can Do to Unlock Your Child's Academic Potential - A Guide for Parents and Professionals* (1st ed.). CreateSpace Independent Publishing Platform.

Shaywitz, S. E. (2012). *Overcoming Dyslexia: A New and Complete Science-Based Program for Reading Problems at Any Level*. New York: A.A. Knopf.

Silverman, L. K. (2002). *Upside-down brilliance: The visual-spatial learner*. Denver, Colo: DeLeon Pub.

Taylor, J. B. (2009). *My Stroke of Insight: A Brain Scientist's Personal Journey (Reprint ed.)*. Penguin Books.

Turner, M. J., & Hope, K. (2010). *Dyslexia, or, Being right-brained*. Sidney, BC: Ardmore Pub. doi:www.dyslexiavictoriaonline.com

Turner, M. J., & Hope, K. (2009). *Teaching the Dyslexic: Spelling and Language Arts*. Sidney, British Columbia, Canada: Ardmore Publishing. doi:www.dyslexiavictoriaonline.com

Made in United States
Orlando, FL
08 June 2022

18616721R00148